Unlocking the Bureaucrat's Kingdom

Unlocking the
Bureaucrat's Kingdom

Deregulation and the Japanese Economy

Frank Gibney
Editor

BROOKINGS INSTITUTION PRESS
Washington, D.C.

This is a Pacific Basin Institute book.

The Pacific Basin Institute at Pomona College is a nonprofit foundation de-
voted to expanding academic and public knowledge of the nations and cultures
of the Pacific Basin. Founded in 1979, it includes a substantial archive of video,
film, and print material. The views expressed in this book do not necessarily
reflect those of the authors' employers or other organizations with which they
are associated.

Copyright © 1998 by

THE BROOKINGS INSTITUTION

1775 Massachusetts Ave. N.W.
Washington, D.C. 20036

Library of Congress Cataloging-in-Publication data

Gibney, Frank, 1924–
    Unlocking the bureaucrat's kingdom: deregulation and the Japanese
economy / Frank Gibney.
        p.   cm.
    Includes bibliographical references and index.
    ISBN 0-8157-3126-4 (alk. paper). — ISBN 0-8157-3125-6 (pbk.:
alk. paper)
    1. Deregulation—Japan.   2. Trade regulation—Japan.
3. Industrial policy—Japan.   4. Japan—Economic policy—1989–
I. Title.
HD4313.G53   1998
338.952—dc21   97-33784
                                                          CIP

9 8 7 6 5 4 3 2 1

The paper used in this publication meets the minimum requirements of the
American National Standard for Information Sciences—Permanence of Paper
for Printed Library Materials, ANSI Z39.48-1984

Typeset in Times Roman

Composition by Cynthia Stock

Printed by R.R. Donnelley and Sons Co.
Harrisonburg, Virginia

Contents

Part Two: The Protective Bureaucracy in Action

Foreword

THROUGHOUT MY TENURE as ambassador to Japan (1989–93) I was obliged to spend much of my time wrestling with bilateral trade problems between Washington and Tokyo. The most vexing and intractable barriers to Japan's market seemed frequently to be embedded in a regulatory system that was extensive, opaque, and often arbitrary—particularly for new entrants to the market. The Bush administration's Structural Impediments Initiative (SII) negotiations were directed toward removing or modifying a number of these regulatory barriers to trade.

Recognizing that requests for change had little prospect of success if they bore a "made in U.S.A." label, we shopped around for reforms proposed by thoughtful and knowledgeable Japanese. We had no difficulty assembling a wide range of recommendations from the Maekawa Commission, the Administrative Reform Council, and various academicians. Some of their proposals were designed to foster greater competition by lowering market entry barriers, some to enhance the clout of the Fair Trade Commission, some to make keiretsu networks more transparent and less exclusive, and some to lower prices and expand the choices available to Japanese consumers. In making the case for these proposals the U.S. Embassy consistently underlined the potential benefits of reform to the Japanese people. This perhaps accounts for the fact that despite a delicate and difficult negotiation, the results were generally applauded by the Japanese press—and even a few politicians. Some of the practical results were laudable, for example, amendment of the Large Retail Store Law. But the bargaining left a sour aftertaste on the Japanese side, and following President Clinton's election in 1992, Washington adopted a different approach to trade negotiations with Tokyo.

In recent years the political environment in Japan for regulatory reform has changed. In the wake of a prolonged recession, deregulation is
widely heralded in Japan as a necessary prerequisite for reviving the
Japanese economy. The Keidanren industrial federation has become an
outspoken proponent of reform, as have other elements of the business
establishment. The press insistently endorses the need for reform. And
prominent politicians—above all, Prime Minister Ryutaro Hashimoto
and the opposition leader Ichiro Ozawa—have made administrative reform and deregulation central elements of their party platforms.

Not only have the number of proponents of administrative reform
increased, their arguments have changed. The Maekawa Report, issued
in the mid-1980s, urged reform in order to mollify foreign critics and to
harmonize Japan's industrial structure and business practices with those
of its trading partners. Today, deregulation is promoted as a means of
enhancing Japan's future growth prospects, preserving the competitiveness of its industry, and improving the welfare of its long-suffering consumers. Clearly, these are arguments that can be presented with greater
conviction by Japanese politicians and endorsed with greater enthusiasm by Japanese voters.

The sense of urgency behind efforts to promote administrative reform
and deregulation has also intensified. The reasons are obvious. Other
policy options for reviving the economy (for example, increased public
works spending) were tried but produced disappointing results. As financial markets have gone global, Japan's costly and heavily regulated
financial sector has been left behind. And there is a growing awareness
within the Japanese establishment that an economy that relies mainly
on a strong manufacturing sector is like a bird flying on one wing. With
this comes grudging acknowledgment that Japan's service industries in
fields like telecommunications, financial services, transportation, construction, electric power, and health care are unlikely to become world
class without more direct exposure to international competition in Japan. And the financial crisis in Asia has reinforced the perceived need to
step up the pace of reform efforts by highlighting the consequences of
lax regulatory arrangements and a lack of disclosure by financial firms.

Yet, while the political climate in Tokyo appears more conducive to
administrative reform and deregulation, progress has been slow. The
Opposition victory in Lower House elections in 1993 seemed to open
the door to change, but the Hosokawa government accorded priority to
electoral reform; the Hata government, which replaced it, was very short

lived; and the Maruryama coalition regime possessed neither the political strength nor policy conviction to push a regulatory reform agenda forward. To its credit, the Hashimoto government seized the issue, promised to "fight like a ball of fire" for reform, and put forward in 1997 an ambitious plan for streamlining the state bureaucracy, restructuring the budgetary process, deregulating the financial sector, and promoting wide-ranging changes, *inter alia*, in the social security and education systems. A "big bang" financial system reform bill passed the Diet in 1997, and its implementation will commence in April 1998.

Though announcements are ambitious, and some progress is being made, there have been disappointments as well. Plans to reduce the number of ministries and government agencies have been described by the press as a mere paper shuffle. Proposals to privatize the mail and postal savings and insurance systems have as yet come to naught. A call to hive off the Finance Ministry's monetary and tax policy responsibilities from its budget and spending policy prerogatives was beaten back by the Liberal Democratic Party finance "zoku" members in the Diet. And despite much public criticism, the *amakudari* ("descent from heaven") system of placing former officials in key private sector jobs, thereby preserving a symbiotic connection between regulators and the regulated, remains essentially intact. Hence, the palpable sense that proponents of reform face an uphill battle against formidable resistance.

And so they do. The business community enthusiastically endorses the principle of deregulation, yet does not necessarily welcome changes in those specific administrative practices that inhibit competitors. The political class remains weak, and LDP attitudes toward regulatory reform remain ambivalent. Many of its most influential Diet members derive direct benefits from the current regulatory system; they help companies find their way through a labyrinthine bureaucratic maze, collecting handsome payments along the way for their services. Of course the most resourceful and tenacious resistance comes, predictably, from the bureaucracy itself. It has little incentive fundamentally to alter a system that enables it to manage the Japanese economy, run the day-to-day affairs of government, and thus "call the tune."

In this connection, several of the criteria that have been introduced for evaluating regulatory reform—most notably transparency of the regulatory process and international comparability of regulatory standards—represent a direct threat to cherished bureaucratic prerogatives. The result has been a certain disjunction between the glacial pace of administrative reform efforts and the growing demands for change from the press, from the business elite, and some officials and politicians.

The American government has occasionally attempted to accelerate the pace of change through private or public encouragement. During my time in Tokyo I was often accused of applying excessive "gaiatsu"or "foreign pressure." Hence, I found it singularly ironic that some of the same individuals who criticized my activities in public, privately solicited such outside pressures to reinforce and facilitate their own efforts to foster reforms. By the time I finished my official duties, I concluded that nationalistic reactions against foreign pressure had grown more rapidly than the ability of the Japanese government to successfully undertake reforms without it. Perhaps that, too, has begun to change.

Today, "gaiatsu" is being applied by market forces. And "naiatsu" or "internal pressure" has grown apace. Both are healthy developments. But it is important for American readers of this volume to remember that Japan's regulatory traditions are different than ours, and that reforms, when they come, will not necessarily emulate an "American model." The Japanese public expects and accepts a greater degree of governmental intervention in the economy than we find comfortable. The business community is more accustomed to regarding the government as a partner than as a referee. Informal processes of bureaucratic direction—for example, the tradition of "administrative guidance" and the substantial role played by trade associations in shaping and carrying out bureaucratic directives—are more deeply embedded in Japan's governance process. The cozy, insider connections among Japanese legislators, regulators, and the regulated, have, to be sure, been somewhat attenuated. But they remain unusually intimate by American standards. Indeed this fusion of public and private interests remains at the heart of Japan's highly protected, highly subsidized, and comparatively uncompetitive service sector. Thus, while change is coming, albeit incrementally, the form it takes will often surprise and not infrequently disappoint foreigners.

Nonetheless, market entry is easing, competition is growing, and in the financial sector particularly, the growing staffs of the foreign banks, securities firms, and insurance companies are perhaps the strongest evidence of their high expectations for "big bang" financial reforms.

So it is a time of ferment in Japan that will bring great challenges and large opportunities. I heartily endorse Frank Gibney's call for a "third opening" of Japan. For the sake of the relationship that is critically important to the welfare and security of the American and Japanese people and the stability of Asia, I hope it will be accomplished with some dispatch and largely through Japan's own efforts.

MICHAEL H. ARMACOST
President, Brookings Institution

Preface

THE CHAPTERS in this volume were originally written as part of a joint study of economic overregulation and its remedies first commissioned by the Sasakawa Peace Foundation in 1995. Taking "Reshaping the Japanese Marketplace" as theme and working title, the Pacific Basin Institute and the Mansfield Center for Asia-Pacific Affairs asked a cross-section of Japanese, American, and European authorities on this subject to state the problems caused by bureaucratic overregulation and offer some prescriptive remedies in the bargain. Much had been written on this subject in the Japanese press, but surprisingly few concerted studies had been made. For deregulation, with the lessening of the ministry mandarins' control that it implies, is in a very real sense the hinge that can swing back the now-anachronistic mindset of the "catch-up economy" and bring Japan's nation-society back to political as well as economic health.

In Japan the study was climaxed by a conference held at Keidanren headquarters in Tokyo on March 3, 1996, before a blue-ribbon audience of Japanese business leaders, journalists, and public officials. The original essays in the study were collected in a book, published at that time by Kodansha in Japanese, *Kanryotachi no Taikoku* (The Bureaucrats' Superpower). Given the passage of time, as well as the inevitable problems of translation, I asked almost all of the original contributors to update and revise their papers for this book. What editing that seemed necessary was provided by other members of the Pacific Basin Institute and myself. For developing the theme concept, as well as the work of organizing and managing the 1996 conference, we are indebted to Tovah Ladier, director of the Mansfield Center and Akira Iriyama, president of the Sasakawa Peace Foundation. Shigeki Hijino, Tokyo representative

xiii

of the Pacific Basin Institute, was also of great help. Particular thanks is owed to our editor, James Gibney, who brought the book to its final form, and to Theresa Walker and her colleagues at the Brookings Institution Press.

Our study was first aimed primarily at the Japanese public, but we believe it will prove equally useful to non-Japanese readers, Americans in particular. A minor but persistent problem in translation and description was presented by the Japanese language itself. As contrasted with the readily adversarial tone of English, the imposed civility of Japanese tends to sugarcoat problems and ease around dilemmas. A variety of misunderstandings in international translation follows. Where English, for example, speaks bluntly of "deregulation," meaning " to get rid of regulations," Japanese uses the phrase "*kisei kanwa*" meaning literally, "to soften regulations." During the various Japanese-American controversies of the Bush administration, for example, American negotiators (and newspaper readers) talked about something called a "structural impediments initiative." By contrast, Japanese negotiators (and newspaper readers) referred to *kozo kyogi*—a phrase which means literally, "conferences about structure."

Part one of this volume offers some historical and cultural perspective on regulatory reform. In Part two the authors consider areas in which the problems of bureaucratic overregulation have been especially acute. Finally, the epilogue offers an overview of Japan's postwar industrial policy. The people who contributed to this study have different backgrounds and offer different perspectives. The views of the political, the economic, and business sectors, as well as journalists, are represented. Their points of view often diverge. No editorial attempt has been made to homogenize them. Some have dealt with the history of government controls in Japan; others have described its workings. Some write with indignation; others are more detached. At least one contributor makes the case for continued regulation and bureaucratic guidance. But all the authors share a concern with the overriding problem, and most strongly advocate the need for change. By highlighting the inequities in the Japanese economic framework, the authors hope in general to show how outmoded such practices have become, how damaging they can be to Japanese consumers and producers, and, finally, how incompatible they are with Japan's stature as a world economic power in a globalized economy.

Introduction

Frank Gibney

A spectre is haunting Japan—the spectre of international capitalism.

—with apologies to Karl Marx

WHEN PEOPLE TALKED of a new "Pacific century" for the Asia Pacific nations, Japan was assumed to be the original role model. With more than four trillion dollars in gross national product, a favorable trade balance that in 1996 exceeded $120 billion, exports amounting to 10 percent of the world total, and productivity figures in seemingly unending ascension, Japan, standing at the edge of the twenty-first century, continues to dominate the statistics. The People's Republic of China has experienced explosive growth, and what the World Bank has christened HPAEs (high-performing Asian economies) continue to make progress, yet Japan is rightly given credit for pointing the way with its growth-oriented public policies. Scholars and journalists, commenting on the rise of popular democracy and an Asian middle class, cite postwar Japan as the great exemplar.

Yet here, at the assumed apogee of their modern history, the people who built the "economic miracle" of the late twentieth century remain caught in the toils of a seven-year-old slump. With Japan's government still a shaky coalition of warring factions, real political leadership has yet to reappear. A bureaucratic establishment once widely regarded as next to omniscient has shown itself unwilling and probably incapable of

1

making significant reforms or changes in the nation's course, politicians' pious statements to the contrary. To complicate Japan's domestic problems a sudden and drastic fall in stock market and currency values, set off by the virtual collapse of Thailand's economy in early summer, had spread by October 1997 through most of the hitherto booming HPAEs in Southeast Asia and Korea. With its strong currency reserves, extensive trading, and heavy investments throughout the region, Japan might have been expected to offer heavy economic support in this crisis—much as the United States had intervened two years ago to forestall a similar breakdown in Mexico's economy. Given Japan's own difficulties, however, supportive action from Tokyo seemed hardly possible. A commentary in the *Economist* on November 15, 1997, noted: "Far from being the answer, Japan is part of the region's current problems." As of November 1997, Japanese banks had lavished close to $300 billion worth of loans on other Asian economies.

The Japanese public, while still proud of recent achievement, is confused and uncertain. The November 1996 elections—with a 60 percent voter turnout, the lowest in Japan's postwar history— reflected the growing apathy of voters alienated to the point of anomie. The hustling, internationally ambitious Japanese businessman, so long the hero of economic case studies, is worriedly facing basic dilemmas—overproduction, underemployment, and the flight of jobs offshore among them— that, caught in the euphoria of past successes, he never thought would occur. Despite heavy government support, the Japanese Dow in 1997 hovers at less than one-half what prices were in the heyday of the 1980s' "bubble" economy. Once-eager foreign investors are hard to find. The pessimistic refrain of "*Nihon uri*—sell Japan" is widely quoted. It epitomizes a national crisis of confidence.

This crisis of confidence has at last exposed the basic contradiction lurking behind the decades of "Japan Inc.'s" high-growth progress. On the one hand, we have had the spectacle of the world's hardest-fighting competitors, vying for market share and profits in the best traditions of capitalist free enterprise. On the other, we have the world's most powerful bureaucrats, regulating economy and polity with a heavy thicket of regulation, guidance, and injunction worthy of the eighteenth-century Tokugawa shogunate's ministers (whose spiritual descendants they are).

The contradiction here has been obvious to all, yet the Japanese have never been overmuch bothered by logical contradictions. The coexistence of competitive private enterprise and public control seemed practical and useful. It worked. It worked, however, only so long as both parties to the contradiction cooperated in a headlong drive, led by selective exports, to catch up with the industrialized West. The drive proved a success, but success was transitory. Paradoxically, the more its brilliant business strategies put Japan at the top of the world's economy, the more the problems in the contradiction began to surface.

For all the brilliance and energy of Japan's postwar economic miracle, the interlocking of business and bureaucracy, with the latter originally in charge, led to a dominion of entrenched interests which makes a mockery of the free enterprise that Japanese spokesmen publicly support. Time and again newcomers to the Japanese market, especially if they are foreigners, have run up against layer upon layer of detailed government regulation designed to support the status quo. Established companies have combined in *keiretsu* groups and powerful trade associations that actually work in restraint of trade. Japan has also perpetuated a kind of "cultural protectionism," which has if anything intensified over the years. Its proponents, widely supported by the public, insist that the Japanese are so different "culturally" from others that only purposefully designed home-grown products and services can satisfy their wants and concerns.

Since the Meiji Restoration the growth of the Japanese economy has been accomplished within the context of the so-called capitalist development state. At its best, this construct represented a triumph of economic innovation.[1] It is irresponsible exaggeration to dismiss the Japanese achievement as the forced lockstep march of something called "Japan, Inc." Free-enterprise competition within Japan is if anything more intense than in the other leading capitalist economies. Nonetheless, capital and labor alike have worked within the framework of a tightly meshed industrial policy. Theirs has been a competition fought out in Japan, within a set of firmly determined ground rules.[2] These rules and regulations cover every aspect of the national life. They are made and enforced by the consistent guidance of a highly concerned government bureaucracy, which has made its support of Japanese business internationally a canon of public policy.

Until recently, at least, Japan's "producer-first" economy has been equally supported by an exceptionally docile consumer population. Japan's consumers were accustomed to paying high prices for locally made products that sold far more cheaply in international markets. Content as they were, however, to submerge personal gain and comfort in the long-range goals of national and corporate interest, they were willing accomplices in the success of the original modern supply siders.

Within the last few years, however, this mindset has been changing. Japan's business leaders have come to realize that the catch-up drives of a capitalist development state are no longer necessary or useful to the world's second-largest economic power in an era in which free international trade and investment have become imperatives even beyond the power of influential national finance ministries to control. Shoichiro Toyoda, the chairman of the Keidanren (and, it should be added, of the Toyota group), has repeatedly underscored the urgency, as he emphasized, "of bold and effective measures to stimulate domestic demand and open Japan's markets. . . . We simply cannot leave reform half-done." [3]

Toward the 'Third Opening' of Japan

Keidanren, the abbreviated Japanese name for the Japan Federation of Business Organizations, is the powerful official spokesman for Japanese big business. Until the mid-1990s, it was also the principal contributor to Japan's majority Liberal Democratic Party. Most recently, in a January 1997 statement, Keidanren summarized no less than 886 separate requests to the government for administrative deregulation throughout the economy. By way of punctuating its chairman's comments, a Keidanren White Paper demanded deregulation, "the linchpin of economic reform," in almost every business field. The implications of its report were clear. Japan can raise productivity and cure its ailing economy only by getting the bureaucracy out of business, thereby enforcing "urgent and drastic reform of the economic structure."[4]

The concern of Japan's business leadership arises not merely from the recession fall-off in consumer demand. The recent successes of emerging supermarkets and cut-rate retail enterprises in Japan bear witness to a new price consciousness among Japanese consumers. They are beginning to behave less like props in a stage-managed economy and more like cost-conscious (and volatile) consumers in other countries.

But before Japan can normalize the domestic side of its now internationalized economy, Japanese voters must understand the extent to which the processes of trade and investment in their country are clipped and truncated by excessive government regulation and barely visible collusion among business, bureaucracy, and often the media. Ubiquitous government regulation inside Japan fostered an overprotected "hothouse economy," insulated from the pushes and pulls of world economic forces. As Japan became one of the world's economic powers, however, with its favorable trade balances swollen and its financial sector at least partly liberalized, the hothouse windows began to break. Foreign trading partners ever more stridently demanded equal rights for their own products to be sold in Japan. Japanese consumers themselves, as they traveled around the world, began to realize that they were paying almost twice as much for most basic consumer goods as the people outside. The need for Japan to become a "normal country," as the opposition *Shinshinto* (New Frontier Party) leader Ichiro Ozawa put it, is thus as compelling in the economic sphere as in the political.

Belatedly, the government has come to acknowledge the problem. In his Diet message of January 1997, Prime Minister Ryutaro Hashimoto promised a comprehensive review of "all administrative areas, without exception." "It is clear," he conceded, "that the current framework (structure) is an obstacle to the vigorous development of this nation. . . . The present system is hindering Japan's development at a time when the world is being integrated, allowing increasing freedom in the movement of people, goods, wages, and information across borders." Having already promised a "Big Bang" package to deregulate a financial system still hopelessly dominated by Finance Ministry bureaucrats, Hashimoto vowed to put teeth in the sweeping Deregulation Action Program first advanced in 1995. But he added a cautious warning: "Changing systems that are deeply rooted in our society will only happen with great difficulty."[5]

Reaction to his statement was predictably skeptical. In an editorial published the following day, the *Mainichi Shimbun* tartly compared the prime minister's objectives with the vagueness of his plans for achieving them—not to mention the conventional political pork-barreling in his 1997 budget. "We would like to believe for the time being that the Prime Minister is 'serious,' " the editorial concluded. "Hashimoto has nowhere to go but ahead." [6]

After a year of highly publicized planning activity, however, the Big Bang—named after the sweeping financial deregulation of the London City establishment a decade ago—seems rather hard to ignite. In September 1997, the Liberal Democratic Party, back in control of the Diet's Lower House for the first time since 1993, reelected Hashimoto as party president and hence prime minister. New laws and procedures have indeed been drafted to permit free competition in Japan's financial and investment markets by the target year 2001. But his concurrent pledges to shake up moss-backed government ministries and eliminate their networks of autocratic bureaucratic "guidance" thus far seem seriously handicapped both by party politicians' factionalism and the bureaucracy's stubborn hold on behind-the-scenes power.

The imperatives for deregulating the bureaucrat-ridden Japanese economy would seem obvious. The unwillingness or, better stated, the inability of successive Japanese governments to deal with this problem was equally clear. Thus far the most significant progress was made during the five-year premiership of Yasuhiro Nakasone, when the swollen national railroad system was privatized and the telecommunications market liberalized. After Nakasone, in the decade beginning in 1987, the country has had eight prime ministers, a fact that makes its own commentary on the current political process. Despite a plethora of recommendations, very little of importance has been done. The mandarinate in the Kasumigaseki ministries has almost invariably deflected the reform initiatives of weak political governments.

Largely as a result, Japan stands out as an unusually one-sided participant in today's global economy. Some 16 percent of world GNP comes from Japan, but Japan harbors only 1 percent of the world's foreign direct investment. More than $350 billion of Japanese investment has gone into the world since 1950, but foreign investment in Japan is equivalent to less than 10 percent of that amount. According to a recent survey by the American Chamber of Commerce in Japan, foreign firms account for less than 2 percent of Japan's domestic sales and assets, as against 15 percent for the United States and 18 percent for Germany.[7] Such disproportions bring on a wave of cumulative criticism from other nations, with threats of retaliation strong enough to disrupt the whole emerging international free trade relationship.

The time is ripe for the Japanese to look at their whole set of business and bureaucratic *mores* to see what needs fixing. The crash of the bubble economy is still reverberating inside Japan. Plummeting from its bubble-boom high of 38,910 at the end of December 1989, the Tokyo Nikkei average dropped to bounce along new bottoms. An all-time low was reached in the 14,485 figure of June 1995. After advances in 1996 and 1997, averages hovered at the 16,000 level. Over the years, falling stock prices have left a legacy of diminishing corporate assets. This includes the assets of Japanese banks, which were among the leading stock and property plungers of the bubble era. Big city land prices dropped precipitately.[8]

Japan's once-vaunted banking system remains in horrible shape. Current estimates of banks' bad debts range from an acknowledged ¥40 trillion to ¥70 trillion (more than $600 billion). This would amount to well over 10 percent of Japan's GNP! (The main reason for the imprecise estimates is the reluctance of the banks to revalue their bad property debts, in the rather illusory hope that values will come back.) American taxpayers will ultimately pay more than $130 billion as public penance for the disastrous savings-and-loan meltdown of the 1980s in the United States. Some analysts conclude that the Japanese public will end up paying four times that to mop up the bankers' part of the bubble. To complicate the problem, the disastrous failures of many mortgage banks (*jusen*) in the mid-1990s disclosed embarrassing connections with Japan's sizable and prosperous gangster underworld.[9]

The obvious villains in this performance are the mandarins of Japan's Ministry of Finance, who have attempted to control both the stock market slide and the banking disasters with conspicuous lack of success. Accustomed to twirl the wheels and turn the levers of Japan's financial system from their Kasumigaseki headquarters, MOF's bureaucrats had failed to reckon with a new freewheeling international financial game whose players have little regard for national boundaries or protective ministries. All their efforts to re-window the hothouse economy failed. It had simply grown too big and too complex for their traditional guidance mechanisms to handle.

Successively weak governments for their part failed to find any political solutions for the bubble disasters. This would have meant publicizing their extent. It was problem enough to have lines of worried depositors standing outside the doors of bankrupt credit institutions to demand their money—a phenomenon new to postwar Japan. Worse yet, banks and businesses were so used to waiting for bureaucratic guidance that they sought few independent solutions themselves. The result was a massive cover-up effort that may leave permanent scars in Japanese business and finance.[10]

Although the Ministry of Finance has taken some hard knocks, the civil servants of other ministries have their own faults of overregulation to answer for. Strict overregulation by the Ministry of Posts and Telecommunications for years handicapped Japanese companies' competitiveness in this area. The Construction Ministry's rigged bidding and sweetheart deals with favored Japanese contractors have long been an open secret. In the 1990s these problems finally erupted in a series of public scandals. Yet for the past quarter-century successive governments have simplistically sought to fend off temporary recessions with vast infrastructure investment. In the process the ministry and its eager corporate collaborators have virtually concreted over the country with dubiously useful dams, highways, airports, and Bullet Train extensions. They are also expensive: construction costs in Japan are a good 40 percent higher than they are in the United States. In his recent book, *The Emptiness of Japanese Affluence,* the Australian scholar Gavan McCormack scathingly outlined the "collusive corruption" of what he ironically calls the "Construction State." "Incredibly," he wrote, "Japan spends more on public works than the United States does on defense and was doing so even at the height of the Cold War."[11]

Early in 1996, after his surprising appointment as minister of health and welfare in the then-coalition government, Naoto Kan, a long-time consumer rights activist, turned the spotlight on an appalling case of collusive oversight by his ministry's bureaucrats. For more than ten years they had knowingly permitted pharmaceutical companies to import tainted blood products into Japan—similar products had been banned in the United States since 1983. As a result, some 2,000 hemophiliacs had contracted AIDS. A wave of demotions, resignations, and arrests followed, after Kan ordered the ministry files on the subject opened.

The tainted blood scandal shook the country. Coming on the heels of disclosures variously involving bureaucrats from the Ministry of International Trade and Industry, the Finance Ministry, and the Construction Ministry, it prompted a wave of media and public criticism of Japan's hitherto sacrosanct officialdom. Politicians took their share of the hard knocks. For the Kan case, in particular, underlined the passivity of party ministers who are normally content to follow the "advice" of their civil servants. None of Kan's predecessors, fifteen in all, had bothered to root out the damaging files, despite lawsuits and press warnings.

Seen in an American context, such cases of bureaucratic corruption would not have raised many eyebrows. Americans hold politicians, not bureaucrats responsible; the very word "bureaucracy" holds a somewhat pejorative connotation. To most present-day Americans, deregulation of bureaucratic controls would seem a good thing. In Japan the opposite is true. For generations Japan's best and brightest have gone into public service, proud of their dignity and responsibilities. Much the same has been true of European countries, whose civil servants, like Japan's, tend to be more respected and more competent than their American counterparts. In our downgrading of bureaucrats, as the economist Peter Drucker once put it, "America is the odd man out."[12]

Here we meet a striking difference in public attitudes. By tradition and temperament most Americans are programmed to question their bureaucracy's regulations. By temperament and tradition, given the Confucian cast of their society, most Japanese are programmed to accept them. Even in the course of normal social and business relationships, there is a pronounced hierarchical tilt to Japanese culture. Despite the modern inroads of democracy and the equals-under-law principle, Japan remains to a great extent a house divided between top dogs and underlings. The national respect for rank is particularly manifest in the popular respect for government authority, as such. Public indignation in Japan has a high threshold indeed.

In Europe as in Japan the traditional credibility of the official bureaucracy has deep roots. France remains the classic example. In his book, *Le Mal Francais*, Alain Peyrefitte caustically noted: "All government functions depend on the Finance Ministry, which is conditioned to forbid everything."[13] The founder of Europe's bureaucratic tradition was Louis XIV's omnicompetent financial controller, Jean-Baptiste Colbert. To this day the generally high-handed directives of French public officials are denounced as "*Colbertisme*." Colbertism, as Peyrefitte defines it, aimed "to make the kingdom prosper by making every individual the docile executant of economic decisions reached rationally at the top. As far as docility goes, he succeeded. Prosperity was something else again."

Colbert's counterpart in Japan was Tokugawa Ieyasu, that master organizer who laid down the guidelines for orderly administration that lasted for 250 years. He set standards for arrogant rectitude that continue to this day. Tokugawa had more power than Colbert, and he was a lot smarter. He allowed the people below him a good bit of latitude for consensus-building discussion. He also thoughtfully reinvented a late Japanese-model Confucianism that turned obedience to authority into a kind of religion.

Even after the Meiji reformers brought about the massive politico-cultural revolution that put paid to the shogunate, they found themselves reincarnating Tokugawa's bureaucracy, albeit in somewhat Europeanized form,[14] so that they could govern their modernized Confucian country. This happened partly from necessity. Faced with the need to duplicate overnight the modern world of banks, businesses, and parliamentary government—a system of nation-state politics and economics that had taken several centuries for Europe to develop—the junior samurai of the Meiji government perforce had to run everything from a centralized headquarters. The close interlocking triangle of politicians, big business, and bureaucracy later memorialized as Japan, Inc., has a lot of history behind it.

After the collapse of Japan's militarists' ascendancy in 1945—and with it most of their hoked-up Shinto imperialism—the bureaucracy was the only respectable authority structure remaining. General Douglas MacArthur needed officials to run a suddenly occupied country. The Japanese people needed them as well. While the militarists were hopelessly discredited, the civilian bureaucrats, their own role in the aggressive war conveniently forgotten, emerged as Japan's only governing and, for a time, only energizing force.

Shigeru Yoshida, Japan's great postwar prime minister, and his finance minister, Hayato Ikeda, who ultimately succeeded to the top job himself, laid down the plans for a peaceful and prosperous economic power. In the process they altered their Meiji predecessors' slogan of *Fukoku Kyohei* (Prosperous country, strong army) into what might be called *Fukoku Kyokeizai* (Prosperous country, strong economy). Both men were career bureaucrats, as were most of their successors, and they directed and inspired others like them. Unquestioning, the Japanese public followed them. The Liberal Democratic Party (*Jiminto*), which held power from 1955 through almost four decades, was itself virtually a creature of the Yoshida bureaucracy. (Its minority opponents, notably the Socialists, proved outstandingly ineffectual.) In contrast to issue-oriented political parties elsewhere, the Liberal Democrats came into being largely as the executor and interpreter of policies already determined by the mandarins in the ministries.

Beyond any doubt, these enlightened bureaucrats gave the impetus to Japan's "economic miracle." They opened the door and charted the way for the high-growth era and successfully weathered a variety of crises in the 1970s and 1980s. Ironically, the postwar bureaucrats took as their model the centralized government economic controls put into place by the wartime regimes for which many of them had worked. Japanese economists familiarly call this the "1940 set-up."

As it happened, their hand-me-down guidance mechanisms managed to mesh oddly well with a new and dynamic postwar business sector, which needed strong government support to get started. Their success-ful collaboration understandably gave rise to the reality and the myth of a Japanese capitalism that is intrinsically different from the American or the European variety. The virtues of this Japanese-style capitalism have been eloquently outlined by authors like Eisuke Sakakibara—him-self a leading Finance Ministry official. Admittedly, there has been a good bit of unpleasant mercantilism, mean-spirited nationalism, and eco-nomic imperialism in Japan's "capitalist development state." Yet on the plus side, its postwar successes brought prosperity and new dignity to Japan's people, hugely raised levels of education and technology, and created new and largely democratic life styles, while avoiding many of the social ills and disparities of income and living standards that plague American society. Life in the "hot-house" has been good for those inside.

Times change, however. A self-secluded society of workaholic pro-ducers, sending their goods and on occasion their factories to the out-side world, has inescapably been dragged into a worldwide web of information sharing, technology revolution, and a kind of enforced in-ternational togetherness. It is a world that Japan's multinational busi-nesses—not to mention the hard-on-heels competition of its former Asian proteégés—have helped to make. Given the lightning moves of world trade, finance, and investment, however, in the new computer-networked society, the once marveled "bureaucratic development state" has become a badly worn piece of furniture. So are the premises of economic nation-alism that once sustained it. So is the trust that politicians as well as the public put in bureaucratic "guidance."

Naoto Kan, now a leader of the newly founded Democratic Party, summarized the current problem well. "Bureaucrats," he said in a recent speech, "are like an airplane put on automatic pilot. When Japan was in the middle of high economic growth, their pursuit of a pre-set goal worked well. But now, we cannot afford to fly automatic pilot any more."[15]

The first order of business is to find politicians who are not afraid to make big decisions on their own. Former Prime Minister Yasuhiro Nakasone, in his article for this book, described the current government imbalance in baseball terms. "Politicians," he writes, "are pitchers, bu-reaucrats their catchers. A good pitcher decides himself if he will throw a fast ball or a curve, but a weak pitcher throws the pitches as his catcher signals."

Admittedly, the best of Japan's postwar economic blueprints came off the drawing boards of middle-ranking ministry officials. But the men in the ministries need both stimulus and strong support from political leaders to make such plans effective. In recent years neither has been forthcoming.

Japan has made two great strides forward toward internationalization in the modern era. First came the dynamic of the young Meiji reformers. In less than two decades, in a nineteenth-century cultural revolution that ranks with the eighteenth-century American and French revolutions, they turned a decaying, semifeudal shogunate into a modern nation-state—or, more accurately still, a nation-society. While some of the Meiji leaders hoped to build a popular democracy, others were authoritarian. The compromise that resulted was a constitutional monarchy guided by a *noblesse oblige* bureaucracy—a Confucian version of Plato's Guardians of the State. In the end, however, the high ideals of Meiji were subverted by military nationalists, who led an all too docile populace into a disastrous war.

Next came the MacArthur "democratization" and its aftermath. As in the Meiji days foreign pressure—what modern Japanese politicians have memorialized with the handy, shrugged-shoulder phrase *gaiatsu* —was the ultimate cause. But instead of the implicit threat of Commodore Perry's offshore gunboats, there marched in the traffic-guiding Military Police and New Deal Constitution-makers of American military occupation. The Japanese people welcomed General MacArthur as readily as they had canonized Emperor Meiji. From the 1950s into the 1970s, a yeasty postwar mix of technocrats and businessmen built on the imposed Occupation reforms to bring about the high-growth "economic miracle."

Each group in turn "opened" Japan to the outside world. Each opening, however, was followed by a variety of nationalist, seclusive reactions. Where the Meiji reforms ultimately gave way to violence and war, the dynamic of the mid-twentieth century economic innovators fell prey to self-satisfied complacency. Just as their grandfathers had done what the military told them, the modern members of the public obediently touched their caps to the Ministry of Trade and Industry (MITI) and the Ministry of Finance and gave their savings up to heavy capital investment, as the bureaucrats reshaped a rich, semimercantilist state. That day is gone. It is time to "open" the country again.

The late Naohiro Amaya, for many years one of the guiding lights of MITI, was a product of Japan's bureaucracy. An imaginative planner as well as a skilled negotiator, he pioneered MITI's work in developing

Japan's "knowledge-intensive" industry. Just before his untimely death in 1994, he wrote a short but incisive book: *An Argument for the Wise Country (Eichi Kokkaron)*. In it he called on his countrymen to overcome an increasingly negative parochialism, if they wish to play a leading role in the twenty-first century.[16]

"The differences between Japanese society and the rest of the world have become serious," he wrote. He found the swollen price mechanism inside Japan and the climate of excessive regulation parts of a vicious circle. They are the result of what Amaya calls excessively "vertical" overcentralized government, which despite its economic power has grossly failed to give Japan's hard-pressed consumers their share of a producer-oriented economy.

Both business and the bureaucracy are nervous about transforming cherished institutions of the high-growth era, like the old-fashioned seniority system, the full employment principle (for big companies only), and the constant "window guidance" of a control-happy bureaucracy. The changes of a thoroughly internationalized economy—of which Japan's domestic depression is merely a symptom—are doing it for them. Japan's "mass machine civilization" *(Taishu kikai bunmei)* has matured, Amaya wrote. It is time for a major transformation in Japan to meet the challenges of an Information Age future.

What his country needs, he argued, is a major "restructuring and re-engineering." This amounts to a third "opening of Japan" *(Dai san no kaikoku)* in the tradition of the Meiji Restoration and the MacArthur "democratization." This third opening, he said, must "cut to the bone." He concluded: "The Meiji Restoration was a paradigm of sweeping change. It represented a systematic change of structure from the Tokugawa shogunate to a modern state. And it was total in its impact—encompassing the polity, the economy and the society of Japan. Now we have come to a similar era in our history. Of necessity the changes to be made must be general and total. This cannot be done piecemeal."[17]

Others have made similar comments about the need for a third "Opening," but few have so well summarized the need for drastic reform. In any such reform, most of our contributors argue, reshaping the economic marketplace is an indispensable factor.

To free its fettered marketplace, Japan must finally solve the contradictions inherent in the coexistence of a highly competitive business sector—a world of multinational entrepreneurship—with the passively powerful nationalism of a "father-knows-best" bureaucracy. The contributors to this volume have attempted to show how pervasive and in its way sinister is the overregulation of Japan's mature economy by a bureaucracy more suited to the high-growth development of thirty years ago. When they argue, along with the big business leaders of Japan's Keidanren, that deregulation is the "linchpin" of economic—and societal—renewal, they do not exaggerate. The loudly promised if still unexecuted Big Bang of Prime Minister Hashimoto's administrative changes would, if achieved, prove far more sweeping than the progressive economic deregulation that unfolds in the United States. For among Japanese the Confucian respect for government authority has long been instinctive. It is part of a society that has traditionally valued form over content, ritual over rationality. Sweeping deregulation is thus not so much a matter of policy as it is a matter of mind-set. And here the Third Opening must be initiated and carried through by the Japanese themselves, for their own benefit. There is no Perry or MacArthur to threaten them into it, but their democracy's twenty-first-century future hangs in the balance.

Notes

1. In his seminal *MITI and the Economic Miracle* (Stanford University Press, 1982) and other later writings, the political economist Chalmers Johnson has trenchantly observed and classified the growth and background of this major postwar phenomenon, tracing its roots to the prewar and wartime past.

2. The influential economic commentator, Taichi Sakaiya, likened business competition to the country's traditional *sumo* contests. While the actual wrestling is done in the ring, everything else about the *sumo* tournaments—rules, procedures, locales, training, and participants included—is determined and rigidly set by the association in charge.

3. Japan Federation of Business Organizations (Keidanren), "Request for Deregulation," proposal (Tokyo: Keizai Koho Center, 1997), p. 2.

4. Ibid., pp. 10–13.

5. Policy speech to the National Diet, January 20, 1997.

6. *Mainichi Shimbun*, editorial, January 21, 1997.

7. American Chamber of Commerce in Japan, *U.S.-Japan Trade White Paper* (Tokyo: American Chamber of Commerce,1995); and Ketzai Koho Center, *Japan: An International Comparison* (Tokyo: Keizai Koho Center, 1997).

8. Ironically, the 1997 economic crisis in other East Asian countries was

caused by appallingly loose bank loans, the lack of adequate law-based government supervision, unwise restrictions on foreign investment, and the tendency of banks and finance ministries alike to hide losses until too late. The virtue of "transparency" in disclosing financial transactions, as in Japan, had been widely discounted. Although the depression was compounded in some countries by rampant official and business corruption, the "bubble" mentality of basing loans and investments on a Micawberish belief in continually soaring growth rates strinkingly resembled what had happened in Japan.

9. In March 1997 the finance minister belatedly announced a government bail-out of some bank bad debt, including that of the *jusen*, despite the government's current budget deficit.

10. An embarrassing case in point was the recent loss of more than $1 billion by a trader in Daiwa Bank's New York office. This loss was reported to U.S. banking authorities only on September 18, 1995. The Finance Ministry, which had heard of this disaster fully seven weeks before that, had made no effort to disclose or correct the scandal, as *Asahi* and other Japanese newspapers were quick to point out.

11. Gavan McCormack, *The Emptiness of Japanese Affluence* (M.E. Sharpe, 1973), pp. 33ff.

12. Personal correspondence with author.

13. Alain Peyrefitte, *Le Mal Francaise* (Paris: Librarie Ploss, 1976), pp. 107ff.

14. The connection between the Japanese and French bureaucracies was more than coincidental. In 1878 Matusuyoshi Matsukata, who became the financial expert among the Meiji reformers, visited Paris in the course of a European tour. His interest in France's financial workings so impressed Leon Say, then France's finance minister, that he invited Matsukata to spend some time in his office. Matsukata was much impressed by his unofficial apprenticeship. He often used France as a model during his eighteen years of service as finance minister, during which he established the Bank of Japan and set the tone for the MOF bureaucracy for years to come.

15. As quoted in Tetsuya Itagaki, "Kan Naoto Stirs the Health Ministry," *Japan Quarterly*, vol. 43 (September 1996), pp. 24–29.

16. Naohiro Amaya, *An Argument for the Wise Country* (*Eichi Kokkaron*) (Tokyo: PHP Kenkyu, 1994).

17. Ibid., pp. 206ff.

PART ONE

The Long Road
to Regulatory Reform

CHAPTER 1

From Wartime Controls to Postwar Recovery

Tetsuji Okazaki

FOR A VARIETY of reasons, the Japanese economy has for some time been the focus of a great deal of attention. From one perspective, Japan's economy is a potential model of economic development for developing nations, including the former socialist countries that are moving toward free-market capitalism. A more critical view addresses U.S. criticism about the closed and nontransparent nature of the Japanese market. Finally, a third related perspective explores whether the existing economic system, given the recent recession and the subsequent slow economic recovery, will impede future economic growth in Japan.

No matter how one views these contemporary discussions, an understanding of the formative events in Japanese economic history is imperative. The success of any attempt to apply the lessons of Japanese economic development to other countries or to reform existing economic structures will hinge greatly on how deeply the current economic system is rooted in Japanese society. If, as some analysts argue, Japan's economic system springs from Japanese culture, or is the product of a certain time and history over the past hundreds of years, it will be difficult to revise or adapt it to the needs of developing countries. Conversely, if the economic system is marked by a relatively short history, revision and transfer become more realistic. In any event, a great deal can be learned from the system's formative processes. With these issues in mind, this chapter examines recent research while attempting to summarize and explain the history of the Japanese economy.[1]

19

The Economic System before World War II

Although the prewar Japanese economy displayed a degree of backwardness, overall the system could be characterized as a classic market economy. As described below, the market functioned freely in many sectors of the prewar economy.

First, flexibility was seen in the labor market, and large corporations did not hesitate to lay off workers during economic downturns. Only after the 1920s did these large Japanese corporations begin to emphasize long-term employment.

Second, market financing was the main source of corporate finance. The average large corporation met more then 50 percent of its financing needs by going directly to the capital markets. Consequently, the ratio of stock market capitalization to national output (the total value of listed stocks as a percentage of gross national product [GNP] was much higher than it was during the postwar period of rapid economic growth. Following World War I, some corporations turned to bank loans. Instead of resulting in continuous corporate growth, however, they often toppled together with their associated financing banks *(kanren ginko),* otherwise known as institutional banks *(kikan ginko).* Banks could undertake this kind of large, high-risk financing because the government did not regulate deposit rates. Those that held risky assets offered high interest rates thus absorbing high-risk and return capital.

Third, along with the aforementioned conditions in the labor and capital markets, the prewar corporate system made the firm the backbone of contracts throughout the economy, in the labor and capital markets and between other agents in the economy. Highly transient workers did not feel a strong sense of commitment toward their employers, and consequently they lacked the incentive or means to speak out against corporate management.

Elsewhere in the economy, while supplying most of the capital and assuming the bulk of a firm's risk, shareholders played a central role in corporate governance. A considerably high degree of stock concentration ensured effective corporate governance because the stock of large companies was concentrated in the hands of large individual shareholders, such as wealthy private investors *(shisanka),* or *zaibatsu* parent companies *(zaibatsu honsha).* These important investors had an incentive to pay the price and build the framework for corporate governance. First *zaibatsu* enterprises systematically monitored their subsidiaries. The proportion of internally promoted executives at *zaibatsu* companies was high; but it was the parent company that provided the institutional structure for the corporate governance of its subsidiaries. The parent company established inspection sections and monitored its subsidiaries' activities. In non-*zaibatsu* enterprises, however, large private investors often served on the board of directors with the intent of monitoring the firm through the activities of the board. Furthermore, shareholders would at times ensure sound management by threatening to agree to a hostile buy-out when management performance was poor. At that point the firm became the prime target of a takeover by the *zaibatsu* or "new *zaibatsu*" *(shinko zaibatsu jitai)*.

Not only did the principal *zaibatsu* companies and influential private investors play a pivotal role in corporate governance, but, based on their importance, they also wielded a great deal of influence over the distribution of funds that were obtained on the capital markets. The main *zaibatsu* companies controlled the distribution of funds on internal capital markets owing to their power to inspect and approve the investment portfolios that were proposed by their subsidiaries. Prominent wealthy investors supplied their own capital with their investments and used their credibility to control the flow of funds on capital markets. Furthermore, these agents also occupied a crucial position in the relationship between the government and private sector as seen in the composition of the membership of the various deliberation councils. In the prewar period, the deliberation councils on the whole had few members. Most positions were filled by executives of the parent *zaibatsu* and by prominent private investors in their capacity as members of the Ministry of Commerce and Industry *(Shoko Kaigisho)*. Thus, before World War II, the deliberation councils served as the conduit for the exchange of information between the government and capital markets by way of these *zaibatsu* and large private investors.

The Wartime Economy and the Transformation of the Economic System

The prewar Japanese economy, which could be characterized as a classic market economy, underwent a dramatic transformation during World War II. In response to the call for mobilization, what had been a market economy became a planned economy, radically changing many of the former market structures.

Mobilization of the wartime economy under the shadow of Allied economic sanctions transformed Japan's macroeconomy over the course of several years. As imports fell dramatically and real GNP stagnated, personal consumption declined markedly. In contrast, because of increased military expenditure, government spending rose and boosted fixed capital formation. Changes in the industrial structure accompanied changes in the composition of macroexpenditures. During the war, the fastest growing industries were manufacturers of components that were used in the production of munitions, aircraft, and warships. The steel and nonferrous metals industries that supplied raw materials to machine manufacturers also grew quickly. Elsewhere in the economy, in response to the drop in consumption, the production of consumer goods such as textiles and foodstuffs declined from the early part of the war. As an export industry at the time, the fiber industry recorded a particularly steep drop in production owing to the decline in Japan's foreign trade. Dependent on personal consumption, the commercial and service industries also shrank. Thus, in terms of economic development the wartime period can be described as a period of rapid industrialization in the chemical and heavy industries.

Government planning and control provided the mechanisms that facilitated this mobilization of the wartime economy for the production of munitions. The government could have used fiscal or monetary policy and directed taxation or an inflation tax to finance its purchases, thereby making use of market mechanisms to direct resources toward the munitions sector. However, it did not choose this method because of taxpayer resistance. Furthermore, the government was concerned that a serious inflation would significantly distort income distribution and thus jeopardize the social stability on which the successful prosecution of the war depended. Besides these practical concerns, military and government officials widely subscribed to the philosophy of planning and controlling. In the second half of the 1930s, government officials began to focus on the remarkable accomplishments of the Soviet Union and Nazi Germany. Both these countries had chosen planned economic systems that resembled Japan's plan for the chemical and heavy industries based around the munitions industries. Their success strengthened official faith in the virtues of planning and controlling the economy.

Around the outbreak of the Sino-Japanese War, the government effectively seized control over all aspects of the economy through a series of legislative maneuvers. These measures began with the implementation of foreign exchange controls in January 1937 and continued with the Temporary Measures Act Concerning Exports and Imports *(Yushutsunyuhinto Rinji Sochi Ho)* and the Temporary Measures Concerning Fund Adjustment *(Rinji Shikin Chosei Ho)* in September 1937, and the National General Mobilization Act *(Kokka Sodoin Ho)* in March 1938. Relying on these laws, the government established a planned economy that replaced the market economy. After 1939, the Japanese economy was managed according to the plans of the government Planning Board *(Kikakuin)*. Finally, when price controls were introduced, supply and demand adjustment mechanisms were suspended.

The most important piece of economic planning during the war was the Goods Mobilization Plan *(Bushi Doin Keikaku* or *Butsudo)*. It allotted specific supplies of each good, which had been calculated based on various other economic plans. The exact allocation of resources depended on the demand for munitions, the need to expand productive capacity (plant and equipment investment), and the demand for exports. In this respect, the plan strongly resembled the plan of the former Soviet Union. The Japanese system, however, favored objectives that were considered important by the Planning Board or military departments that exercised substantial influence over the board. The strategic variable in the Goods Mobilization Plan and the binding constraint on the entire wartime economy were the amount of inputs that could be imported. Through the first half of 1941, while trade with the Allies was still possible, import potential was determined by Japan's stock of foreign reserves (import capacity). After trade with the Allies was cut off, however, the import bottleneck was the physical limitation of maritime tonnage capacity to transport resources to and from areas within Japan's sphere of influence.

To manage the wartime economy within these constraints, the government exercised its sovereign and increasingly concentrated authority to alter economic policies that impeded progress, and designed and implemented new policies to replace them. Most reforms were systematically implemented in the New Economic System *(Keizai Shintaisei)* in 1940–41. Most important, the New Economic System established organizations known as control associations *(Toseikai)* in each industry. The control associations facilitated the flow of information between the public and private sectors. Each association maintained its own internal organization and several full-time staff members and derived its authority from the Important Industrial Groups Law *(Juyo Sangyo Dantai Rei)*. The Planning Board then used the control associations to gather information from the enterprises and incorporate this information into its own economic planning. The Planning Board would provisionally allocate limited common resources, namely, maritime transport tonnage capacity, to each control association. Based on these figures, the control associations would respond with their provisional production plans. The Planning Board would then review and compare the provisional production plans from each control association and revise the allotment of transport capacity. Through an iterative process, the Planning Board was able to implement the Goods Mobilization Plan effectively. By establishing the control associations, the government gathered information from individual firms in each industry and created a framework for coordination among various industries.

Furthermore, the New Economic System precipitated corporate reform. Smooth operation of a planned economic system assumed that the Planning Board would both monitor the industries by way of the control associations and revise the objectives and functions of firms. In other words, the Planning Board attempted to change the primary objective of firms from the pursuit of profits to the fulfillment of production quotas. The separation of capital and management became the method for achieving this goal. Until that time, many firms had failed to meet the Goods Mobilization Plan because they were still seeking profits, not following production plans. Deciding that the intervention of shareholder management encouraged the pursuit of profits, the Planning Board set out to reform the system of corporate governance and limit shareholder power.

The Planning Board's attempt to separate capital and management weakened slightly after it sparked strong resistance from the private sector. The Outline on the Establishment of the New Economic System, which was enacted at a Cabinet meeting in December 1940, clearly stated that a firm was "one organic body comprised of capital, management and labor" *(Keizai Shintaisei Kakuritsu Yoko)*.[2] This corporate vision, however, differed dramatically from the prewar concept of the Japanese corporation in that it now treated managers and workers, particularly the latter, as members of a firm on equal footing with shareholders. Practical reforms in the financial system and labor-management relations were thus based on this new philosophy.

In the financial system, by reorganizing the system of indirect financing, the government was able to reduce stockholder control that had been exercised through the capital markets. Under the New Financial System *(Kinyu Shintaisei)*, as the new indirect financing system was called, a bank that had conducted commercial relations would became a managing bank *(kanji ginko)*. Through the intercession of the National Financial Control Association *(Zenkoku Kinyu Toseikai)*, which was effectively administered by the Bank of Japan, the managing bank could then establish a loan syndicate *(kyocho yushidan)*. As the head of the loan syndicate, it also conducted investigations and monitored borrowing firms. In response to the expansion of their new roles, banks allowed their inspection divisions to operate independently and strengthened their inspection mechanisms. The Bank of Japan, which was responsible for monitoring banks, also elevated its investigations division to departmental status. The government further decreased the role of the suppliers of capital in management by increasing labor participation in management activities at each level of a firm's stratified internal organization. This was accomplished by organizing workers into industrywide patriotic organizations *(sangyo hokoku kai)*.

As reforms in the financial system and the labor relations system advanced, shareholders retreated from management activity. Before the war, large shareholders had occupied a considerable proportion of managerial positions in large corporations, but that proportion declined during the war. Managers who had been promoted from within the company began to fill the majority of the positions formerly occupied by large shareholders. The enactment of the Munitions Company Code *(Gunju Kaisha Ho)* of 1943 confirmed this trend. It severely restricted the authority of the general meeting of shareholders that was enshrined in the Commercial Code *(Sho Ho)* and expanded the scope of discretion and authority of company presidents who became the "persons responsible for production" *(seisan sekininsha)*. Accompanying the Munitions Company Code, a system was introduced that assigned a single bank to each corporation. This considerably decreased bank inspection of firms. However, because it also made firm discipline remarkably lax, at the conclusion of the war, yet another systematic reform required designated banks to monitor firms to whom they had lent. Thus, the structure of corporate governance that is characteristic of contemporary Japanese corporations, with its emphasis on employee profits, its minimal role for shareholders, and its important monitoring role delegated to the banks, was established during this phase of the wartime economy.

In these respects, Japan's wartime economy was essentially a planned economy. The bold systemic reforms required for this style of management were undertaken in a variety of areas under the auspices of the strong authority that the government exercised under unusual wartime conditions. These reforms went on to form the basis for today's so-called Japanese-style economic system. In short, the postwar economic recovery was built on the foundations of the wartime economy.

The Postwar Economic Recovery and the Japanese-Style Economic System

The roots of postwar relations between the government and firms can be traced directly back to the wartime economic system, the changes brought about by postwar economic reform, and inflation that continued to equalize the distribution of income and assets begun during the war. The government also dismantled the capital markets that had operated before the war. In other words, postwar changes destroyed the foundations of the prewar economic system. Consequently, reverting to the prewar economic system was no longer an option, and the wartime economic system became an attractive alternative in efforts to rehabilitate the economy. From 1945 to 1948, a wide range of economic controls was implemented, and the planned and controlled wartime economy continued without any major changes. The well-known priority production system, derived from the Plan Concerning the Supply of Goods *(Busshi Jukyu Keikaku),* was essentially the same as its wartime predecessor, the Goods Mobilization Plan.

Furthermore, many postwar reforms advanced the changes in corporate governance that had begun during the war. Though enactment of the Labor Union Law *(Rodo Kumiai Ho)* dramatically strengthened the voice of workers, dissolution of the *zaibatsu* parent companies, concentration of shares in the Holding Company Liquidation Commission *(Mochikabu Gaisha Seiri Iinkai),* property tax policy, and an inflation that contributed to the demise of wealthy private investors all reduced drastically the amount of influence that shareholders wielded over corporations. To maintain the flow of private capital to firms under these conditions, the government reorganized the institution of governance by banks through the Business Reconstruction and Adjustment Law *(Kigyo Saiken Seibi Ho)* and Corporate Accounting Emergency Measures Law *(Kaisha Keiri Okyu Sochi Ho).* The Bank of Japan assisted in forming cooperative financing through loan facilitation as it had done during the war. Economic controls were sporadic, however, and under conditions that virtually guaranteed the existence of the firm, bank regulation did not deter the growth of inefficient corporate management as was indicated by excess employment.

This situation was changed by the move toward a market economy that was precipitated by the Dodge Mission to Japan, which was sent to Tokyo in 1949 to advise on economic policies. Numerous economic controls were rapidly dismantled as Japan faced many of the same challenges confronted today by the former socialist countries. The main bank-centered loan syndicates, which the Bank of Japan had helped form, responded to the changing conditions by intervening in corporate management and forcing greater management efficiency. In the course of the war and shortly thereafter, the balance of the system of corporate governance, which had earlier verged on infringing upon workers' autonomy, was maintained by the intervention of the banks. In response to the changes made to the market economy, the corporate system born during the war was revised and became the foundation of Japan's market economy.

Government intervention in the economy continued in the form of various regulations and industrial policies in areas that did not conflict with the fundamental nature of the market economy. One of the principal tools of postwar industrial policy was the system of foreign exchange allocation. National administration of international trade ended and, as part of the reversion of administrative authority over foreign currency from the Allied Occupation, the Foreign Currency Control Law *(Gaikoku Kawase Kanri Ho)* was enacted in 1949. Using the law, the government supervised foreign currency transactions until it liberalized international trade in the 1960s. Thus, the government exercised its control over foreign currency to carry out its industrial policies.

Moreover, the framework that supported the government's industrial policy was also inherited from the wartime and early postwar periods. Trade associations, which were the direct descendants of the previous control associations, were authorized under the Businessmen's Group Act *(Jigyosha Dantai Ho)* of 1948. This in turn spurred the formation of a wide-ranging network of trade associations. The membership posts of the Economic Reconstruction Planning Committee *(Keizai Fukko Keikaku Iinkai),* which were to be filled by representatives of the private sector, were already occupied by representatives of each trade association. To meet the goal of economic rationalization as set forth by the Dodge Line, however, many of the representatives from the different trade associations also participated in the Industrial Rationalization Screening Association *(Sangyo Gorika Shingikai),* which had been created by the Ministry of International Trade and Industry.

This system of deliberation councils and trade associations played a crucial role in government efforts to coordinate the rationalization of complementary industries (for example, iron and steel and machinery or iron and steel and shipbuilding), thus paving the way for Japan's strong international competitiveness in these areas. Needless to say, the success of this effort hinged largely upon the quality of the information that was used in the selection of strategic industries and the coordination of development policies. The deliberation councils and trade associations responded to these needs by gathering information at the enterprise level, relaying it to the government, and then finally disseminating it to the firms.

Thus postwar Japanese industrial policy took advantage of the distinctive features of the financial system as discussed above. Representatives of financial institutions had participated in the Industrial Rationalization Screening Association from its inception, but, with the establishment of the Industrial Fund Section Committee *(Sangyo Shikin Bukai)* within the association, financial institutions carried out industrial policy even more systematically. The Industrial Rationalization Screening Association Industrial Fund Section Committee worked with the Ministry of Finance's Financial Institution Fund Council *(Okurasho Kinyu Kikan Shikin Shingikai)* and the National Bank Association's Fund Coordinating Committee *(Zenkoku Ginko Kyokai Shikin Chosei Iinkai),* which were established in 1956 and 1957 respectively, to coordinate the funding of investment in factories and equipment. While supplementing the capacity of financial institutions to inspect individual industries and the latest technologies, this system also facilitated financial evaluations of industrial policy as a whole.

Conclusion

Indeed, the modern Japanese economic system has a surprisingly short history. The prewar Japanese economy differed significantly from today's and possessed many characteristics of a classic market economy. In an environment that featured a highly fluid labor market and large capital markets, corporations operated under a system of corporate governance that resembled the classic joint-stock corporation. The main actors in this system, namely the *zaibatsu* and prominent private investors, also played an intermediary role in the relationship between the government and the private sector.

In the end, the economic mobilization that accompanied World War II upset and changed Japan's economic system insofar as the government introduced planning and control systems to manage the wartime economy. A number of systemic reforms thus lay at the root of these structural changes to the economy. What is intriguing here is that most of the systems introduced as part of the institutional base of the wartime planned economy were maintained in the postwar period. After the changes seen during the transformation to a market economy, these systems functioned as the systemic base of the new market economy. There are two possible explanations for this outcome. The first explanation is that the multiplicity of systems introduced during the war possessed a mutually supportive character (systemic complementarity), known as one cause of path dependence. The second possible explanation is that the many postwar reforms dismantled the systemic base of the prewar economic system. When the two explanations are considered together, one is led to conclude that a return to the prewar economic system following the war was impossible. The Japanese market economy can therefore be considered unique because, although it is certainly a market economy, certain key elements of its systemic foundation were introduced under a planned and controlled economic system.

Notes

1. For a more detailed explanation, see Tetsuji Okazaki, and Masahiro Okuno, ed., *Gendai Nihon Keizai Shisutemu no Genryo* (Historical origins of the contemporary Japanese economic system) (Nihon Keizai Shimbunsha, 1993); and Tetsuji Okazaki, *Nihon Seido Kaikaku to Keizai Shisutemu no Tenkan* (Japan—System reform and changes in the economic system); [Shakai Keizaishigaku] (Social Economic History), vol. 60, no.1 (1994).

2. Bureau of Research, Bank of Japan, ed., *Nihan Kinyushi Shiryo* (Materials on the financial history of Japan), vol. 34 (Tokyo: Ministry of Finance,1973), pp. 147–48.

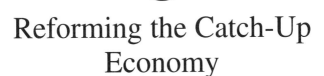

CHAPTER TWO

Reforming the Catch-Up Economy

Iwao Nakatani

NATHAN ROSENBERG of Stanford University, in his extremely valuable work with L.E. Birdzell, argues that innovation originates from the extent to which society permits individual autonomy and diverse values.[1] Because innovation tends to come from recently established firms rather than from entrenched ones, innovation in any society will depend upon how easily firms are created and how easily they enter the market. Therefore, he concludes, under authoritarian social systems, efforts by leaders to sponsor and promote innovation will ultimately achieve limited success.

This argument is extremely persuasive in light of the Western experience. Western popular revolutions, though painful, have brought about an unprecedented level of individual liberty. Moreover, many Western societies have achieved tremendous political and economic success. However, it is important to remember that it took a long time to build liberal economic systems with the market mechanism undeniably at their core, and many complications have arisen in the course of liberal economic development. Nevertheless, Western societies have amassed unrivaled wealth and achieved a high standard of living. What are the implications of this for the many developing countries that follow in the footsteps of the Western experience?

Rosenberg's argument is, in all likelihood, correct for those countries that have led the world economy. However, for the many countries that are still pursuing rapid economic development, perhaps only half of the argument is valid. Rather than developing cutting-edge technology by themselves, they can achieve much faster results by absorbing advanced technology and knowledge from the advanced industrial economies. Then, they can leverage this technology by commercializing it at relatively low cost. This method can be described as "studying and absorbing" the technological and organizational fruits of the advanced economies. When supported by conscious public policy choices, this method of "studying and absorbing" is more rational for developing countries seeking to catch up with Western economies than attempting basic research. In this sense, almost all contemporary, developing economies can be said to be "learning societies" rather than "innovating" societies.

Anthropologist Karl Polanyi argues that for the market mechanism to work, a minimal amount of social preparation is indispensable. He suggests that such preparation include a system of laws as well as a certain concept of individuality.[2] In the real world, the framework for a market economy does not simply appear overnight. Rather, a well-designed infrastructure, which is necessary to the success of a market economy, must be built and firmly established in society. Only then will a market economy begin to function.

From this perspective, for two important reasons, the role of government in developing countries and the significance of regulatory and industrial policies are essentially different from those in advanced industrial economies. First, the type of regulatory policy must change with the economic development of the country. Any regulatory policy can be evaluated only on the basis of that country's level of economic development. Second, only if a country has industrialized does Rosenberg's argument become appropriate. In other words, because innovation is the source of economic development in advanced economies, the only method of promoting innovation is maximizing the potential of market forces by guaranteeing freedom of choice and the freedom to enter and exit the market that is at the heart of individual economic enterprise. Thus, for an industrialized economy, retaining the regulatory policies of its period of economic development is not simply undesirable. It is counterproductive because it will prevent the creation of knowledge necessary to maintain a high level of income.

Therefore, when analyzing the effect and the significance of regulatory and industrial policy, it is important to understand clearly the following: If the market mechanism is to work, preparations must be introduced gradually. Industrial policy compensates for the incompleteness of the market and must correspond with a country's level of economic development. It should change as a country develops economically.

The Role of Industrial Policy in the Economic Development of East Asia

Industrial policy can be defined as the overall set of policies that correct and compensate for market failures that cause problems in the distribution of resources or the distribution of income as a result of deficiencies in the structure of a competitive market.

The nature and scope of these structural deficiencies change not according to the sectors involved but rather with the stage of the economy being considered. For example, in developing countries, capital markets do not allocate capital as efficiently as they do in advanced economies because capital accumulation is difficult. Therefore, the number of investors who can participate in the market is limited. In situations in which trading in capital markets cannot take place widely, even if capital markets are fully liberalized, these markets will not distribute their capital efficiently. In this kind of economy, an industrial policy must first liberalize the capital markets partially to build the infrastructure necessary for capital to be allocated efficiently.

Accordingly, the usefulness of government intervention in some sectors of the economy as a means of implementing industrial policy will likely decrease as an economy develops. Because the scope of the "deficiencies of the market structure" decreases as an economy develops, the extent of government intervention required to compensate for these deficiencies will also decrease. Therefore, industrial policy needs to be sensitive to the changing needs of a maturing economy. It must be tailored to the needs of the targeted industries, and it must take into account the extent of incentives that are available to guide the distribution of resources.

In the past ten or more years, the East Asian region has assumed a central role in the economic development of the world. Why is it that neither Africa nor Latin America has taken off economically? Why has only East Asia experienced tremendous economic growth? The fundamental factor may have been the "information link." In other words, the information that is indispensable to economic development—technology, production management techniques, and marketing know-how—has flowed through the region along with capital, and it has been this flow of information that has become the source of East Asia's dynamism. Economists often refer to this phenomenon as the "flying geese development pattern" or as the "multilayered pursuit" of capital.[3]

Just as the lead goose blocks the wind for the geese that trail it, Japan was the first country to succeed in doubling its international competitiveness by introducing advanced technology from the West and transforming that technology into manufactured products. Following on Japan's successful strategy, the Asian newly industrialized economies (NIEs) industrialized, and their vitality spread to the Association of Southeast Asian Nations (ASEAN) countries and then to the coastal regions of China and Vietnam. As a result, Asia is now the center of global economic growth exhibiting a dynamism of historic proportions.

In Africa and Latin America, the "information chain" mentioned above has broken. It has been difficult for African countries to absorb the advanced technology of Europe and to link it to their own economic development. One reason for this is that the technological gap is striking and that there has been no effective way to transfer the technology as there has been in Asia. Latin America, unable to resist the influx of capital from the United States, has accumulated external debt because it has been unable to link American technology constructively to its own economic development. In both of these regions, no industrial policy has created the proper framework for propagating the information that accompanies advanced technology. Rather, these regions have become well integrated into the market mechanism of the Western economies but have been unable to cultivate the "seeds" of independent growth. In contrast, the countries of East Asia have implemented an industrial policy that compensates for the "inadequacies in the market" depending on their respective levels of economic development. Furthermore, they have artfully absorbed foreign technology and capital in a form appropriate to their own capacity. In fact the economic liberalization of each of these countries has been gradual precisely because each country has taken the time to build the infrastructure required, such as the appropriate legal framework and tax system, and the requisite social capital. Because these countries have selected this type of strategic industrial policy in accordance with their respective level of economic development, they have forged the information link that is required to make the transition from developing economy to developed economy. This approach toward industrial policy has helped East Asia achieve the highest economic growth rate in the world.

Even with an abundant supply of information, technology, and capital, the recipient country will not be able to absorb these factors of production effectively without adequate preparation. If a country ignores the level of its economic development and decides to transform itself quickly into a laissez-faire market economy, in many cases this endeavor will simply end in failure. The reason that the Russian plan to move to a market economy has not succeeded is that there is no program for moving toward a market economy that takes into account Russia's current level of economic development. In short, without the prerequisites of a market economy, that is, the various systems—capital markets, financial systems, tax systems—needed to support it, and without the ethical and spiritual preparation of participants in the market, the market will not function properly no matter how much effort is made to promote it. The Russian case has revealed that insufficient technology for increasing agricultural yields, insufficiently prepared financial and labor markets, and an insufficient accumulation of technical experience undermine the attempt to create a market economy.

Despite being a socialist country, China has achieved striking economic success in recent years because it has adopted an orderly program of economic reform that requires a "staged" process of transformation to a market economy by encouraging market reforms in special economic zones. The Chinese government's recent articulation of its concept of a socialist market economy suggests that it does not aspire to the kind of market economy that Russia has attempted. Although maintaining its central political authority, the Chinese government is moving toward a market economy in a staged process. Recently, China has encountered basic problems, such as inflation, associated with moving too quickly toward a market economy without sufficient infrastructure to sustain the market.

The Current Need for Economic Reform in Light of the Postwar Development of the Japanese Economy

Given the postwar economic history of Japan, I would like to analyze the current Japanese economy and consider what role the Japanese government should assume in the future.

In the fifty years since the end of World War II, Japan has become a leading economic power as a result of repeated government efforts to increase economic growth. Four basic characteristics have defined the Japanese economic system during the postwar period. First, there have been close relations between government and business. Second, the government has deliberately created a system of indirect financing that distributes resources well. Third, the "catch-up model" strategy adopted by Japanese firms has aimed at absorbing technology from the advanced economies rather than at innovating. The Japanese firms have built on this base of imported technology by adapting and improving it. Finally, the fourth characteristic of Japan's economic system can be identified as a commitment to social equality.[4]

The Close Relationship between Government and Business

There are a variety of arguments about the effectiveness of the industrial policy of the Ministry of International Trade and Industry (MITI). From their empirical research on the impact of Japan's industrial policy, many economists have come to negative conclusions about MITI's performance. However, some care needs to be exercised in the interpretation of these results. In much of their statistical analysis, they have focused solely on the variables and data that can be quantified. There is a possibility that they have overlooked the major impact of MITI's policies.

The so-called priority production method of the late 1940s was a typical industrial policy because it concentrated economic resources on targeted sectors of the economy. However, as the standard of living improved and a diverse range of consumer goods was required, this policy lost its efficacy. The tax incentives for investment in plant modernization and the strict capital controls of the late 1950s and early 1960s were a typical industrial policy designed to protect infant industries, specifically the automobile and computer industries. But when these industries reached a certain level of competitiveness, these policies were gradually abolished.

Many regulations or special tax measures and subsidies also become unnecessary as the desired target is met. MITI has changed its industrial policy as Japan has grown economically. As a mature economy, Japan has no need for industrial policies aimed at specific sectors of the economy today. Many regulations, special tax preferences, and subsidies should be abolished now with few exceptions. The spirit of the argument for liberalizing Japan's economy as presented in the Hiraiwa Report[5] should be respected. Moreover, the regulations that assist "weaklings"—like the Foodstuff Control Law and the Large-Scale Retail Store Law—should be modified to reflect a more comprehensive income redistribution policy such as a system of progressive taxation on consumption or a social insurance policy. An industrial policy that attempts to limit competition by restricting the distribution of resources should not be implemented. However, the largest problem for Japan is that despite its high level of economic development, elements of the old policies that were created for a developing economy still remain in place. Japan should now build the infrastructure needed for the market to function fully, including abolishing regulations, reassessing the government-business relationship, strengthening the antimonopoly law, and requiring information disclosure.

Even if Chalmers Johnson's assertions about the strength of MITI's influence are debatable, more detailed evidence is needed to support the argument that MITI's postwar industrial policy, a policy that drew in the powerful industrial groups, was, in fact, meaningless. More important, if a given policy that was useful at a certain stage becomes ineffective, or even detrimental, at the next stage of development, will the political climate always support the will that is necessary to abolish these kinds of policies? Even if regulations or industrial policies have outlived their usefulness, forces that fear a loss of their special privileges often oppose the termination of industrial policies or the abolition of regulations. Contemporary Japanese politics reflects this sort of dilemma. Consequently, the Japanese economy cannot respond appropriately to the demands currently being placed on it, and thus it has experienced a prolonged recession.

A System of Indirect Financing

The Japanese financial system depends on indirect financing, including public financial institutions such as the Japan Development Bank. For some time, the government has supplied capital mainly to targeted industries. In fact, at present the financial systems of the countries of East Asia that are in the midst of this rapid catch-up process have similarly organized financial systems. In terms of supplying capital, indirect financing is the most effective means of supporting the development of specific industries. In contrast, financing systems, where the capital is supplied by many investors and supply flows through stock or bond markets, are controlled by the market. Thus they are not conducive to industrial policy.

At its current level of economic maturity, the Japanese economy needs the basic preparations for a direct financial system that can provide less risk-averse capital, like the venture capital available in the U.S. financial market. In this sense, the Japanese financial system needs to be overhauled. Current efforts at financial reform by the Ministry of Finance have made little, if any, progress because they rely too heavily on past experience in simply making adjustments in existing privileges and not fundamental changes. Perhaps for this reason, Japanese capital is rapidly losing its substance, because there are many aspects of the financial system that inhibit competition and there is absolutely no sign of a supply of less risk-averse money. Even without drawing a comparison to the U.S. example, it is clear that it is not major industries that stimulate growth in a mature economy. The stimulus comes instead from new ventures (that is, the enterprises that lead the global information industry such as Intel, Microsoft, and Silicon Graphics, were all nurtured by U.S. venture capital). In recent years, the percentage of new industries in the Japanese market has been quite low relative to the demands of the time.

The Japanese Firm's "Catch-Up" Strategy

The strategy of Japanese enterprises has most often been to catch up. In other words, rather than aiming at revolutionary innovations, these enterprises have essentially pursued a strategy of quickly absorbing Western technological advances and then adapting and improving that technology to increase their competitiveness. All developing countries practice this strategy. The difference is that Japan has been extraordinarily effective in implementing it. However, this catch-up strategy works only for developing countries. The means by which the people of the country with the world's highest income can maintain its competitiveness is by continually innovating.

However, the nature of Japanese enterprises is not conducive to innovation. The reason for this is that the philosophy of equality discussed below has permeated these firms "excessively." Rather than individual creativity, these firms have emphasized the learning capacity of the group. The incentive mechanism that Rosenberg argues is indispensable to innovation is produced in an enterprise culture that allows individuals to engage in creative projects. This mechanism does not exist in many major Japanese firms. Japan's performance in the computer game industry can serve as an example. While Japan's traditional large firms that deal in computer software cannot hold a candle to their venture-backed competitors from the United States, Japanese companies have dominated the games-software field. They have done so by abolishing the organizational principles that have characterized Japanese firms in the past, creating a nonhierarchical environment conducive to innovation.

"Excessive" Egalitarianism

The strength of Japanese firms to date has been their egalitarianism: all company employees are treated as equally as possible. Lifetime employment and the seniority system are just one aspect of this philosophy. Among those who enter a company at the same time, differentials among wages or salary are kept to a minimum. Egalitarianism has the effect of, on the one hand, dampening the ambitions of those employees who are noteworthy and, on the other hand, heightening the group spirit of the entire company and raising the overall morale of company employees. So long as the company employee makes no major mistakes, does not display any presumptuous behavior, supports seniors, and makes an effort, he will gradually ascend the company ladder along with those who enter the company at the same time. Without a doubt, this pattern has been a major source of corporate morale in postwar Japan.

Nonetheless, egalitarianism is becoming a barrier to the innovative capacity of Japanese firms in today's mature economy. The dangers of an egalitarianism that hinders exceptional human resources are quite obvious for a country that must meet the challenge of developing new concepts and lead the global economy rather than imitate the developed economies. To encourage new concepts and progressive innovation, individuals must be encouraged to challenge the limits of their own capability.

Under the current form of egalitarianism this explosion will not be forthcoming. To encourage those individuals who are likely to engage in the tremendous task of shaking their companies' profit structure at its very foundations, an enterprise culture and incentive system that will provide the deserved appreciation and rewards are necessary. In this sense, the evaluation system found in Japanese firms that reflects an egalitarian philosophy will need to be fundamentally overhauled.

Conclusion

Over the past fifty years, the Japanese economy achieved phenomenal success using the catch-up model of economic growth. However, that economy is today facing one of its greatest economic challenges. Since it entered the 1990s, Japan's economy has been in a persistent state of decline. In recent years, its economy has been one of the worst performers even within the Organization of Economic Cooperation and Development. Japan has surmounted such difficulties in the past. After experiencing fifty years of political and economic success after the Meiji Restoration, the Japanese economy entered an economic downturn that lasted longer than ten years. Economic systems thrive or lose their relevance and power based on whether their rules of competition, organization structures, and fundamental relationships among individuals can evolve fast enough to keep up with changing times. If a country loses its capacity to change, at some point its economic system will no longer maintain its vitality. Without a doubt, this will produce a long period of economic stagnation. The Japanese economy of the 1920s could not respond to the "second industrial revolution" that was unfolding in Europe and the United States. The Japanese economy of the 1990s is missing the massive "third industrial revolution" (or the information revolution) being led by the United States. So long as Japan fails to make a rapid shift from the economic system of the catch-up model to a system that is open to the world and allows the freedom and diversity that will facilitate the emergence of creative innovation, Japan's prospects will not be bright.

Reforming Japan's social structure—abolishing regulation, opening markets, reorganizing capital markets, and reforming the character of Japanese companies—should not be undertaken because of pressure from outside Japan. Rather, it is an indispensable task if Japan is to improve the prospects for its own future.

Notes

1. Nathan Rosenberg and L. E. Birdzell, *How the West Grew Rich* (Basic Books, 1986).

2. Karl Polanyi, *The Great Transformation* (Beacon Press, 1944).

3. Kaname Akamatsu, *Sekai Keizairon* (Tokyo: Kokugen Shobo, 1965); and Toshio Watanabe, *Seicho no Ajia, Teizai no Ajia* (Tokyo: Toyo Keizai Shinbunsha, 1985).

4. Yukio Noguchi, *1940-nen Taisei* (Tokyo: Toyo Keizai Shinbunsha, 1985).

5. Gaishi Hiraiwa, *Hiraiwa Report* (Tokyo: Advisory Group for Economic Structural Reform, December 1993).

CHAPTER THREE

Politicians, Bureaucrats, and Policymaking in Japan

Yasuhiro Nakasone

IN A DEMOCRACY, sovereignty rests with the people and public opinion is integral to decisionmaking. The positive input of public opinion in the political process relies critically on the people's capability to make sound judgments on policy, and on fair and clean elections. Thus, importantly, journalism must be without bias. Yet how have political policies actually been shaped in Japan? Of course, the government implements policies and is in turn overseen by parliament, while the role of political parties is to mediate between these two institutions. But, as I see it, the whole process is influenced to a large degree by institutionalized interests: special interest groups, *zoku giin* (politicians who specialize in the policy area of specific ministries), and especially the bureaucracy.

The state bureaucracies of Japan and France have been called the most competent in the world. The Japanese bureaucracy, through its cumulative knowledge and experience, works like a giant think tank for the nation. In the aftermath of World War II, Japan's bureaucrats, who had previously answered directly to the emperor, became civil servants and were expected to look to elected government figures for direction. Partly because of the inability of the political parties to formulate viable policy programs, however, this leadership was not always forthcoming. To the

This chapter originally appeared in the *Asia-Pacific Review,* vol. 2 (Spring 1995), published by the International Institute for Policy Studies, Tokyo.

extent that the politicians were weak policymakers, the Ministry of Finance, the Ministry of International Trade and Industry, and recently the Ministry of Posts and Telecommunications, expanded their powerful influence on policymaking.

Politicians are pitchers, bureaucrats their catchers. A good pitcher decides himself if he will throw a fastball or a curve, but a weak pitcher throws the pitches as his catcher signals them. I have always believed that our politicians should make, and take responsibility for, their own decisions. In this chapter I outline the basic character of political decisionmaking as it has developed over the course of postwar history; factors that have influenced this process; and how the shortcomings of policymaking in Japan in the future can be overcome.

The Postwar Pattern of Bureaucratic Decisionmaking

The period from the latter half of the Allied Occupation through the early 1950s has been called the Yoshida era. It was a time when Japan laid the foundations for the reconstruction of its war-devastated economy, and the presence of the United States exercised enormous influence on the political process. Prime Minister Shigeru Yoshida (1878–1967) made full use of American authority to consolidate his leadership. At the core of the power structure he built were bureaucrats. The Ministry of Home Affairs of prewar times had been dismantled, but the Ministry of Finance remained intact, exerting tremendous influence on policymaking through budget control and other means. Not coincidentally, the finance minister at the time was Hayato Ikeda, one of Yoshida's closest confidants.

In 1955 conservative political forces united to form the Liberal Democratic Party (LDP), while socialists from the right and left merged to organize the Japan Socialist Party (now known as the Social Democratic Party of Japan, or SDPJ). Under the "1955 regime," the LDP formed the government while the Socialists perennially remained in opposition. This two-party system flourished during the cold war years mainly because it reflected the bipolar ideology in the international arena. Achievements in foreign and security policy showed that Japan clearly sided with the West and participated in the free world economically as well as politically.

The stability of this arrangement enabled bureaucrats to orchestrate Japan's period of rapid economic growth. Japan's bureaucrats are inherently growth oriented. Politicians depended heavily upon the planning and executive know-how of the bureaucracy to pursue economic growth. At the center during this period were a group of former top-level bureaucrats, Nobusuke Kishi, Hayato Ikeda, and Eisaku Sato—all of whom became prime ministers.

During this period, the business community and the Ministry of International Trade and Industry (MITI) held tremendous sway. Behind the prime ministers, most notably Ikeda, were business leaders such as the famous "four kings" (the chief executives of New Japan Steel, the Japan Development Bank, the textile giant Nisshinbo, and the media group Fuji Sankei), who wielded a great deal of influence over Japanese politics. Moreover, since the prime ministers themselves were ex-bureaucrats, they were able to mobilize the necessary bureaucratic talents to achieve high growth rates. At the time, career politicians—whose main experience was in politics, not bureaucracy—had a weak standing. This did not change even during the administrations of Kakuei Tanaka (1972–74), Takeo Fukuda (1976–78), and Masayoshi Ohira (1980).

The Japan Socialist Party (JSP), for its part, was heavily dependent on support from *Sohyo* (General Council of Trade Unions of Japan). This national center of labor, the largest in Japan until its dissolution in 1989, consisted mainly of unionized government and public corporation employees, which put the JSP under the rather strong influence of lower-echelon bureaucrats. Thus the two major political parties in Japan were, beneath the surface, heavily reliant upon the bureaucracy. This structure enabled the LDP and JSP to work together on occasion, reaching compromises on many issues, such as the National Personnel Authority recommendations on wages for government and public enterprise workers.

Importantly, however, while the bureaucracy did indeed acquire a great deal of power, its influence was exercised mainly in administrative implementation. It is also true that the bureaucracy did in effect set policy in some areas, principally those that required economic vision and expertise—such as Japan's participation in the International Monetary Fund and the Organization for Economic Cooperation and Development, and Japan's transition from an industrial to a post-industrial state. But the important political decisions and policies of the time were made by politicians and their parties: Shigeru Yoshida—the peace treaty and the original security pact with the United States; Ichiro Hatoyama—the Russo-Japanese peace talks; Kishi—the revised security treaty with the United States; Ikeda—the income-doubling policies of the 1960s; Sato—

the return of Okinawa; Tanaka—the restoration of diplomatic ties with China; and my administration—political reform, the privatization of the national railways and the national telephone monopoly, and trade talks with the United States. The first administrations formed by career politicians were Takeo Miki's (1974–76) and my own (1982–87). In the wake of the money-tainted Tanaka government, Miki stressed reform and clean politics. I sought to decrease the power of the bureaucracy through administrative reform.

My Days as Prime Minister

Before and after the war, I was a bureaucrat in the Ministry of Home Affairs. But since my days as a member of the opposition Democratic Party in the 1950s, I have been critical of the bureaucrat-centered political system created by Yoshida because I feel policymakers should be publicly accountable. As a member of the Commission on the Constitution, I engaged in a thorough review of the Constitution and proposed a system of popular elections for the office of prime minister instead of Diet (parliament) elections. Then, and later when I became prime minister, I tried to take my cues from the U.S. presidential system.

Inspired by the account in Theodore White's *The Making of the President, 1960*, which told how John F. Kennedy created the famous Kennedy machine and made himself U.S. president, my administration mobilized many of the best and brightest in Japan to advise us on both domestic and foreign affairs.[1] Personally, I benefited a great deal from relationships formed during my time in the Imperial Navy during the war. Many of these outstanding young men later went on to important careers in business or government, and their assistance helped me in the formulation of policy and in the persuasion of party and Diet members.

As prime minister, I insisted on a bold program of reassessing postwar politics in three areas: Japan's inward-looking attitude on foreign policy; the excessive scope of the national bureaucracy; and the lack of power in the office of prime minister. First, I looked at foreign policy. Japan had become preoccupied with its own peace and prosperity, pursuing a course of unilateral pacifism made possible by continued dependence upon the United States following the Allied Occupation (1945–52). In the LDP, a strong tendency to adhere to outmoded, introverted attitudes toward national security and foreign policy prevailed, even when international circumstances began to call for a more active role by Japan. These attitudes, essentially a holdover from the Yoshida era, no longer mesh with the international environment.

Second, with help from private sector leaders, I set up many councils to deal with administrative reform. I felt that it was necessary to scale down the size of government agencies and organizations that had grown excessively during the course of rapid economic growth. The tendency toward centralization of state authority, which dated back to the Meiji period (1868–1912), had to be reversed. Under a powerful central government, Japan vigorously moved forward to catch up with the West. Meanwhile, government agencies vied with one another to increase their spheres of jurisdiction. Japan has caught up, but excessive government regulations and control are inhibiting the continued development of free-market-style capitalism and slowing the growth of the Japanese economy.

We are now in an age of information and computerization, an age that values individualistic, broad-minded, and flexible ways of thinking. The concept of restrictive, centralist control by an oversized bureaucracy—which developed from the Meiji through the high-growth period—can no longer provide the necessary leadership. This explains the exigency of governmental reform in Japan today.

Finally, it was necessary to reconsider the *primus inter pares* concept as it applied to the office of prime minister and the cabinet. In the prewar days, the prime minister's position was that of assistant to the emperor, and because the prime minister was no more than first among equals, he could not even discharge one of his cabinet ministers. Resignation of one minister meant resignation of the entire cabinet. After the war, under the new Constitution, the emperor became a symbolic figure. The prime minister was invested with supreme command over the armed forces and the power to dismiss ministers. Together with his cabinet, he also recommended the appointment of justices to the Supreme Court. Furthermore, because the LDP controlled the majority of parliamentary seats, LDP prime ministers controlled the Diet. Thus, theoretically at least, Japan's prime minister holds greater power in domestic politics than even the president of the United States. During my time in office, I tried to use this power in practice.

New Challenges

The 1955 regime supported by the two major parties weakened and finally broke down owing to the drastic global changes that culminated in the collapse of the Soviet Union. As both Moscow and Washington quickly lost their respective hegemonic status, their "magnetic power" to coalesce other nations declined perceptibly. As a result, peoples and nations became exceedingly aware of their autonomy, and individuals, ethnic groups, states, and regions began to assert their own identities. The Japanese, too, have come to a time of contemplation, of pondering how the nation should move from the regulatory and ideological structure sustained by the U.S.-Soviet confrontation to a new era of greater diversity. During the years from the Takeshita to the Hata administrations, centrifugal forces exerted greater strength than centripetal forces. It became difficult to get anything done through established procedures. The breakup of the 1955 regime led to the spread of anti-LDP sentiment both among the public and in the media, a trend encouraged by revelations of corruption and bribery.

The caliber of politicians themselves has changed today. In *Japan's New Global Role*, Brookings Institution senior fellow Edward Lincoln presents a fascinating study of how much the demobilized military contributed to Japan's postwar economic growth, especially in its early stages.[2] College-educated young men, discharged after the war, returned to take up positions in business, government, journalism, and academia. Their experiences gave them a much better perspective of the country as a whole, and they gave serious thought to how the nation's unity might be maintained. Having endured hardships, they set about the rehabilitation of their war-ravaged country with determination and energy.

In 1993 the emergence of the coalition government led by Morihiro Hosokawa brought an end to nearly four decades of LDP rule. Born in 1938 and educated after the war ended, Hosokawa essentially belongs to the *après-guerre* generation. People of this generation do not know poverty and war. They have been raised in relatively affluent circumstances, are accustomed to watching TV, driving cars, eating good food, and enjoying many kinds of leisure activities. They are now rising to positions of leadership in national politics and in the political parties, as Lincoln points out. These younger and often less experienced politicians have more difficulty in asserting themselves vis-à-vis the bureaucracy. Like a horse that recognizes his rider's ability and accordingly behaves either in an obedient or intractable manner, bureaucrats are most cooperative when led by strong politicians.

Although the coalition between the LDP and SDPJ has brought back some stability to Japanese politics, mainly by putting veteran politicians back into positions of control, certain irreversible changes have taken place. Yet other changes need to be made. The continued dependence on nonelected bureaucrats for information and policy know-how is fettering the democratic development of our nation. Political decisions must be placed firmly in the hands of elected politicians. They bring not only democratic legitimacy but also conviction and historical perspective to the policy process. Let me outline what I consider to be important ingredients of decisionmaking by politicians and parties.

Political Decisionmaking: Factors That Influence the Process

The crucial factor in politics is the relationship between the office of the prime minister and the party or coalition that supports him. Disharmony makes the cabinet weak, while harmony allows the prime minister—both in his official capacity and as party president—to make the personnel appointments crucial to effective political decisions. Next to personnel decisions, public support for the cabinet is most important in determining this power relationship.

This is an age of television politics. In Japan, new programs such as "News Station," or internationally, the news channel CNN, wield enormous influence on political decisionmaking. In some ways, the scrutiny of the media has a democratizing effect. Although the media should not be mistaken as an exact reflection of public opinion, the media are useful as a gauge to measure public support. Public support ratings have great impact on the prime minister's ability to carry out key policies.

Party primary elections are meaningful in choosing the party president, as are popular elections for the office of prime minister. A primary election was held when I ran for the LDP presidency, and after one month of nationwide campaigning I won by a wide margin. Direct, enthusiastic support from the people enabled me to ignore sometimes unreasonable demands from the party bosses. Unfortunately, many of Japan's recent prime ministers have been chosen by *dango*—backroom agreements among party bosses, be they LDP faction leaders or coalition party heads. This selection process has made it difficult for them to obtain strong support bases, and as a result they have served short terms. This is reminiscent of the Fourth Republic in France, where, until de Gaulle, there were twenty-two prime ministers in twelve years, and France relied on able but unelected bureaucrats for continuity in government.

A given administration's public support is particularly sensitive to foreign policy, especially to the prime minister's performance at summit meetings, his contribution to or criticism from the Group of Seven (G7), and to negotiations with other countries. The public's attention to foreign policy problems has sharpened considerably since the advent of television. Should we stand by, for example, as SS 20 missiles are removed from Europe only to be reinstalled in Siberia? Can anything be done to counter the appreciation of the yen? If these issues are left to the bureaucrats alone, Japan may be unable to earn the respect of other nations and to voice its concerns in the world.

The human element is the other decisive factor in determining a prime minister's policymaking ability. Selection of a person of outstanding caliber as party secretary general is decisive, for it is the secretary general that the prime minister (party president) consults on key policies and appointments. Examples of successful teams are Prime Minister Sato with Kakuei Tanaka as secretary general, Shigeru Hori as chief cabinet secretary, and Shojiru Kawashima as vice president of the party or Prime Minister Ikeda and his vice president Bamboku Ono.

In the case of a coalition government, the presence of point men capable of bringing different parties and viewpoints together is crucial. In my administration's coalition with the New Liberal Club (NLC), LDP Secretary General Rokusuke Tanaka and the NLC's Toshio Yamaguchi performed this vital function. Behind the Hosokawa and Hata administrations were the Shinseito's Ichiro Ozawa and the Komeito's Yuichi Ichikawa. Noboru Takeshita has been rumored to have brokered the Murayama coalition. No coalition, much less an eight-horse team, will work without such point men.

Another example of the importance of highly capable personnel concerns crisis management. Of the various unexpected developments in the past decade, let me single out the Korean Airlines incident (1983) and the Persian Gulf War (1990). What the prime minister needs most in such cases is the able assistance of the chief cabinet secretary and the ruling party's secretary general. They are the first to get information, using the Cabinet Intelligence Office, the Foreign Ministry, and all other available agencies and sources. Timing makes all the difference. During the Korean Airlines incident, I relied heavily on efficient teamwork among the secretaries to develop prompt responses. Such teamwork has been missing in recent years. During the Gulf War, the chief cabinet secretary's position was weak, and Japan responded poorly to the situation. This lack of a crisis management system represents one of the country's principal weaknesses. Bureaucrats cannot set up a crisis management system until the political leadership on which it depends is forthcoming.

Overcoming the Shortcomings of Policymaking in Japan

What can we do to boost our nation's decisionmaking capability? Increasing power in the hands of politicians is not a simple matter. The parties and politicians have to improve their policy know-how and decisionmaking abilities. Although most members of the Diet today are career politicians, they have come to think and act like bureaucrats. But politicians should be different: they must have both insight and courage. Courage comes from morality. Once politicians become aware of what path Japan ought to take, they should be ready to commit their whole person to steer in that direction. Politicians must have this sort of spiritedness and responsibility and must be willing at times to go against the consensus. What needs to be done? Six points come to mind:

First, it is vital to review and restudy the basic rules of politics and remind ourselves of the importance of these rules. There are almost no newspaper editorials that argue for certain positions from the point of view of political values and principles. The reluctance of journalists in Japan to take a firm stand looks very irresponsible in comparison with the writing in the *New York Times* or the *Washington Post*. Journalists and scholars alike should raise their voices on questions of basic political principles and warn the public of the danger associated with the absence of principles in Japanese politics today.

In the past, there was an expression: *kensei no jodo* (the way of constitutional government). This expression embodied the old rules of constitutional government, which provided Japanese democracy with an ethical guidebook for political behavior for a long time. But today, there is no morality in sight. No one is surprised any longer if the prime minister says one thing today and the opposite tomorrow. The weight of works and speeches, of political responsibility, is gone. One would expect newspaper editorials to furiously denounce this moral bankruptcy of democratic politics. Why are they silent?

Second, alignments among politicians should be determined by their principles and policy goals, not by old grudges and personal feelings. Personal matters should not interfere with the representation of the people's will. In these times of social disintegration, selfish opportunism seems to prevail, but politicians must have foresight and act courageously, guided by political philosophy. If everyone puts up his banner openly, debate in the Diet can be more meaningful and represent different views. So-called consensus decisionmaking is nothing but an excuse for backroom deals by men who do not have the confidence to take a stand openly.

Third, political funding should be secured. Because the Japanese prime minister has the right to dissolve the House of Representatives at any time, the unstable governments of the past year made younger members of the House of Representatives especially live in constant fear of a sudden general election. Being chronically short of political funds they could not fight an election campaign that routinely costs tens of millions of yen. Even senior Diet members may have to sell long-treasured family assets to obtain funds for campaigns. Some parties have institutional sources of funding: the Soka Gakkai Church supports the Komeito, the labor unions help out the SDPJ. In the case of the LDP, the business community traditionally performed the same function, but their contributions have all but dried up. Because unstable sources of funding are a major cause of corruption, the Diet passed a new law in January 1994, which stipulates support for politicians from national coffers.

Let us hope that this decision will indeed create some security. Nevertheless, I believe democracy is still best served when it is supported by the people, not by the state. Max Weber's *Politik als Beruf* showed how political parties developed from loose associations of local notables who commanded the respect of their constituents to strictly bureaucratic organizations of professional politicians. Although I believe that professionalism and expertise are very important for responsible politics, politicians should not become like bureaucrats. They should always remember the ideal of the local notables.

Fourth, the despotic tendencies among party leaders we have witnessed of late must be controlled. If political funds from national coffers go to political parties, this means that power will be concentrated in the hands of those in charge of such funds, namely, the party secretary general. Lawmakers will be reluctant to express opposition to a given policy, or anything else the leadership proposes, if their position on certain committees, for example, is at the mercy of party executives. Integral party structures have to be made more democratic to ensure that a diversity of opinion sustains the party. The vigilance of the media and the general public is crucial in this respect.

Concentration of power in the party's top executives is likely to be decisive with the introduction of the single-seat constituency system. As long as the Japanese people are included to think that "might is right" and to follow and further empower the strong, the result might be worse than the wartime Imperial Rule Assistance Association set up to support the totalitarian regime. What I fear most is that the atmosphere of liberalism, in which minorities are considered worth listening to because they have something to say, may evaporate. As I once told a colleague, numerical superiority may afford power, but it does not guarantee authority.

The SDJP's recent policy reversal is another example of the dangers of party despotism. As much as I welcome the substance of Prime Minister Tomiichi Murayama's recognition of the constitutionality of the Self-Defense Forces, of the U.S.-Japan security treaty, or of official visits by government ministers to the Yasukuni Shrine on Japan's Memorial Day, I cannot find much good in the *procedure* by which this reversal of policy was carried out. Unlike the German Social Democrats who made fundamental changes to their platform at their Bad Godesberg party congress before taking up governmental responsibility, the SDJP's changes were made unilaterally by the party leadership without prior consultation with the party base, and only after the party had already joined the coalition government.

Fifth, I would like to call more attention to the question of how to help political parties become better organized and individual politicians gain more experience and widen their perspectives. Politicians walk a tightrope of human sensitivities every day. Humor your constituents too little and they will vote you out of office; humor them too much and you will eventually work against their interests. The number of people who want to run for political office in the Diet or prefectural assemblies is very, very small. Many refuse, saying that it would be meaningless to invest immense effort and funds in a campaign—and win—only to come under vicious attacks from the media. This is a clear sign of the decline of our democracy. Legislators need adequate resources and support if they are to commit themselves to political activities more freely.

Finally, I think steps must be taken to reform the bureaucracy so that it can efficiently administer policy, as devised by elected representatives of the people, rather than formulate policy on its own. Bureaucrats should be selected and dispatched to the various ministries by a central authority (the cabinet); the ministries should not select their own personnel. Moreover, for promotions to the rank of head of division (*kacho*) or above, the candidate should be required to have served in two other ministries for a certain number of years. These two measures would help to ensure that bureaucrats focus their loyalty on the nation or the civil service as a whole rather than one particular ministry, and thus reduce the interministry rivalry that characterizes Japanese governmental decisionmaking today. A third reform would be to have a significant percentage of mid-level and senior bureaucrats, such as bureau chiefs, councilors, and administrative vice ministers, be political appointees recruited from outside the civil service, not only from the political world but from business and academia as well.

Reforms in political decisionmaking such as those I have outlined are indispensable if Japan is to maintain prosperity and a healthy democracy for its people and make the contribution to the international community that its economic power demands.

Notes

1.Theodore White, *The Making of the President, 1960* (Atheneum, 1961).
2. Edward J. Lincoln, *Japan's New Global Role* (Brookings, 1993).

CHAPTER FOUR

Deregulation in Japan and the United States: A Study in Contrasts

Edward J. Lincoln

DEREGULATION REMAINS a buzzword in Japan, with discussion reinvigorated by Prime Minister Hashimoto's personal endorsement in 1996 of major changes in the next several years. Many Japanese point to the example of the United States when they talk about deregulation, and many Americans assume Japan must be doing something akin to what has happened in the United States when they read about deregulation in Japan. But the record of deregulation—conceptualization of the issue, debate, and action—remains fundamentally different in the two countries. Recognizing those differences is important, and delineating some of the salient contrasts is the purpose of this chapter. Those differences imply that the ringing rhetoric in Japan has not been matched by much real deregulation, and future progress is likely to be slow and incomplete in comparison to the United States.

The United States

Economic regulation in the United States grew out of rising concern in the second half of the nineteenth century over competition problems in rapidly emerging new industries. The emergence of modern financial institutions, railroads, steel, and other industries raised serious concerns about the "excesses" of capitalism. Some of the new industries were characterized by very high fixed costs and relatively low marginal costs (such as the railroads or electric power generation) and appeared to be headed toward natural monopolies or oligopolies with monopolistic or unstable pricing.

Such problems in these rapidly growing industries led to political movements to bring industry under some form of government control or regulation. The popular press (epitomized by the yellow-journalism book *The Robber Barons*) fed the notion of rapacious capitalists hurting society, a view further popularized by novelists (especially Frank Norris and his devastating view of railroads in *The Octopus* and financial speculators in *The Pit*). New political groups, such as the Populists, brought mounting pressure to bear on state legislatures and Congress to regulate specific industries. Creation of the Interstate Commerce Commission (1887) to control railroad rates, passage of the Sherman Antitrust Act (1890) and the Clayton Antitrust Act (1914), the Motor Carrier Act (1935), the Civil Aeronautics Act (1938), and other measures resulted. By the end of the 1930s, federal or state regulation of prices and other aspects of competition (entry of new firms or the offering of new services) was applied to all major forms of domestic commercial transportation (railroads, trucking, river barges, and airlines), electric and gas utilities, financial services, telephone service, broadcast telecommunications, and natural gas markets.

On the health and safety side of regulation, change emerged from a similar concern over the excesses of capitalism. Driven by profits, firms were assumed to willfully ignore problems of product safety or working conditions for their workers. Upton Sinclair's powerful novel *The Jungle,* for example, spurred Congress to pass legislation establishing a regime for meat inspection. But the real surge in noneconomic forms of regulation is much more recent, arising out of the social concerns of the 1960s and thereafter, which brought a wide variety of laws covering employment discrimination, workplace safety, product safety standards, defective product recalls, and others.

For economic regulation, the American system favored independent government regulatory bodies that were supposed to act in a quasi-judicial manner to insulate regulation from partisan politics. Institutions such as the Interstate Commerce Commission (ICC)—regulating railroads, trucks, and barges—or the Civil Aeronautics Board (CAB)—regulating airline routes and fares—had commissioners appointed by the president for fixed terms, who were to act as judges, rendering decisions on requests for changes in rates or other regulated aspects of service after exhaustive public hearings. Decisions on these matters, similar to those in regular judicial decisions, were accompanied by extensive explanations by the commissioners justifying why they made a particular choice. In this way, it was hoped, decisions would be based on careful, impartial assessment of objective facts and carefully grounded in the specific regulatory mandate of the law.

Having responded to the desire of society to curb the excesses of unbridled capitalism, why did the United States embark on a path of deregulation? The process began with a vigorous intellectual debate, among both academics and various private-sector groups affected negatively by regulation. Economists and businesses began to question the rationale and effects of regulation. Economists identified four major problems with the existing framework of economic regulation:

First, in contrast to the popular notion of regulation created from public pressure to curb the excesses of capitalism, some economists argued that the creation of regulation and its operation were actually controlled by the affected industries. Thus, while the Populists led the political charge against the railroads in the 1870s and 1880s, the railroads themselves—tired of rate wars and frequent bankruptcies—were eager for regulation so they could jointly fix higher prices and thereby raise profits throughout the industry. This view is now widely accepted. Thus laws intended to protect consumers from the depredations of industry accomplished exactly the opposite effect.[1]

Second, economists argued that regulation promoted inefficiency and distortions despite the best efforts of the regulators to be fair. In industries such as electric utilities or telephone service, for example, regulators allowed firms to achieve a specified return on their assets as a means of determining permissible prices for their products or services. This, however, simply led firms to overinvest; the larger their capital base, the higher the prices they could request in order to earn the allowable rate of return. Furthermore, the quiet life of a regulated industry had a depressing effect on technological change, in the view of many economists, creating further losses through relative inefficiency.[2]

Third, over time, shifts in technology and market conditions may eliminate the need for regulation. Railroads, which had a monopoly on long-distance inland transportation in the nineteenth century, now face fundamentally different market conditions, in which they compete with other forms of transportation. In a number of regulated industries, therefore, economists argued that regulation was no longer necessary because new conditions implied that market competition would work properly without the heavy guiding hand of government.[3]

Fourth, in other industries, economists began to argue that the original conception of the need for regulation was flawed. The fear that the airline market would demonstrate unstable prices and a tendency toward monopoly, which provided the official rationale for regulation of the new industry in the 1930s, was widely viewed by economists as wrong by the early 1970s.[4]

These changing views of economic regulation fed into a vigorous political process in the 1960s and 1970s, led by both business and consumer interests. New entrepreneurs and businesses saw regulation frustrating their desire to compete, and in some industries (such as the airlines) consumers saw deregulation as a way to lower prices. This political debate led to new legislation in Congress, beginning during the Carter administration, to deregulate or restructure the regulatory framework for specific industries. Major pieces of legislation included the Airline Deregulation Act (1978), the Natural Gas Policy Act (1978), the Motor Carrier Reform Act (1980), the Staggers Rail Act (1980), the Cable Television Deregulation Act (1984), and the Telecommunications Act of 1996.

The impetus for deregulation of telecommunications was enhanced by the decision to break up AT&T in 1982, reached in a seminal antitrust case brought by the Justice Department. Although this change preserved the regulated monopoly of local phone companies, it accelerated the changes toward more open competition in long-distance phone service and removed controls on Bell Labs.

In some other cases, efforts at deregulation have come directly out of the regulatory agencies themselves. Telecommunications deregulation began with decisions beginning in the late 1960s by the Federal Communications Commission (FCC) that permitted competitors to AT&T in long-distance telephone service for the first time and permitted consumers to attach non–AT&T equipment to phone lines. Similarly, the ICC, CAB, and FCC made decisions on specific cases or altered their decisionmaking criteria in a way to permit more competition. Appointment of noncareer commissioners provides the opportunity for moving these commissions in innovative directions over time. However, the ability of the regulatory agencies themselves to carry out extensive change has been limited. The Civil Aeronautics Board had experimented with a variety of small changes in regulation from the 1950s to the 1970s, but was not in a legal position to undertake the major changes that came from Congress in 1977 (which eliminated the CAB as an institution). Similarly, the ICC had gradually liberalized truck and railroad rates in the late 1970s, but legislation was essential to permit real decontrol of railroads and trucking.

Continuation of the process of economic deregulation has been underwritten by broad public and academic belief in its success. Airline fares have fallen and the number of passengers has grown rapidly; long-distance telephone rates have fallen; railroads are more competitive and have increased their market share in domestic freight transportation (since regulation had held their rates up rather than down). Economists estimate an overall increase in national welfare of tens of billions of dollars a year owing to the lower prices and increased economic efficiencies that have come with deregulation.[5]

Social regulation or deregulation has been far more controversial. Concerns over the tendency of business to behave poorly on safety and health issues absent regulation have been widespread in society. Federal regulation of pharmaceuticals, for example, has long had public support, driven by fears of harmful side effects from drugs. But the lengthy and expensive process of obtaining approval for new drugs has been heavily criticized for reducing innovation; the expense reduces the number of new drugs that firms can afford to develop. Furthermore, the government is criticized for using outdated testing techniques and standards that may keep potentially valuable drugs off the market. The solution for an area as critical as drug regulation, though, lies not in simple deregulation but with careful revision of the regulatory process.

Similar arguments underlie debate over other aspects of health, safety, and social regulation. Do federal standards for worker safety promote job safety or simply raise costs for industry? Do federal rules mandating recalls of defective products protect consumers or force firms to absorb costs imposed by arbitrary federal researchers? Do environmental laws benefit the public or go too far in imposing high costs for marginal improvements? Do affirmative action rules open job opportunities or hurt productivity? Because there is great room for disagreement about regulatory mechanisms and their costs and benefits, this area of regulation remains politically controversial, and properly so. When this degree of debate exists over the facts and their importance, no group of career government officials can make decisions; only the political process can resolve these questions.

Regulations in the United States will remain numerous and important, especially in the area of health and safety. Society is clearly better off with many of the regulations that exist: no one wants elimination of sanitary requirements for restaurants, elimination of building codes, or relaxation of standards and inspection for commercial aircraft. In that sense, all societies—including the United States—will remain regulated. But the large gray area of regulation described above implies that on many issues, American society will debate and alter the nature of health, safety, and social regulation, and in the current political environment, further movement toward deregulation or restructuring seems likely. On the economic front, the picture appears even clearer; the trend toward deregulation, buttressed by strong support from economists, appears to be well in place.

Japan

Regulation and deregulation in Japan have evolved in very different ways. To generalize broadly, regulation has been more pervasive, more intrusive, more arbitrary, and more accepted by the public in Japan. By the time the nation emerged from World War II, much of its economy was heavily regulated with price controls and other mechanisms. Although many of the wartime price and output controls disappeared in the early postwar period, the government was left with far stronger powers in the economy than was the case in the United States.

Laws establishing the basic regulatory framework have generally been less precise in Japan than in the United States, and enforcement was left to officials in the ministries rather than granted to independent regulatory agencies. Thus licenses to operate a trucking business are granted by the trucking bureau of the Ministry of Transportation (MOT); approval of railroad rates is the province of the MOT's railroad bureau; and approval of airline routes and rates is in the hands of the MOT's aviation bureau. All of these offices are completely staffed by career bureaucrats.

Decisionmaking by the officials charged with regulatory powers is opaque. In most cases, the process does not involve open hearings and the decisions are based on no published set of criteria. Furthermore, the reasons for particular decisions need not be explained publicly, nor is there any regular route of appeal. All of this means that the process of decisionmaking on regulatory matters is quite arbitrary and depends on the integrity and common sense of the individual bureaucrats responsible.

In the Japanese context, the public acquiesced in delegation of such arbitrary power to the bureaucracy partly because the bureaucrats were supposed to be highly trained products of elite educational institutions who were acting out of a strong sense of selfless national responsibility. One could equally argue that the public was never asked if it wanted such a strong bureaucracy, since much of the postwar system of heavy bureaucratic power was established before or during World War II (or even descends from the premodern system in which the samurai bureaucrats were at the top of the official social hierarchy).

With the economy growing at an average annual rate of 10 percent in the 1950s and 1960s, there was relatively little reason for the public to complain. Whether regulation and industrial policy were helpful or unhelpful, the economic record was so positive that the bureaucracy could feel confident in the public trust. Nevertheless, the overall system has contained some potentially serious problems.

First, despite the public trust in the integrity of its officials, the lack of transparency implies ample room for arbitrary decisions that are detrimental to the interests of the public and the economy. Who is to know why a decision was made? The process does not ensure an opportunity for all affected parties to present their views to the regulators in an open forum, nor are the regulators required to explain the rationale for their decisions. The 1995 disclosure of malfeasance in the Ministry of Finance, where an official who was instrumental in the decision to bail out two small failed credit cooperatives was discovered to have been wined and dined (including a trip to Hong Kong) to an unusual degree by the institutions in question, illustrates the nature of the potential problem in opaque systems. And a 1996 scandal exposed bribes to Health and Welfare officials from a nursing home company seeking licenses for its facilities.

Second, public officials all retire at relatively early ages (still age 55 for the most successful handful in the relentlessly narrowing pyramid of ministerial management). When they retire, the ministry bears a responsibility to find bureaucrats postretirement jobs (with the movement to postretirement jobs known as *amakudari*–descent from heaven). Many of these jobs are in the very industries that the officials previously regulated. This phenomenon varies across industries, and weak controls to lessen the problem exist, but it remains pervasive. This creates an obvious strong incentive for bureaucrats to work cooperatively with industry rather than upholding any broader public interest. The scandal concerning HIV-tainted blood (in which the Ministry of Health and Welfare kept imported heat-treated blood off the market until the Japanese pharmaceutical industry developed its own heat-treatment technology, a decision that resulted eventually in the death from HIV infection of several hundred people who were recipients of blood transfusions in the interim) involved *amakudari* connections between the regulators and the pharmaceutical industry. *Amakudari* is pervasive, and its impact on policy not yet well studied.[6]

Third, some regulatory activities themselves provide large numbers of jobs for bureaucrats and retired bureaucrats. The Ministry of Transportation is reported to have over a thousand officials engaged in work related to automobile inspections. Many MOT officials involved in administering the system also take positions working in private-sector car inspection facilities after their retirement. The inspection system has imposed heavy unnecessary costs on Japanese consumers (because cars are subjected to unnecessary replacement of parts at artificially high prices). But it should be no surprise that MOT fiercely resisted any change in the overall framework for car inspections during the prolonged U.S.-Japan automotive negotiations from 1993 to 1995.

Fourth, the Japanese regulatory system for establishing safety has generally relied on detailed specification of designs rather than performance standards. In such an approach, the opportunity for manipulation is high. Rather than specifying, for example, that a product withstand an impact of a certain intensity, the tendency is to specify the materials and required thickness. Such standards can be manipulated to favor certain products (for example, domestic ones) while automatically excluding others (for example, foreign ones) that might perform as well.

Finally, vigorous use of the courts to resolve problems arising from health and safety problems is lacking, and thus the tendency of bureaucrats charged with regulation is to err on the side of caution. Career bureaucrats who rotate among divisions do not want their careers spoiled by the emergence of a problem while they are in charge of some regulatory issue, so they overreact in setting standards.

These problems yield a distinction between the reality and the ideal of Japanese regulatory practices, much as Americans eventually learned that their own regulatory practice was different from the ideal. Given the general dominance of the bureaucracy and the opaqueness of the system, though, one could easily argue that the dilemma of reality versus ideal is considerably worse in Japan than the United States.

In a broad sense, the social or political environment in which regulation exists is quite different from that in the United States. This difference is sufficiently substantial to cast some doubt on how far deregulation will proceed.

First, to make a broad generalization, Japanese have been more skeptical of competition than Americans. The notion of *wa* (harmony), which pervades Japanese society is, in many ways, the antithesis of market competition. Japanese economists and bureaucrats frequently have worried about "excess competition" or "confusion in the marketplace," notions that hardly exist in American economic thought. The frequency of market failure in capitalist systems is a debatable point; a strand of economic thought extending at least back to the German economist Frederick List in the early nineteenth century favored cartels and regulation on the assumption that markets frequently fail. Modern economic theory, as taught in American universities, certainly includes the notion of market failure but has generally viewed these problems as relatively unusual aberrations and not common conditions. Given the stronger suspicions about market outcomes, the Japanese government has been willing to go much further in regulating competition, even in industries that no American economist would think needed regulation. For many years, for example, the government regulated the location of liquor stores, so that each would have a fixed territory, thereby minimizing direct competition among them. Talk of "confusion in the marketplace" continues unabated, and articles emphasizing harmony or discussing coordinated industry action (even in supposedly unregulated industries) are a daily occurrence in the press.

Supporting this view of the need for the guiding hand of government is the belief that unfettered competition implies increased job insecurity and higher unemployment. Deregulation may sound attractive in the abstract, but the fear of personal insecurity or joblessness resonates with the public. Articles in the press have conveyed the notion that turmoil in labor markets—job losses in deregulated industries and higher unemployment levels—was a consequence of deregulation in the United States (a conclusion that American economists dispute).[7]

Second, the public is taught to acquiesce in detailed regulation of their lives from an early age. Many schools control their students' hair styles, length of skirts, length of pants, use of cosmetics, choice of book bag, shoes, and other aspects of their appearance and behavior. Corporations control their employees' choice of clothing, provide group calisthenics, and teach young employees complex and rigid hierarchical routines for proper bowing. While pressure to conform with sets of arbitrary rules designed to maintain uniformity and social control varies across schools, families, and corporations, one can argue that people are used to a much higher degree of regulatory intrusiveness in their lives than Americans. Therefore, they are more likely to acquiesce in extensive and intrusive government policies for both economic and social regulation.

The kind of petty regulation by schools or corporations described above has existed in the United States as well. But this sort of interference in personal affairs has largely disappeared because of a blizzard of successful lawsuits over the past thirty years. Few such lawsuits have occurred in Japan, and when they do, the courts have generally been sympathetic to schools, corporations, and others doing the regulating. In 1994, for example, the courts upheld the right of a city government to refuse registration of a newborn child's name on the grounds that the name was inappropriate. The relative difficulty of bringing lawsuits in Japan, combined with the record of the decisions, sends a strong message through society about the inevitability of intrusive and arbitrary regulation.

Despite the fact that the Japanese public seems less likely to press for vigorous deregulation, dissatisfaction has clearly increased during the 1990s with the general state of regulation, and some real moves in the direction of deregulation have begun. Why?

Some members of society have become more outspoken about arbitrary and foolish aspects of regulation. Former Prime Minister Hosokawa made much of his experience while serving as a governor of a three-year battle with the Ministry of Transportation to move a bus-stop sign a few meters down the street.[8] Many people have experienced similar sorts of arbitrary displays of power by government officials and appear to be more willing to write about them, exemplified by the outspoken books attacking the bureaucracy by Ministry of Health and Welfare official Masao Miyamoto (fired in 1995 for his outspokenness).[9] The fact that, for example, the Ministry of Transportation was approving increases in regulated taxi fares and highway tolls in 1994 despite generally falling prices in the rest of the economy was widely decried in the press (but to no avail). Dissatisfaction arising from such individual episodes has led to a general sense of "get the government off my back." Government careers still attract the top students in Japan, and bureaucrats still occupy a privileged social position, but at least some of the luster is gone from their reputation.

Some analysts also began to question the underlying economic and social rationale of regulation. Having believed earlier that regulation was an integral part of the economic success of the postwar period, some economists began to argue that regulation was now holding the economy back. In this group are some prominent scholars, including Haruo Shimada (a labor economist at Keio University), Iwao Nakatani (an economist at Hitotsubashi University), and Yukio Noguchi (another economist at Hitotsubashi). This new interpretation was fueled by the period of very low growth that began in 1992, in which average annual growth in the four years from 1992 to 1995 was only 0.6 percent. With the stagnation so prolonged, concern arose that the problem was structural, and, in particular, that overregulation was preventing the economy from expanding in new and important industries (such as telecommunications), thereby holding back overall economic growth.

The public has also become somewhat more aware of differences between Japan and other countries because of the explosive growth in foreign travel. After expanding only marginally from 4 million in 1980 to 4.9 million in 1985, the number of Japanese traveling abroad jumped to 13.6 million by 1994. With over one in ten Japanese traveling abroad each year, awareness of lower prices abroad grew. For prices that are regulated in Japan, such as airline tickets, highway tolls, rice, and telephone calls, people are now more aware that government regulation is holding prices high.

Finally, any industry in Japan involved in exporting faced severe price pressure in the first half of the 1990s imposed by the appreciation of the yen. As a result, a chorus of voices calling for deregulation arose from organizations such as Keidanren (the major association representing the voice of big business), hoping that deregulation would reduce production costs. However, industries would like markets for their inputs deregulated, but not for their own output. As a result, the voice of industry is not unified and is often ambiguous. Keidanren, whose chairman in 1993, Gaishi Hiraiwa, headed a government advisory commission on deregulation, helped to initiate real action on deregulation but was unable (or insufficiently interested) to keep the bureaucrats from controlling the process once begun.

The differences with the United States in the nature of public dissatisfaction are subtle but noticeable and important. American discussion of deregulation originated in industry-specific arguments about high prices or inefficiency, not from a broad concern over poor performance of the economy. Certainly Americans have a low opinion of bureaucrats, and the broad notion of "overregulation" has popular appeal, but the bulk of the real discussion in academia, the press, and politics in the past quarter century has been centered on particular industries or specific issues. To bring about change, analysts and interest groups needed to demonstrate convincingly the costs, inefficiencies, or distortions owing to the regulatory framework for a particular industry or issue and to present an alternative framework. In contrast, the discussion in Japan has been broad and vague, and particular industries or issues have been used largely as examples to illustrate the general problem.

The distinction between concerns over economic and other forms of regulation is difficult to decipher in the case of Japan. The overall issue of deregulation appears not to discriminate since both economic and noneconomic (health, safety, and social) regulation has been heavy and intrusive. But when discussion becomes more specific, the pressure for changes in the noneconomic forms of regulation seems muted at best. Consumer groups do exist in Japan, but they have been vocal defenders of strong government regulations or controls on such issues as chemical additives in food products, residual pesticide levels on fruits and vegetables, or approval of drugs. These are issues of particular interest from an international perspective since health and safety regulations have often been manipulated to keep foreign products (approved as safe under U.S. or European regulations) out of the Japanese market. The decades-long dispute over American apples, the delays in obtaining approval for drugs long used outside of Japan (including Tylenol, still unapproved in 1997), or the infamous aluminum bat case (in which concerns over safety of bats led to an overlapping set of design standards and approval processes that eliminated safe, sturdy American-made bats) all reflect this problem. But the notion that the bureaucracy should continue a strong regulatory framework for these kinds of issues appears to remain intact at the same time that the overall notion of deregulation has become popular.

Nevertheless, as dissatisfaction with regulation surfaced, the Japanese political process responded. Prime Minister Hosokawa established a special committee to report on deregulation (the Hiraiwa Commission), and the subsequent Hata, Murayama, and Hashimoto administrations moved forward with policy changes. After the Diet elections in the fall of 1996, Prime Minister Hashimoto (leader of a somewhat strengthened Liberal Democratic Party) renewed the call for vigorous deregulation over the rest of the 1990s. However, the process for implementing deregulation bears little resemblance to the process in the United States.

These differences reflect the underlying nature of public debate. Rather than addressing deregulation in an industry-specific fashion, with legislation introduced to the Diet to establish new, less regulated regimes for each industry, the politicians turned the responsibility for change over to the bureaucracy. The mandate given to the bureaucracy in early 1994 by the Hosokawa government was quite vague, stemming from the fairly unspecific concerns noted above: a sense of bureaucratic arbitrariness in many regulatory areas, the notion of over-regulation slowing the economy, and the observation that prices are higher than abroad in many areas.

Given a mandate for action, the bureaucracy focused on numbers. If the economy is "overregulated," then the solution is to reduce the number of regulations, in this conception of the issue. Therefore, the bureaucracy issued a list of items to be deregulated or modified in April 1994, and invited lists of requests from both the Japanese business community and from foreign governments or businesses. Further announcements of lists of regulations on which action would be taken or "studied" appeared later in 1994, 1995, and 1996. This process was slated to continue for five years, dominated by the bureaucracy acting on its own with only cursory oversight.

The fundamental problem is the inherent weakness of any process of deregulation controlled by career officials. Faced with a mandate to reduce the number of regulations, any well-trained bureaucrat can discover a variety of small, inconsequential items to stick on the deregulation list that do not substantially change regulation in any meaningful sense. No bureaucracy dominated entirely by career officials can move very far in deregulation because the competent officials are those whose *raison d'être* depends on the existence of regulations. During 1994–95, the predictable response of various bureaus of the different ministries tasked with producing lists of items to deregulate was resistance on the basis that most regulations were vital.

The contrast with the United States is striking. Some regulatory change in the United States originated in the regulatory agencies themselves, aided by the ability of administrations to pick the commissioners—and in so doing pick outsiders (not retired bureaucrats) who might bring in new and innovative ideas. Similarly, for health, safety, and social regulations administered directly by federal departments, the ability of administrations to put political appointees in place provides an opportunity to move the bureaucracy in new directions. With Japanese regulation centered in a career bureaucracy, and only a marginal political presence in each ministry in the form of the minister and political vice-minister, the possibility of innovation from within is greatly lessened. The career bureaucrats are certainly not totally inflexible, and changes do occur over time, but the system is less likely to move vigorously toward deregulation than the U.S. regulatory commissions or the U.S. bureaucracy.

Furthermore, the process of deregulation in the United States has relied heavily on legislative action. Even in the somewhat more flexible bureaucratic system of the United States, the scope and speed of regulatory change were constrained either because of past legal mandates or bureaucratic inflexibility. As discussed earlier, the legislative process produced important new laws revamping the regulatory framework for various industries, buttressed by an informed political debate and detailed analysis. In Japan very little of this has happened. Since the bureaucrats control much of the relevant information about the industries, the politicians have very limited staffs, and many of the knowledgeable academics serve on ministry advisory commissions, it is unlikely that an independent, politically driven effort could dislodge the bureaucrats from their dominance of the deregulation issue.

Over the past two decades, a few episodes of legislative action have occurred that give the appearance of movement in the direction of deregulation. In the mid-1970s, the Diet voted to delegate railroad rate approval from itself to the Ministry of Transportation, a move that shortened the process of granting approvals but left basic regulatory control in place. The "privatizations" of the Japanese National Railways, NTT (Nippon Telegraph and Telephone), and Japan Tobacco in the 1980s were also significant legislative steps but were not really moves toward deregulation. The process of railroad rate approval remained unchanged, and the only significant accomplishments were to weaken the power of the railroad's unions and fob off all JNR pension obligations on the

Finance Ministry. NTT remains largely owned by the government, and the overall state of regulation of telecommunications remains very far behind the United States (the breakup of NTT into three companies proposed in late 1996 aroused considerable skepticism). Privatization of Japan Tobacco provided a means to allow foreign firms independent access to retail cigarette outlets in Japan, but ownership of the corporation remains in the hands of the government. Overall, legislative action in the Diet has had a very small role in the overall process of deregulation in Japan.

Conclusion

Deregulation remains a major topic for advanced capitalist nations. Having toyed with various regulatory or government ownership regimes over the past century to combat assumed problems or evils of competition, many nations are moving to overhaul and reduce government regulation of economic activity. Japan is certainly a part of this process, but the contrasts with the United States are sharp and significant. Those differences all imply that deregulation in Japan is unlikely to proceed as far or as fast as in the United States.

Little of the debate over regulation in Japan has focused on particular industries; the discussion has not progressed very far from the vague notion of overregulation. Whereas the U.S. process has been centered in legislation, the Japanese approach has been to delegate the effort to the bureaucrats themselves. These are critical differences.

Despite this weakness in the process, some real deregulation will occur. With slow economic growth and fear that excess regulation will hobble the international competitiveness of some industries, the bureaucracy will ease some economic regulations. Similarly, modest change may occur in the areas of health, safety, and social regulation, although without the pressure of international competition, the process seems even weaker than for economic regulation. The public is unlikely to press the political system for bolder change and probably does not really want bolder moves. Finally, the process will be clearly producer oriented—the alterations will be crafted as carefully as possible to preserve producer interests. This is not necessarily in the best interest of Japanese consumers, the economy as a whole, or foreign firms desiring to do business in Japan.

Notes

1. Paul W. MacAvoy, *The Economic Effects of Regulation: The Trunkline Railroad Cartels and the Interstate Commerce Commission before 1900* (MIT Press, 1965), was among the seminal works presenting this view.

2. The main theoretical underpinning for analyzing such problems was presented in Harvey Averch and L. L. Johnson, "Behavior of the Firm under Regulatory Constraint," *American Economic Review,* vol. 52 (December 1962), pp. 1052–69, which spawned numerous other theoretical and empirical works.

3. This was the essence of the argument presented in a path-breaking book, John R. Meyer and others, *The Economics of Competition in the Transportation Industries* (Harvard University Press, 1959), which was one of the first strong calls for a reduction in transportation regulation.

4. See Steven Morrison and Clifford Winston, *The Evolution of the Airline Industry* (Brookings, 1995) for a review of these arguments.

5. Clifford Winston, "Economic Deregulation: Days of Reckoning for Economists," *Journal of Economic Literature,* vol. 31 (September 1993), pp. 1263–89, reviews the work of economists measuring the economic benefits of deregulation.

6. One of the few academic studies of *amakudari* is Ulrike Schaede, "The 'Old Boy' Network and Government-Business Relationships in Japan," *Journal of Japanese Studies,* vol. 21 (Summer 1995), pp. 293–317. See chapter 10 in this volume.

7. Prominent among these is a major piece written by a "committee" of anonymous authors, Group 2001, "Kisei Kanwa to Iu Akumu" (The nightmare of deregulation), *Bungei shunju,* vol. 72 (August 1994), pp. 134–146, and (November 1994), pp. 318–30.

8. Morihiro Hosokawa and Tetsundo Iwakuni, *Hina no Ronri* (The logic of the countryside) (Tokyo: Kobunsha, 1991), pp. 19–21.

9. One of his books has been translated into English. Masao Miyamoto, *The Straitjacket Society* (Tokyo: Kodansha International, 1994). See chapter 5 in this volume.

CHAPTER FIVE

Deregulating Japan's Soul

Masao Miyamoto

WORDS AFFECT THE inner consciousness. Because I was trained in psychoanalysis, I pay a lot of attention to a person's choice of words and subtle differences in nuance. Moreover, I know from my ten years of experience in the Japanese government that Japanese bureaucrats attach great importance to words and the nuances they convey. So when representatives of the Mansfield Center first approached me in the fall of 1994 to write a piece on deregulation, I was struck by their use of the Japanese expression *kisei kanwa*, which literally means "to undertake a relaxation of the regulatory environment." While the Japanese media regularly use *kisei kanwa* to mean deregulation, I immediately became curious about whether these two expressions in fact had the same meaning.

Some time later, I was asked to speak before the Tokyo chapter of the Chambers of Commerce of Australia and New Zealand. A representative of the New Zealand embassy presented me with a brochure entitled "Deregulation in New Zealand." According to this brochure, New Zealand was once the most regulated of the OECD group of nations, and its economy performed dismally. It went on to explain that by privatizing public corporations, abolishing subsidies to agriculture and industry, unilaterally lowering tariffs, abolishing the import licensing system, liberalizing areas such as transportation, electricity, and telecommunications, which used to be operated by government monopolies, and drastically cutting income and corporate taxes, the nation was able to achieve a real economic growth rate of 6.1 percent. These measures improved competitiveness, helped expand exports, lowered the unemployment rate in New Zealand, and moved the fiscal budget from deficit to surplus.

While reading this brochure, I asked myself, "Why is it that Japan is trying to achieve *kisei kanwa* (deregulation), rather than simply promoting *kisei teppai* (to abolish or repeal regulations) altogether?"

The Japanese press almost always uses the expression *kisei kanwa* over *kisei teppai*. So I looked up the word *kanwa* in the dictionary and found that it is the equivalent of "relaxation" or "alleviation" in English. Next, I looked up the word *teppai* in the *Kojien,* the most authoritative Japanese dictionary. The entry read, "to abolish and discontinue; to remove." It defined the word *kanwa* as "to loosen; to relax." The dictionary also noted that deregulatory policy means the same thing as "a policy of appeasement" (*yuwa seisaku*). The word *yuwa* means "to forgive and forget." To appease means to exhibit a conciliatory attitude, in order to break the deadlock.

After completing this research, I came to realize that the words "abolish" (*teppai*) and "relax" (*kanwa*) have meanings as different as night and day. "Deregulation" means that the status quo will be maintained, but that the parties involved are willing to make concessions so that they can continue to get along. The existing regulations will simply be relaxed.

In short, *kisei kanwa* is just one of many expressions used by Japanese bureaucrats engaged in a delicate effort to maintain the status quo. They have developed dozens of different ways of saying no without directly resisting calls for change.

Consider some of the phrases contained in an unofficial handbook used by myself and my colleagues to prepare ministerial responses to questions from the Diet. The phrase *maemuki ni,* which means "positively" or "constructively," is calculated to give listeners faint hope that something may possibly transpire in the distant future, although there are no immediate prospects. The expression *hairyo suru,* literally to give something your "careful consideration," actually means letting it stay indefinitely on your desk without ever taking any action. Similarly, *kento shimasu* ("investigate, look into") means to kick something around but do nothing. Finally, *shincho ni,* or "cautiously," is used when things are virtually hopeless, but one can not come right out and say so; it means that nothing will be done. These expressions can be interpreted to mean exactly what the bureaucrats want. The word *kanwa* is used for the same reason. In other words, a bureaucrat chooses the word *kanwa* to mean that he has no intention of doing anything about the regulation.

Preserving the status quo. That is the responsibility bestowed upon the bureaucrats who manage "Japan Inc." Not long after I joined the Ministry of Health and Welfare (MHW), my boss me gave the following piece of advice: "No matter how trivial your job may seem, you must not let your organization become subject to downsizing. As long as you are a bureaucrat, this is the most important thing to remember. Even if you feel that the work of a certain department is useless, you should not let it disappear. Rather, you can count on a promotion if you help it grow."

About three months after I was assigned as a director at the Pharmaceutical Affairs Bureau that oversees the operation of government-run national hospitals, there was a meeting of ministry-affiliated technical specialists, all of whom were graduates of the same medical school as myself.

"So Masao, how do you like your new job?" my superior asked.

"Boring. I have so much time on my hands," I responded. "I think we can do away with this position. I also think eliminating the local pharmaceutical affairs bureaus would go a long way toward revitalizing the national hospitals. Also, aside from a few exceptions, all national hospitals should be privatized. It is as if these hospitals were put under a command economy run by the ministry, and because this system is a communist one, there is no free competition. This has become an obstacle to improving the quality of medical care. I'm sure the public will benefit if the principle of free competition is allowed to prevail."

My superior looked somewhat uncomfortable. Then he responded, "What you say may be true, but never let anyone hear you say that in public. By saying that your position is useless, you will only be denying your value to the organization." That is when I realized, "Bureaucrats are much more concerned about preserving their *mura* (literally "village" or tight-knit group), than about being of some service to the public." As long as a bureaucrat can justify his actions by saying that he is doing something to preserve the organization, then no one questions him, although he may be wasting taxpayers' money.

To be fair, I do not think most Japanese bureaucrats really believe that preserving or enlarging their organization is more important than improving the people's standard of living. Many of my friends who work for the bureaucracy seriously feel that Japan's bureaucratic system needs to change. But these people live by a code that allows them to speak about the problems only in the system, not to make comments in public about the shortcomings of the particular organization to which they belong.

If a bureaucrat were to say that he was in favor of restructuring, that would mean that he could accept the potential downsizing of his organization. And that would mean that he broke another code that says, "Expanding the organization is considered virtuous."

Bureaucrats are evaluated according to a scoring system in which points are deducted for misconduct. Violating either of these codes immediately results in a demotion. Once one becomes part of a Japanese organization, public criticism from within, though it may be constructive, is considered taboo.

Let us try to find out why the word *kanwa* meaning "to relax" came to be used instead of *teppai* or "to abolish; to repeal." Part of the responsibility lies with the press. After all, the media are characterized by "the village mentality," with a thicket of regulations that prevent economic competition and reporting clubs that follow strict if unwritten rules designed to preserve their relationship with the subjects they cover. The net result is that much of the Japanese media may disappear if regulations are abolished. So when the bureaucracy encouraged the media to translate "deregulation" as *kisei kanwa*, it is not surprising that the media went along. The press unconsciously backs up the bureaucracy because they have the same interest in maintaining the status quo.

The thinking behind *kanwa* and *teppai* is totally different. *Teppai* is sought by those who want to part with the old ways and to introduce the concept of freedom to Japanese society. This freedom would bring major changes to the current social system.

However, by supporting *kanwa*, it is possible to maintain the status quo, in which organizations believe that "having no principle is the principle." This attitude is very typical of Japanese groups. No major social changes are observed as long as the people remain under the control of the bureaucracy. *Kanwa* is a rather ambiguous word; this enables the group to preserve its *wa,* or "harmony," which is most valued by Japanese organizations. In short, Japanese society can continue to practice protectionism.

Many Japanese have asked me why one should become so preoccupied with terminology if the Japanese people are enjoying a better standard of living. As far as they are concerned, it does not matter if one is talking about *kanwa* or *teppai*. These are the very people who fail to realize that by allowing government officials to hide behind the rhetoric calling for "deregulation," the people remain under the thumb of the bureaucracy. Japan is said to be one of the world's largest economies in terms of per capita GNP, but in fact Japan's quality of life lags far behind that of the United States.

When I was a bureaucrat, we worked by the golden rule, "The public should neither be allowed to live or die." Because the bureaucracy has recently been subject to criticism on the need to reform, officials may say, "In principle, we support the flexible operation of regulatory schemes." But as soon as they regain confidence and power, the same officials will say, "The regulatory environment will be tightened." Because the officials used the phrase "flexible operations," there is no recourse when they turn around and say, "The schemes will no longer be flexible." Furthermore, if they really want to keep the regulation intact, the bureaucrats can, as a last resort, claim, "We are dealing with a policy, not a regulatory issue." As long as the Japanese public allows the bureaucrats to play these rhetorical games, it will be impossible to wrest control over the regulatory environment from these officials.

Deregulation does not mean simply to relax existing regulations. The ultimate objective is to take away authority from the bureaucrats. However, the bureaucracy will have to be downsized if regulations are removed, and people accept the new principle of free competition. Not only will this make it impossible for the bureaucrats to continue to practice protectionism, but the spirit of free competition, which they view with the greatest distaste, will permeate the entire society. Competition will lead to a collapse of bureaucratic control. These officials do not use the term *kisei teppai* because this is exactly what they want to avoid.

In a nutshell, *kisei kanwa* is nothing more than the kind of deceptive behavior at which bureaucrats excel. To understand the emptiness of the term *kisei kanwa,* one needs only to examine the slow speed at which administrative reform has been carried out thus far. The bureaucrats are doing their best to "put the mouse in a labyrinth," as the Japanese expression goes.

I support the use of the term *kisei teppai* because I think that will give us better insight into the nature of the bureaucracy. The people of Japan have become too meek. The more inquiring people become, the more difficult it will be for the bureaucrats to respond ambiguously. *Kisei teppai* is necessary to break the power of the bureaucracy and to put a stop to the sacrifices that are being made for the sake of the system.

The place to begin is in Japan's educational system. Perhaps more than any other factor, the regulated schooling provided by the Ministry of Education is responsible for the overregulated nature of Japanese society and its inability to break out of this bind.

In 1995, the term "mind control" became very popular in Japan because of the activities of the religious cult, Aum Shinrikyo. The cult's leader has been arrested, and the cult is about to be disbanded. Many people believe that peace will return to Japan now that all of the suspects have been rounded up. But I would caution those who are giving a sigh of relief. That is because this incident, which rocked the entire nation, was a product of Japan's education system, and the Aum sect was merely a manifestation of the distortions found within this system.

"Mind control" and "regulations" have something in common: they both restrict human behavior. Japanese organizations seek people who can be manipulated to obey the rules of "the village" or organization. And the bureaucracy ideally wants its citizens to behave as if they had been castrated, like a gentle flock of sheep. School is the place where such ideal people are created. There students are placed under "mind control" so that they become masochistic and begin to believe that suffering equals pleasure. Personal sacrifice becomes a virtue. This basic thinking was prevalent during World War II.

The Aum incident resulted from the inability to distinguish between reality and illusion, as the cult's followers pursued self-sacrifice in its purest form. Just as the people of Japan were brainwashed by the government during the war, the Aum victims were found to be in the same psychological state. This prompted the victims to see fiction as reality, just as the kamikaze pilots were tricked into believing that they would prefer an honorable death to surrendering.

Once the facade is removed, one finds that far from being a democracy, Japanese society begins to exhibit characteristics of a totalitarian society where the group comes first and there is a strong sense of community. However, socialism or communism à la Japan is somewhat unusual in that it calls for the equitable distribution not only of wealth but of people's abilities.

It is not easy to communize or share abilities. That is because every human being is different. However, the Japanese sense of the group is built on the commonly held illusion that all Japanese are the same. That illusion begins with the denial of the individual, because recognizing the individual would lead people to realize that not all Japanese are the same.

My friend has a child that was about to begin kindergarten. The teacher told her and the other parents to make sure that the children brought only white rice for lunch. Not understanding why the teacher insisted on white rice, she asked the teacher, who replied, "If one child were to bring a different sort of rice or a sandwich, other children would envy him. That's why we decided that all children should have the same thing for lunch." Even at such an early age, when children have not developed as individuals, abilities are shared through self-denial, which is fostered by having the children eat, act, and think the same.

Rules and regulations are indispensable to promote communism of the mind. Communist nations such as the Soviet Union were regulated—but regulations in Japan delve into the deeper conscious. And the rules that govern students grow stricter as the students grow older. People sent to prison are forced to have their hair cropped closely, but many Japanese junior and senior high schools require their students to get a crew cut because they see it as a symbol that the student has been "castrated." This hairstyle forces students to follow the regulation that they be symbolically castrated. Of course, the bureaucrats reject this reasoning and claim that it is to keep the students from becoming delinquent. They act as if they are really thinking on the students' behalf.

The education system that aims to castrate and instill obedience in the students does not stop with uniformity of appearance and style. Junior and senior high school students in Japan are not even allowed to use a vending machine on their way home from school. Even on hot days, they are supposed to endure thirst until they get home.

Many schools in Japan require students to wear uniforms. June 1 is the day for switching from the winter to summer uniform, and October 1 is the day when students switch back to their winter uniforms. It does not matter how hot or cold it is on these days: the schools are not allowed any flexibility. The bureaucrats see this system as an opportunity to teach the students how to persevere in hot and cold weather and to instill in them the values of Japanese groupism. In this way, school uniforms are used as a means to achieve uniformity of spirit.

The officials offer the following explanation about the importance of the ministry-led education system, which strives to castrate its citizens: "Recognizing the differences in students' abilities will hurt less capable students. This is what we absolutely must avoid. So the gifted students need to learn to persevere." Furthermore, the officials claim that by ignoring individual differences, it will be possible to create a "kinder, gentler society." Conversely, this objective means that such a society is one in which gifted people make sacrifices. No matter how one looks at it, this is not normal. I believe that real kindness can be found only after a person has suffered and overcome repeated setbacks. The students are bound by school codes, and the education system robs them of a opportunity to let their talents or capabilities blossom. The students are always on the defensive; they are most concerned about how they can keep themselves from being hurt, never mind trying to be kind to others.

One can see by examining Japan's education system that almost no attention is paid to the importance of challenging the status quo or criticizing the establishment. Rote memory is emphasized. That is why Japanese students excel at answering the types of questions that require memorization of details. This is another result of the education system that has so thoroughly castrated the students.

This characteristic of Japanese education can also be observed in the relationship between politicians and burcaucrats. Although the bureaucrat recognizes that a politician has been elected by the people, he also knows that, if the politicians begin truly to debate the issues, then the bureaucracy will no longer be able to manipulate the Diet and the *raison d'être* of his organization may be on the line.

Once castrated, humans become less aware of what is going on around them and stop questioning what they see. Even if they feel that something is not right, they do not raise doubts, complain, or act to do something about their grievances. That is why it is so hard in Japan to nurture creativity and individuality. Naturally, it becomes hard to generate the will to bring about change. So the status quo continues in a virtual bureaucrats' paradise.

This education system has a great impact on the development of people's personalities in that it discourages the individual from discovering himself. Many observers have pointed out that the Japanese are ambivalent about saying yes or no. This kind of behavior can again be explained by the fact that the education system has castrated the people.

When competition is introduced into a society where communization of abilities has become the norm, people become very insecure when they realize that they may no longer be able to depend on others. Furthermore, people do not know how to deal with competition because the development of self has been discouraged. Thus people try to alienate themselves from the competitive society.

I do not endorse the totalitarian society depicted in Plato's work, *The Republic*. I can, however, compare the situation in Japan and the relationship between freedom and regulations with people living in caves, as described by Plato.

The people are enslaved in chains, deprived of the right to move about. With the sun shining brightly from behind, they look at their shadows on the walls as if these shadows represented life itself. They are led to believe that the shadows are reality. But one day one of the slaves manages to free himself from his bondage. Once freed from the confines of the cave, he begins to accept that the world as he had known it while living in the cave was merely an illusion. And as his entire body is showered with sunshine, he learns to enjoy his newfound freedom.

Once the former slave enjoys the splendor of freedom, he is determined never to return to the cave. However, he decides to go back into the cave to explain to his comrades that it is pitiful for them just to look at their shadows and let their lives go to waste. But the slaves, who had grown accustomed to looking at their shadows, are too frightened to accept freedom. So they end up killing their former comrade.

By substituting "regulation" for "shadow," it is possible to see the similarity between Plato's depiction of these men in the cave and the current state of Japanese society. The public, on the one hand, hopes that regulations are lifted. Yet on the other, they are afraid of freedom. While calling for deregulation, they are afraid of the freedom to become independent, so they end up preferring something ambiguous like *kisei kanwa*.

And the people's fear of freedom is just what the bureaucrats are counting on. They do not want people's lives to be free of regulations and for them to be liberalized. That is because people who have come to enjoy freedom do not want to lead lives with parameters set by bureaucrats. Obviously, no one wants to live like a slave who has been banished to a cave for the rest of his live. That is why the bureaucrats insist that people should live within the regulatory environment they have set up.

What has to be done to transform a state that is of, by, and for the bureaucrats into a state that is of the people, by the people, and for the people? The first step is to take a long, hard look at the fact that the self is managed and controlled in an absolute sense. In other words, it is important to liberate one's self from the regulations that have become a part of the inner self.

It is not so difficult to achieve *kisei teppai*—that is, to remove regulations altogether. Having a mind of one's own, and taking the initiative to act, no matter how trivial this action may be, will lead to *kisei teppai.*

Eliminating regulations will be for the good not only of the citizens of Japan but the global economy as well. Only a handful of bureaucrats think that this move would be negative. There is a saying, "The frog in the well doesn't know the ocean." If the Japanese continue to listen to the views of a small minority of bureaucrats, then the society will never be able to break out of the mentality of the Edo era, when the country closed its doors to the outside world. Only by realizing a society free of regulation can the nation hope to replace Japanese groupism and a communist system with a democratic one. Today the people of Japan need an environment in which they can be responsible for their own behavior rather than one in which bureaucrats are allowed to maintain control over them.

CHAPTER SIX

Reform, Japanese-Style

Eisuke Sakakibara

BOTH INSIDE AND OUTSIDE of Japan, a consensus has developed that the 1990s are to be a decade of profound change—for our nation and for the rest of the world. Yet the question of what direction and shape this change ought to take has produced tremendous confusion, creating expectations of change for its own sake that have not only failed to improve matters but made them worse.

Old Bromides by New "Reformers"

Japan in particular has spawned a plethora of ill-conceived proposals, under such rubrics as "structural reform" or the dreadful "Heisei revolution," which purport to address the need for reform of the current system. None of these proposals, however, goes much beyond an expression of pique at such present-day sins as excessive government intervention or excessive emphasis on corporate priorities. The reference model for reform in these critiques is nothing more than a classical interpretation of individualism or the 1980s version of laissez-faire doctrine.

Excerpted from *Bunmei to Shite no Nihon-Gata Shihonshugi* (*Capitalism Japanese-Style*) (Tokyo: Toyo Keizai Shimposha, 1993). Translation by Alan G. Gleason for the Pacific Basin Institute.

Unfortunately, many of the problems that confront us today have arisen precisely because of the advent in the 1980s of an extreme variety of individualism (dubbed "me-ism" in Japan) and a rigidly classical form of laissez-faire policy that would leave everything in the hands of the market. Inevitably, the hysterical brandishing of old bromides at new problems not only brings us no closer to a solution but exacerbates the problems. Rather than press for quick remedies or flail away with outmoded policy proposals, it behooves us instead to take a long hard look at where we stand now in the context of our own history.

For the past half-century, we Japanese have been too preoccupied—first with recovery from the war, then with sustaining economic growth—to pay proper attention to our history and culture or to our identity as a nation. Throughout the postwar era, the primary challenge for every Japanese citizen has been to ride the wave of the technological revolution, learning from Europe and America and struggling to keep up with them. Even now, with Japan's recovery a fait accompli and the fruits of postwar economic growth ready to be savored, we still look to the West, prattling about individualism and consumerism and attempting, as before, to continue Westernizing our country. In this respect few recent proposals for reform represent any departure from the tendencies of the past. Most, in fact, would only accelerate those tendencies, pushing Japanese society further and further from its "Japaneseness."

Just so there is no misunderstanding on the part of the reader, I wish to stress that I am not a "nationalist" in any sense of the word. However, I do take strong exception to the current fashion of advocating national policies that are merely extrapolations of the philosophy of Western corporate consultants or of our own consultants in the heady "bubble" days of the 1980s. It was the pseudorationalism and shallow "innovations" of the business school style of management that distorted the liberal economic system of the 1980s. What we now see in the 1990s is the collapse of a grand scheme to unify and transform the world in obeisance to the logic of capital, or more precisely, of financial deregulation, without regard for the intrinsic nature of economics or for the historical background and identity of individual sociopolitical systems. It is therefore all the more bizarre to see the Japanese media fawn upon proposals to alter the Japanese sociopolitical structure in accordance with the very tenets of unbridled individualism and laissez-faire that have so distorted Japanese society over the past decade.

How Did the Pursuit of Desire and Profit Become the Norm?

The frenzy of the 1980s not only created a "great divide" (as Studs Terkel often says) in American society, it irrevocably warped the social fabric of the entire world, including Japan. As the Japanese bubble expanded, it did not merely send stock and real estate prices soaring. Its influence went much deeper, penetrating the hearts of men, dramatically altering the moral codes and conventions that govern human behavior. Bemoaning the excessive yen-worship of Japanese corporations in recent years, novelist Saburo Shiroyama writes:

> It is depressing to see the number of boorish corporations and boorish executives who will go to any lengths in their pursuit of profit these days. Do these individuals even deserve to be called executives? Are they anything more than money-mad zombies, leading their minions in one frontal assault after another under the flag of profits? . . .The spectacle only grows more desolate when the mass media extol these individuals as heroes.
>
> Reisuke Ishida, prewar vice president of Mitsui and Co. and postwar president of Japan National Railways, was famous for his remark, 'I may be crude, but I'm not vile.' While the first half of this quip is merely a bit of self-deprecating humor, the latter half is significant, for it sums up his aesthetic of management with dignity. Indeed, Ishida practiced what he preached throughout his life. He was the model of the dignified executive, without a hint of vileness.
>
> What a contrast with the recent crop of pseudo-managers who are not merely crude, but carry vileness to the extreme in their obsession with self-aggrandizement and success at any cost! Inevitably, they surround themselves with vile subordinates all too eager to imitate the boss. In this stifling corporate atmosphere, no thought is given to the selection and training of worthy successors. What has become of this country?[1]

This is a harsh critique of the corporate profit-first principle. Shiroyama goes on to say that the same mentality has corrupted Japanese politics, from where it has spread to the bureaucracy and the financial sector as well. The credo of "private sector vitality" has been twisted into the canard that greed is good, and the infatuations with the new financial engineering techniques known as *zaitech* have even infected segments of the public. Clearly, the Roaring Eighties juggernaut has wreaked havoc on both corporate and private life in Japan. But exactly what happened during this decade, and why?

The 1980s were a time when the neoconservative point of view, bolstered by the conservative revolutions of Ronald Reagan and Margaret Thatcher, made deep inroads not only among Japan's intelligentsia but within the general public as well. On the one hand, the ideological justifications of leftist and progressive intellectuals had exploded in their faces; at the same time the shackles were being removed from the long-suppressed desires of the individual citizen. Gradually these desires, in the form of "me-ism" and the profit-first principle, became legitimized as valid social objectives.

Because neoconservatism is so inextricably linked with neoclassical economic doctrine, it had a profound effect on Japan that went well beyond the purview of simple conservatism. The push for liberalization in the form of deregulation and privatization versus bureaucratic regulation, local autonomy versus centralized power, and the primacy of the individual versus the organization of community tipped Japan's traditional balance (one that had survived even in postwar Japan) between *tatemae* (principle) and *honne* (true intention) heavily in the direction of *honne*. The pursuit of self-interest and money-worship became more pronounced than ever. On the individual level, morality is what provides a balance between the *tatemae* of altruism and the *honne* of egoistic desire. On the societal level, regulations and discipline are needed to maintain an equilibrium between freedom and order. But disregard for morals and rules in pursuit of one's own desires and profit became the norm for life in the Japan of the 1980s.

This trend was exacerbated by the administrative reforms of the Nakasone cabinet, which centered on economic policies of privatization and deregulation. I will not argue here about whether privatizing the Japan National Railways and the Nippon Telegraph and Telephone Corporation was a good idea or a bad one. The problem is the assumption behind the privatization of these public corporations that all regulations are bad, the public sector is bad, and the contemporary society can be sustained on the pillars of freedom and the entrepreneurial spirit alone. The 1980s were truly the age of the entrepreneur, but it is no coincidence that so many heroes of the age—men like Recruit chairman Hiromasa Ezoe and Sagawa Kyuubin president Kiyoshi Sagawa—became embroiled in scandals in the 1990s. The appearance of the Ezoes, Sagawas, and others of their ilk was inevitable in an era that championed the free market and the pursuit of corporate profit with an un-bridled ambition and energy that held no regard for the ethics of entre-preneurship or the rules of society.

Yet the lesson has yet to sink in that the problem with these tainted heroes was not their own behavior but the mores of the times. To be sure, the unrestrained freedom of expression and the entrepreneurial spirit are priceless assets in an economic system like Japan's, which tends to find its comfort level in a cocoon of vague yet protective regulations. But the "freedom" of the 1980s was a force without a compass, a will-ful, undisciplined creature steeped in the desires of a mass consumer society. The scruffy, sleazy entrepreneurs that Japan has spawned over the past decade bear little resemblance to their forefathers, men like Soichiro Honda and Akio Morita. But the problem, as I said before, is not with the individual entrepreneur but with the mood of the times and with the public policies that nurtured this mood.

Do We Want to Pass America in the Debt Race, Too?

The primary focus for these policies of liberalization was deregula-tion of the financial sector. Financial deregulation began to catch on with the advent of the Euromarket in the late 1960s and spread from there around the globe. By the 1970s it had taken root in America and by the 1980s had gained a footing in England, Japan, and continental Eu-rope. The U.S.-Japan Yen-Dollar Commission that convened in 1984 spurred the rapid deregulation of Japan's finance industry during the latter half of the 1980s.

I do not intend to attempt a comprehensive evaluation here of the financial deregulation policies of the 1980s. Suffice it to say that de-regulation was central to the frenzy that overwhelmed the decade. Di-rect financing overtook indirect financing in popularity, while nonbanks sprang up to replace (or serve as fronts for), banks which remained saddled with regulations. That the nonbanks were allowed to expand their financial activities in this fashion was a consequence of the ideol-ogy of liberalization that dominated the era. It was obvious that the nonbanks posed a problem in terms of risk management and financial regulation, but in the antiregulatory atmosphere of the day, efforts to impose new regulations on them were virtually unthinkable.

Adept at crunching numbers and operating computers, the graduates of America's business schools flooded the market with financial products geared to specific customer needs, expanding the business of finance in new directions. This in turn spurred the proliferation of *zaitech*—sophisticated financial transactions unrelated to business operations—on a global scale. Everything became *zaitech* fodder: stocks, bonds, exchange rates, and in Japan, even golf club memberships and works of art. Although somewhat different in character from *zaitech*, the explosion in real estate investments both in Japan and overseas was another logical consequence of financial deregulation and the rapid expansion of the finance industry.

Like the United States, Japan saw a substantial rise in individual and corporate debt during the 1980s. Outstanding corporate debt at the end of 1990 was 134.6 percent of Japan's gross national product, while individual debt was 63.2 percent. These rates were respectively 47.5 percent and 20.2 percent above their 1981 levels. Thus in ten years, corporations and individuals taken together increased their debt relative to GNP by 67.7 percent. During the same period (from the fourth quarter of 1980 to the first quarter of 1989), American companies and individuals increased their debt by 25.6 percent of their GNP—far less than the Japanese.

Japanese corporate debt as a percentage of GNP has been higher than that of the U.S. throughout the postwar era; individual debt, however, has ballooned only in the last ten years. When Japanese individual debt reached 63.2 percent of the GNP in 1990, it had passed the U.S. level of 62.3 percent recorded at the end of the first quarter of 1989. In 1978 individual debt in Japan was a mere 17.5 percent of GNP; in 1970 it was only 4.6 percent, while in the United States it was close to 50 percent that year. To make a long story short, Japan's individual debt had been less than one-tenth America's twenty years earlier. But Japanese consumers allowed their debts to burgeon in those two decades, particularly in the 1980s, and ultimately surpassed American consumers in the race to borrow.

The above figures on individual debt include housing loans, but the results are the same for consumer credit outstanding when housing loans are excluded. The ratio of nonhousing consumer credit outstanding to disposable household income in 1990 was 20.1 percent in the United States and 22.5 percent in Japan. The equivalent figures for 1985 were 20.9 percent and 12.5 percent respectively—a graphic illustration of the degree of debt piled up by Japanese consumers in those five years.[2]

These figures show us that Japanese corporations and consumers, no less than their American counterparts, have saddled themselves with some serious balance sheet problems through a combination of rapidly accumulated debt and depreciated assets. Americans and Japanese alike borrowed too much and spent too much during the 1980s.

Japan Requires Japanese-Style Reform

Awareness is starting to spread that the Japanese economy—or in a larger sense, the Japanese socioeconomic system—currently suffers from structural problems against which conventional countermeasures, or policies offering symptomatic relief, are utterly ineffective. Meanwhile, the endless parade of political scandals that began with the Lockheed incident has finally forced a consensus on the urgent need for political and administrative reform. At the root of these developments is a widening gap between *tatemae* and *honne*, a gap caused by the process of Americanization that had been going on since World War II but accelerated in the 1980s. Under these stresses, the system I have described here as Japanese-style capitalism has gradually deteriorated and now shows signs of severe structural fatigue. The *tatemae-honne* gap also signifies a loss of the philosophical underpinnings of our society.

This underlying philosophy (in American society, Protestant morality; in Japan, the samurai ethic coupled with the spirit of the Edo merchant class) is referred to by Japan's great historical novelist, Ryotaro Shiba, as the "core" of a society. As we approach the end of the twentieth century, Japan's social core appears on the verge of a meltdown.

In response to this state of affairs, many a self-styled reformer has urged a radical revamping of the political and economic system. Kenichi Omae, for example, discusses the need for drastic reform as follows:

> The Heisei Revolution is not about mere reform. The paradigm transformation I have described above cannot be accomplished through fine-tuning alone. This is an attempt to wipe the slate clean, to zero-out the past and build from the ground up a new, more authentic Japan as befits one of the advanced nations of the world. . . .
>
> In this sense the Heisei Revolution is more than just a few political and administrative reforms. It demands a change in the consciousness, values, and worldview of the Japanese people, unifying all these elements under a single credo: the sovereignty of the *seikatsusha* (consumer).[3]

Omae may well be correct in arguing that Japan's closed political and economic system needs to be forced open through radical reform or "revolution." Since the war ended a half-century ago, the political and administrative life of the nation has continued with virtually no changes in the framework of Japanese law—from the Constitution itself to the basic laws on public finance, local government, the Diet, building standards, agricultural land, and so on. It is certainly high time Japan reexamined that framework. But what Omae demands—a change in the "consciousness, values, and worldview of the Japanese people"—is not only impracticable, it is hardly a job to ask of the political or administrative agencies of the country. The role of the enlightened philosopher and the role of the politician or bureaucrat are two utterly different things.

If a fundamental reevaluation of the current system is in order, what direction should it take? What model should we adopt for a new system? While Omae, Taichi Sakaiya, and other members of the "reformer" school do not always clearly articulate what they stand for, their favorite catch phrases included "decentralization of power" and "the sovereignty of the consumer." Decentralization of power means reducing the central government's role to the bare minimum—diplomacy and defense, basically—and the transfer to prefectural and local governments of most administrative functions (in which Omae includes tax collection) that affect the lives of the populace. The sovereignty of the consumer is a concept based on classical liberalism or laissez-faire philosophy. This is the proposition that if economic adjustments are left up to the market, the consumer will benefit most of the time. Omae makes this position clear in his discussion of free competition:

> The problem is, who pays the balance when a land purchasing agency is created? Who pays the balance for the National Railways Liquidation Corporation? If a bank fails due to its own errors in risk management, it should be allowed to fail.
>
> The reason we have economic cycles in a liberal economic system is to eliminate weak companies during downturns and preserve the strong. Those strong companies will then raise the economy to a new peak, and once again, those who took bad risks will drop by the wayside.
>
> Without this economic principle at work, prices will not fall, and quality of life will not improve.[4]

But does it really work that way? The laissez-faire doctrine espoused by Omae came close to being realized in its fully orthodox form in the America of the 1980s. But the distribution of income and assets grew increasingly unequal, and the quality of life for American consumers did not merely fail to improve, it worsened at a pace unprecedented in U.S. history. If Japan decides to play by the same rules, who can guarantee that the same thing will not happen here? The law of survival of the fittest lowers the quality of life of most citizens, who do not belong to the ranks of the "fittest." And it is a fact that the only remedy for this inequity is to be found in the redistribution of income and establishment of a welfare system by the government. Competition and market mechanisms are essential, indeed are the foundation of a capitalist society. But no capitalist state can achieve stability or run efficiently without the establishment of a healthy balance between competition and government regulations that protect the weak, the wage earner, and the consumer.

The same problem arises with the transfer of power from the center to the provinces. Our way of thinking as a nation, our culture, has a far greater affinity for a decentralized system than even the United States or Europe; indeed, such a system has already evolved over the course of Japanese history. It is natural, then, that the decentralization thesis would carry an instinctive appeal for most Japanese. However, our nation's experience demonstrates that the most efficient system is one in which decentralization is offset by the centralization of some functions. Decentralized power itself functions more efficiently when balanced by power at the center.

My purpose is not to describe how to "rebuild" Japan; therefore I will not go into the specifics of how to achieve (or restore) the balance between competition and regulation, or between centralized and decentralized power. Still, it should be clear that reforms based on the doctrine of Western-style individualism or Anglo-Saxon free market capitalism cannot be implemented in Japan, or, if implemented, are destined to fail. Critics who arrive belatedly on the scene extolling the virtues of foreign ideologies no doubt have some sort of role to play in the debate. But Japan requires a distinctively Japanese type of reform (or revolution, if you will), and critics who look only to Europe or America for inspiration and hastily conclude that the answers lie there must be taken to task for failing to do their homework.

What we need now is a reaffirmation of the samurai spirit and merchant ethic that form the Japanese philosophical "core" spoken of by Shiba. We must then reexamine our system and our laws in light of the new global environment in which they must function, and, based on this Japanese core, construct a distinctly Japanese form of capitalism. The last thing we need is to alter our "consciousness, values, and worldview" only to replace them with the Anglo-Saxon model of capitalism. Although it is essential that we learn from other countries in the internationalized world of today, we ignore our own history and culture at our peril. Pronouncements and policies that only look outward for guidance can at most succeed in destroying the old system and fomenting chaos in its stead. Destruction and chaos are certainly one sort of "revolution," for which reason we must not take the activities of the self-styled reformists lightly. But in the meantime, we must get on with the work of creation and construction, or we may discover too late that our core has been extinguished.

Notes

1. Saburo Shiroyama, "A Lament on Mammonism," *Yomiuri*, July 3, 1992.

2. Masanori Masuda, "Recent Trends in the Consumer Loan Market," *Chosa Geppo* (Monthly Survey) (Tokyo: Nissei Research Institute, September 1992).

3. Kenichi Omae, *Gekiron: Kaisoron* (A controversial plan for rebuilding Japan) (Tokyo: Tokuma Shoten,1992), pp. 212–13.

4. Omae, *Gekiron.*

PART TWO

The Protective Bureaucracy in Action

CHAPTER SEVEN

Who Has Obstructed Reform?

Taro Yayama

REGULATED INDUSTRIES ACCOUNT for about half of all industry in Japan. Here is a classic system of nontariff barriers. It contributes to Japan's current account surplus, which in turn has spurred the yen appreciation of recent years. The bureaucracy for its part seems completely unaware of this connection. Virtually all bureaucrats publicly maintain that Japan's markets are open. They find no difference between them and the markets of other major industrialized economies. In April 1995 the Murayama administration hammered out a three-year plan for deregulation as an emergency measure to counter the appreciation of the yen. Yet because the plan contained nothing of any substance, the market realized that the Japanese government had not yet changed its fundamental stance. Traders continued to buy yen, causing the yen to appreciate further.

According to a survey by the Japanese Economic Planning Agency, Japan's overall cost of living in 1994 was much higher than that of New York, London, or Paris.[1] With the cost of living being 40 percent higher in Japan, why haven't worldwide goods, money, and services rushed in and driven down the cost of living to an international level of equilibrium? Why has the trade surplus continued to increase? There is no choice but to conclude that this mysterious phenomenon is due to the closed nature of Japan's markets.

A Brief and Checkered History

Despite these complaints, change comes slowly. The support base for both the Liberal Democratic Party (LDP) and the now diminished Japan

Social Democratic Party (JSDP) consists of industries that are protected by regulation. To understand why the course of structural reform since World War II has been so tortuous, one must begin by examining the year 1964. In 1964 the First Provisional Commission for Administrative Reform submitted a report on administrative reform to Prime Minister Eisaku Sato. Although the report suggested government changes for the new era it envisioned, the report was completely ignored by the Sato administration for several reasons. First, the report ran counter to the prevailing bureaucratic thinking of the day and thus seemed too idealistic to be of use. Second, Japan in 1964 was at the peak of an economic boom. The need for administrative reform was not strongly felt.

The word "deregulation" was heard in Japan for the first time in 1979, when an Organization of Economic Cooperation and Development (OECD) report strongly advised deregulation. At that time Japan's Economic Planning Agency and Fair Trade Commission formed a joint study group to consider whether or not deregulation was needed in Japan.

In 1979 the Carter administration advocated its "open sky policy," which called for the deregulation of the airline industry in the United States. The Reagan administration continued this policy by deregulating the airlines and a broad range of other industries. Following the U.S. lead, the Thatcher government in Britain also responded by privatizing various government enterprises and abolishing numerous industry controls.

Japan, going along with this trend, convened the Second Provisional Commission for Expediting Administrative Reform, chaired by Toshio Doko in 1981. The Doko Commission, learning from the failure of the first commission, assembled representatives of the various government ministries and agencies to serve on its committees. Its goal was to create a practical proposal that might be put into effect. The Doko Commission achieved moderate success through the consensus it formed by compiling the report with the cooperation of these various agencies. But this very cooperation also detracted from the commission's proposal, inasmuch as its reforms were too lenient.

In a curious turn, the commission avoided altogether the use of the term "deregulation." Given the fact that the government was running a huge deficit at the time, the commission had first to "restore fiscal balance without increasing taxes." The commission also had to consider the scope of "administrative protection." Although the government has often protected private industries, the widespread protection of the public sector was seen as even more of a problem. Three public corporations symbolized the issue at hand: Japanese National Railways (JNR), Nippon Telegraph and Telephone (NTT), and Japan Tobacco and Salt. JNR's annual losses of a trillion yen made restructuring especially urgent for improving the national budget. Yet, when JNR's operations were analyzed, it became clear that the reason for its inefficiency lay in its structure as a public corporation. The commission thus concluded that JNR should be privatized along with NTT and Japan Tobacco and Salt.

Although JNR was considered a public corporation, it operated almost exactly as it had in the days when it was under the direct jurisdiction of the Ministry of Railways. Railroad cars were ordered in equal numbers and for the same price from various railroad car manufacturers. There was no competitive bidding. During the JNR era, railroad cars were purchased at a price that was 30 percent higher than under the bidding system after the railroads were privatized. Fluorescent lights, with a market price of ¥500, were purchased for as much as ¥8,000, ostensibly because they had to conform to special "JNR standards." Furthermore, all products were purchased through Tokyo, which resulted in excessive transportation costs. After JNR's privatization under Prime Minister Yasuhiro Nakasone, special standards were abolished. The railroads now use ordinary commercially available products. As a result, fluorescent lights can now be purchased for ¥500 from ordinary electrical appliance stores.

The biggest change since JNR was privatized and became Japan Railways (JR) is the productivity of its workers. The JNR used to employ close to 400,000 people, but the number of employees of the seven JR companies created from JNR (after privatization the railways were partitioned into seven companies) has fallen dramatically to a present total of 180,000. Owing in part to a marked improvement in employee efficiency, the trillion-yen deficit has been reduced to zero. In fact, the JR companies now even pay stock dividends and taxes. A separate account was set up to cover past losses that have not yet been fully absorbed.

Similarly, the privatization of NTT introduced competition into the long-distance telecommunications market. With the price war that ensued, the highest rate for a telephone call fell from ¥400 to ¥180.

JNR and NTT each supported 2,000 "affiliated enterprises." These companies profited by using their political connections to force the public corporations to purchase their products; it was not uncommon for politicians to receive political contributions from these affiliated enterprises. Needless to say, the affiliated enterprises strongly opposed privatization, knowing that it would expose them to competition. They enlisted Diet members who faced the prospect of losing cash gifts to argue their case for them. Anti-privatization sentiment rose accordingly on the political scene.

Nevertheless, political skill allowed Prime Minister Nakasone to overcome this sentiment. From the president on down, he dismissed eight JNR executives who opposed the partition and privatization of the corporation. He then appointed a member of the reform faction to lead the Ministry of Railways, which controlled JNR. Nakasone clearly conveyed his intentions. It was expected that his administration would be in power for a long time. Bending to the wind, the bureaucrats in the Ministry of Railways refrained from speaking out. If the Nakasone administration had stayed in power for only one or two years, the bureaucracy would no doubt have paid only lip service to privatization, all the while stalling until the administration changed and the plan could be scrapped.

As it happened, the Nakasone administration stayed in power for five years. Since then, Japan's leadership has changed almost annually. Instituting deregulation or administrative reform means confronting the bureaucracy—an utterly impossible task for a short-lived or weak administration. Three major reforms, however, have been implemented since Nakasone: electoral reform, the partial opening of the rice market, and tax reform. The first two were carried out by the Hosokawa administration. Though incomplete, the first steps toward tax reform were also taken under Hosokawa.

Nakasone was the first prime minister to position Japan clearly in international politics as one of the "Western powers." In the economic arena, he was also the first prime minister to grapple seriously with the opening of Japanese markets. Beginning in 1985, Nakasone unveiled his "action program" plan for market liberalization. This step marked the first Japanese attempt to reform institutions and practices that act as import barriers to international standards. The aim of this effort was to make Japanese markets, with a few exceptions, free in principle. Nakasone met with foreign ambassadors in Tokyo to hear their complaints on trade with Japan. As a first step, he attempted to eliminate nontariff barriers. This effort made Nakasone acutely aware of how much he needed to restructure Japan's economic system. Accordingly, Nakasone established the Advisory Group on Economic Structural Adjustment for International Harmony. He appointed Haruo Maekawa as its director.

The Advisory Group presented its findings in 1986. Commonly known as the Maekawa Report, this historic paper established the necessity of reform in the Japanese economy.[2] It was essential, the report concluded, to plan for economic growth led by domestic demand. At the same time, Japan was urged to transform radically its foreign trade policies and industrial structure. Until the Maekawa Report, Japanese industrial policy had always required the government to play a leading role in protecting major industries, while nurturing the small and medium enterprises that grow up around large enterprises. As the yen appreciated in line with the 1985 Plaza accord (among Japan, the United States, the United Kingdom, France, and West Germany [the G5 powers] on the yen-dollar exchange rate), major corporations forced subcontracting parts manufacturers to sell their products at lower prices. The only government policy to palliate the effects of a strong yen in this sector was one to extend low-interest loans to small- and medium-sized parts manufacturers that were hit hardest. In other words, Japanese policy was aimed at maintaining the existing relationship between major corporations and subcontractors. Without question, this encouragement of the status quo was antithetical to the concept of structural adjustment.

The effective adjustment of a nation's industrial structure means forgoing the development of goods that can be provided by other countries and concentrating on backing local producers like Kyocera that possess proprietary technologies and goods. Yet for a century Japanese industrial policy has sought to include every kind of industry in Japan's economy. Thus each Japanese tariff in the past was initially designed to protect a particular domestic industry. Once industrial promotion—going further—takes the form of nontariff barriers, the lives of domestic industries that should have left Japan are prolonged.

The first attempt to deal squarely with the problem of controls in structural reform was made by the Second Administrative Reform Promotion Council. This was in session from 1987 to 1990. In 1987 the council presented a report on deregulation that advocated easing or abolishing Japanese specifications in all industries to fit the standards of the United States and Europe. Unfortunately, the Takeshita cabinet, which received this report, was slow to act on it. Thus the trend toward deregulation failed to gain momentum.

The Third Administrative Reform Promotion Council, which deliberated from 1990 to 1993, continued the work of the second council. The third council reported on the causes of the disparity between domestic and overseas prices; deregulation for the purpose of revitalizing industry; and measures to increase the standard of living. Despite these findings, the Miyazawa cabinet in power at the time seemed in no way eager to promote deregulation and administrative reform.

Nonetheless foreign pressure on Japan began to increase rapidly. Previous complaints about economic and trade issues had been directed toward Japan during the cold war. As a member of the political anti-Soviet alliance, however, Japan was treated leniently. (With reference to Nakasone, President Reagan once reportedly remarked to a legislator calling for a hard-line policy on Japan, "I can't be tough on a friend." When the Soviet Union finally collapsed in 1991, however, the economic floodgates opened. Japan was deluged with criticism from around the world.

In the summer of 1993, Morihiro Hosokawa rose to power as the first prime minister of a non-LDP administration in four decades. Following a "consumer-first" agenda, Hosokawa made deregulation the centerpiece of his policy. An Economic Reform Study Commission hastily established by Hosokawa presented its findings at the end of 1993. Known as the Hiraiwa Report (from its chairman, Gaishi Hiraiwa), it set forth four goals for economic reform: a transparent economy, open domestically and internationally; a creative, vital economy; an economy that gives priority to consumers; and an economy in harmony with and respected by the world.[3] To achieve these goals, the report laid out deregulation policies for all sectors. As mentioned, the Hosokawa administration instituted political reform, partially opened the rice market, and took the first steps toward tax reform. Though the JSDP participated in Hosokawa's administration, it opposed each of the proposed reforms, causing the administration to lose momentum. For this reason among others, Hosokawa was forced to step down after only eight months in office. The succeeding administrations of Tsumotu Hata and Tomiichi Murayama did little to further regulatory reform. The Hashimoto cabinet, which returned power to the LDP in 1996, has demonstrated some awareness of the problem, but it remains to be seen whether its slogans and ambitious plans for deregulation will be translated into reality.

Case Studies

There still exist no fewer than forty-two laws running counter to the Anti-Monopoly Law, saying in effect that Japan need not have free competition. Indeed, an open-ended and wide-ranging regulatory system is still in place. The regulatory net spreads over 40.8 percent of all Japanese industry. When we add to this such "invisible" controls as *dango* (collusive bidding resulting in price fixing), the *keiretsu* networks of affiliated companies and "administrative guidance," the total easily exceeds 50 percent. I have applied the term "semisocialist" to Japan's economic structure. Another commentator has referred to Japan as the country having "the most successful socialist system." Japan is different.

Over the past twenty years I have been tracking the various systems that came into being in Japan in the period before and after 1950. Based on this research, one inevitably concludes that the complex of regulations and trade barriers should be abolished. Although there has been some progress that even outsiders would recognize as deregulation, Japan's systematized coalition of politics, bureaucracy, and industry remains largely intact, undermining the living standards of its people, causing friction with its trading partners, and weakening the global economy. What follows are some examples of Japan's "semisocialist" economy in action, beginning with its infamous system of auto inspections.

Auto Parts and the *Shaken* System

Japan has one of the lowest penetration rates of foreign-made products among the industrialized economies. The import rate for auto parts is 60 percent in the case of England, 40 percent for France, and 33 percent for the United States. Even in Italy, which is said to be particularly closed to auto imports, the rate is 16 percent. Japan, by comparison, imports only a tiny 2.4 percent. Opening the Japanese market in this product category would be highly beneficial to the narrowing of America's deficit with Japan—of which automobiles and auto parts constitute the single largest component. Such an opening would also promise great benefits for Japan's long-suffering consumers.

The primary reason for this country's low level of auto and auto parts imports is the system of compulsory inspection and repair called *shaken* (in full translation—"official automobile check-out"). This system is based on the Road Vehicles Act promulgated in 1951. It mandates the checking of motor vehicles by a government agency, but with Japan now producing the world's best cars, the very basis of the law has changed.

A comparative look at the inspection system of Germany, said to be second in its rigor only to Japan, is instructive. First, under the German system the owner takes his vehicle into the inspection station (half private, half public) and has a maintenance professional point out any defective areas. The areas covered by this inspection are restricted to a total of five that relate to the exhaust system, the brakes, and so on. If no problems are discovered, the car is okayed as is, and the cost for inspection runs about fifty to one hundred dollars (U.S.). When something is found wrong, the owner has the car repaired at one of the garages lined up near the inspection station. Finally, he has his papers signed and sends them back to the inspection station.

The garages are divided according to specialty, such as electrical system or brakes. With all kinds of parts on hand, the shops can meet a variety of needs. They purchase from any supplier that has good quality and low prices, including overseas sources. When inspection-related repairs are made, owners need not be concerned about using "genuine parts." As long as standards are met, they use a part even if it is not the same manufacture as the original .

In principle this applies in Japan as well. But manufacturers and dealers who want people to use parts they themselves make have created the myth that owners must use original parts—in other words, "genuine parts." There are also superior-grade parts, which are the same as genuine parts. Although the two types are made by precisely the same manufacturers, the labels of the "genuine parts" carry such names as Toyota and Nissan. Even though the parts are identically standard when they leave the factory, those whose wrapping shows the name of a car manufacturer sell for 10 percent to 15 percent more. Parts makers advertise the fact that "genuine" and "superior-grade" components are the same, but repair shops affiliated with car makers and dealers carry only genuine parts in stock.

If selling generic parts made by the same Japanese manufacturer is difficult, selling those made overseas is even more so. One needs first to dispel the "genuine parts" myth prevalent among car owners, but the parts makers lack the publicity power of the auto companies.

Thanks to the myth of genuine parts, it is expensive to maintain a foreign-made car in Japan. The *shaken* system requires inspection when a car becomes three years old, then at two-year intervals, just as in Germany. In Japan, however, the average cost per inspection is about U.S.$670 (Transportation Ministry figures), whereas Mercedes Benz–class inspections of foreign cars cost from $3,000 to $4,000. Because of the insistence on genuine parts, components for German cars are brought in from Germany, American from the United States, and so on. Given a choice of two similar cars, the Japanese consumer will understandably buy a domestic make. When *shaken* is factored in, this means a saving of hundreds of dollars. Thus the strict *shaken* system is, in effect, another kind of nontariff barrier.

The Japanese system requires inspection of sixty-five different parts of the vehicle and involves disassembly. Carrying this work out nationwide are 8,030 authorized repair facilities. Authorized by the Transportation Ministry, each facility must be capable of performing all kinds of inspections. It is much like telling a neighborhood clinic to equip itself with everything from an X-ray unit to Catscan and MRI. "We've got inspection equipment we've never used sitting in a corner gathering dust," says a shop employee with a wry grin. If a facility is to recover its investment in all this equipment, its management has no choice but to increase sales by installing as many replacement parts as possible.

This ulterior motive of the repair shops naturally fits the desire of car makers to earn money by selling lots of parts. The manufacturers specify eight to ten parts that must be replaced regularly, such as brake hoses, master cylinders, boots, and rubber parts. According to one expert, all of these parts have life-spans of ten years or 100,000 kilometers—in other words, from the time the car is bought new until it is junked. Although car makers claim for their parts a useful life of four to five years, some garages replace them at every *shaken* inspection. Strangely, Japanese makers do not specify replacement parts for the cars they export. Were they to do so, Japanese cars would be given a wide berth. In short, we Japanese are being forced to spend money needlessly.

One conspicuous difference in the Japanese system compared with that of Germany is that in Japan, before a car is taken to the government inspection station, its owner must have it taken apart and repaired at a garage. This is called the "fix, then inspect" method, but it is the opposite of the German way. As a result, while the repair shops employ first- and second-class mechanics, those at the inspection stations are third class. If they lack the ability to inspect cars already fixed by first-class garage mechanics, there is also no necessity for the extra step. At a station's reception counter one finds a few people applying official seals to documents brought by maintenance personnel with the cars. In reality, then, inspection stations are there not so much to inspect as they are merely to stamp documents.

The Provisional Council for the Promotion of Administrative Reform, which advises the prime minister, has strongly proposed the streamlining of *shaken*. As a result, in 1994 the Ministry of Transportation approved a system of "inspect, then fix" like that of Germany. This allows owners first to take their cars in for inspection, then have only specified trouble spots repaired or replaced. But after that it is still necessary to go once again to the inspection station for yet another checkup. This not only doubles the owner's inconvenience, but the presence of third-class mechanics at the government stations provides no reassurance to owners that repairs have been done properly.

As it happens, each prefecture has only about two inspection stations. This means that a trip to the station is a day's work. Only those with plenty of leisure time could readily make the needed two trips. The new method can hardly be called an improvement or a streamlining. It would be better to adopt the German system of one inspection (which would require additional stations) or to make authorized commercial stations wholly responsible for inspections. The latter option would introduce price competition. Accordingly faith in the "religion" of genuine parts would disappear as well.

The Type Designation System administered by the Transportation Ministry is another reason why foreign cars are excluded. Under this system, piston displacement, height, width, and so on are fixed. Naturally, domestic vehicles are manufactured in accordance with those standards. But since it is not feasible for foreign makers to build cars in line with such standards, often they do not conform. For a long time, for example, because Japan's Type Designation System permitted only cars with side mirrors, Western makes with inside mirrors were excluded. They were allowed only after objections were raised against the practice as a nontariff trade barrier .

Many Americans replace shock absorbers to make their cars ride better. Japanese can do this, too, for about $200, but this raises the height of the car one or two centimeters, above the Type Designation standard. Permission to deviate from the standard then costs an additional $1,000 in fees. This means a cost of $1,200 to replace a set of shock absorbers. How can American-made shock absorbers be expected to sell in this situation?

Every car owner abhors this rigid, costly system. The Transportation Ministry, however, insists, "It is precisely because we have *shaken* that the accident rate is so low." The ministry says Japanese police put the number of accidents clearly attributable to "bad maintenance" at 0.035 percent of the total. The necessity of *shaken* is publicized in pamphlets stating that by comparison, the percentage in the United States is 0.5 to 3.5, in Germany 3.0 to 3.5 percent. What these statistics are grounded on, however, is not made clear. Both countries have federal systems of independent states. It is difficult to imagine that the federal governments gather statistics on accidents because of poor maintenance from every state or land. Even if the figures for Germany and the United States are true, no matter how thoroughgoing the maintenance, it is impossible to bring the accident rate virtually to zero. A car can be involved in an accident the day after inspection. In any case, no system that imposes such a heavy burden on owners can be justified.

In 1951 some mediocre automobiles were being produced by Japanese car makers. For safety's sake, a strict *shaken* system was undoubtedly necessary. But today, with Japanese companies having attained the world's highest levels of technology, ordinary citizens feel there is almost no need for it. So why does the Ministry of Transportation cling to the system? The reason is clear: to protect the Japan Automobile Service Promotion Association (GASPE). And it is doubtless for this purpose that ministry bureaucrats are sent upon retirement to serve at the core of that association, where government and industry become as one.

In 1993 the automobile service industry reported sales of well over $6.28 billion. Maintenance related to *shaken* and regular inspections represented a 45 percent share. Only in Japan can one find what should be called a "*shaken* industry," where even if there were no accidents or breakdowns, there would still be a constant "demand" for maintenance services. According to my own survey, limited to passenger cars alone, the cost of maintenance and repair averages about $500 more per car in Japan than in Germany and America. With almost 20 million cars going through the system annually, Japanese owners are treating the *shaken* industry to a feast of some $1 billion a year.

During the past decade the streamlining of the system has ended up in the politicians' laps many times. In every instance, however, the majority Liberal Democratic Party took a staunch stand and crushed the effort. Why does the LDP protect the *shaken* industry? The mechanism works like this.

At the end of 1994, the electoral system changed to one based on 300 small electoral districts. For seventy years previous to that, elections were held according to the medium constituency system, under which three to five persons were elected in each district. Politicians received contributions from 83,000 repair facilities nationwide, and their votes to boot. In a single medium-sized constituency district, there were about 700 repair facilities. By taking these businesses into their support groups and collecting a $1,000 political contribution from each, they were able to rake in $700,000 a year. And they received the votes of those firms' employees. For the LDP, having 195 of their members (out of a total of 511 parliamentarians) on close terms with the "auto family" meant that, come election time, gaining the support of an industrial group like GASPE netted money and votes. In exchange, they protected the *shaken* system. Here is a classic example of the amalgamation of politics, bureaucracy, and industry, familiarly called "the iron triangle."

With the reform of the electoral system, however, it is hoped that the political posture of "industry first" will gradually change. Under the system of small electoral districts, the number of repair businesses will be reduced to about 200 per district. In the past a candidate could be elected with 40,000 to 50,000 votes, but now he must top all entrants. Consequently, the number of votes needed will rise to between 100,000 and 150,000. Political parties, it is hoped, will thus give priority to policies that benefit consumers and owners, rather than industry, and pledging to do so will enhance their chances of getting elected.

Rice and the Food Control System

November 1, 1995, will likely be long remembered as the day when Japanese agriculture policy was greatly transformed. This was the day when the Food Control Law of 1942, enacted during World War II, was repealed and replaced by the new Food Law of 1995. The 1942 law had regulated the production and distribution of rice for fifty-three years.

Japanese rice producers were enslaved by the old food control system. In addition to forced acreage reduction programs, which the government enforced nationwide, producers had no recourse to alternative distribution systems. They were forced to sell to the centralized system controlled by the *Nokyo,* or agricultural cooperatives. Under the old system, rice was collected by certain designated entities and sold by licensed sellers; this system did not allow other players to enter the market. The new system encourages producers to reduce rice production voluntarily. They will be allowed to sell rice directly to wholesalers and retailers. Both collectors and sellers merely have to register. Another important change that the law brings is with respect to the handling of "black market" or independently distributed rice. This is said to account for 20 percent to 30 percent of total rice distributed. Such rice has now been accepted into the system as "rice which has been produced outside of the regular production schedule" *(keikaku-gai-iyutsu-mai).*

These features of the new law may be interpreted as a great accomplishment in the overall drive to reform Japan's food control system. Indeed, they can be seen as a second step toward liberalizing Japan's rice market, following the partial opening that occurred in December 1993. Despite all the rhetoric calling for "deregulation" and "the introduction of market principles," however, a detailed reading of the laws and government ordinances reveals that the government has taken the teeth out of the lofty goal of liberalization.

The following is just one example. As just noted, under the new system, rice collectors merely need to register in order to participate in this activity. In reality, however, newcomers seeking to enter the rice-collection business must meet several conditions, including participation in production adjustment–related activities. This requirement means giving advice to farmers who join participating acreage reduction programs, attending acreage allocation meetings, and participating in the coordination of these plans. Furthermore, although producers can bypass rice collectors in order to distribute rice produced outside of the regular production schedule, the government still maintains control over such rice by requiring that producers report the amount of rice that they have shipped.

Why was such an anachronistic system introduced in the first place? Because the new system is a product of behind-the-scenes maneuvering by the Ministry of Agriculture, Forestry, and Fisheries (MAFF), the Food Agency, agricultural groups like the *Nokyo,* and the agriculture "family" *(zoku),* that is, Diet members from both the ruling and opposition parties who have a vested interest in agricultural matters. These are the same groups that controlled the old system.

Bureaucrats from MAFF and the Food Agency publicly acknowledged that deregulation of rice production and distribution is inevitable. They hope, however, to keep the framework of the food control system intact. That is because they want to protect the vested interests of the *Nokyo,* which is the largest beneficiary of the system. These bureaucrats are also concerned about the possible loss of at least 10,000 jobs at the Food Agency, which would result from an increase in the amount of rice that can be distributed outside the system.

The *Nokyo* are cooperatives adamantly opposed to letting newcomers participate in the system for collecting rice. After all, they monopolize 95 percent of rice collection and receive 17 billion yen yearly in fees. In recent years, *Nokyo* has seen its influence wane. Losing this "sacred ground" could call into question its *raison d'être.* More *Nokyo* members could be alienated if the percentage of independently distributed rice increases.

How did the bureaucrats and *Nokyo* react? A senior bureaucrat with the Food Agency had a secret meeting with a senior member of *Zenchu* (Central Union of Agricultural Cooperatives), the central governing body of *Nokyo.* The bureaucrat urged *Zenchu* to put a halt to moves to reform the Food Control System, to which the *Zenchu* representative responded that big capitalists (such as trading companies and supermarkets) who have not contributed to Japanese agriculture should not be allowed to enter the market freely. The representative also threatened to block Diet ratification of the Uruguay Round agreement, which called for the partial liberalization of the rice market.

Here the *zoku* enter the picture. The project team, consisting of representatives from the Liberal Democratic Party (LDP), the Socialists, and *Sakigake,* which was in charge of agricultural, forestry, and fisheries issues, listened to the views of the Food Agency and *Zenchu.* This resulted in the new obligation of engaging in production-adjustment activities, which has nothing to do with rice collection, and reporting the quantity of rice shipped.

That is how decisions were made regarding the substance of the new Food Law. This law will guide agricultural policy into the twenty-first century. Can we afford to let this absurdity go unnoticed? As the new system stands today, Japanese consumers will continue to pay four to five times the international market price for domestically produced rice. After 2001, the Uruguay Round will be up for review in the context of the New World Trade Organization. Japan will probably only make an equivocal response when given the choice of tariffication of rice or making some other additional, yet acceptable, concessions.

Nonetheless, Japanese agriculture may find some way out of its current dilemma. That is because the old food control system mainly targeted part-time farmers who earned more nonfarm than farm income; the survival of Japanese agriculture is now at stake because of the problem of aging part-time farmers and young farmers who are unwilling to take over these farms. The only way to solve this dilemma is to convince farmers who are dedicated to rice production to take the initiative in pushing ahead with modernization of Japanese agriculture and the shift toward larger farms. Here, too, the iron triangle of government—in this case MAFF and the Food Agency, *zoku* politicians, and industry (agricultural organizations), which refuse to let go of the food control system—must immediately be dismantled. A radical revision of the Agricultural Land Control Law and the law governing *Nokyo* is required to truly deregulate the market and give autonomy to rice producers.

"Designated Bidders" and the Construction Industry

In March 1995, the Fair Trade Commission brought charges against an organization that brought to light the collusive nature of the construction and civil engineering market in Japan. Nine companies, including Hitachi, Toshiba, and Mitsubishi, had formed an association called the Nine Company Club, which allocated electrical engineering work contracted with the Japan Sewerage Contractor's Association, a group affiliated with the Ministry of Construction and staffed in part by former ministry bureaucrats. Not only that, but the association leaked out information concerning the price at which it expected to award a contract. The association involved itself in the allocation of work among the companies. This incident was a typical case of bureaucracy-led collusive behavior.

The Japanese system of bidding by private sector companies for public works projects contracted out by national or local governments is said to be a hotbed of collusion. On paper is the open bidder system in which anyone is invited to bid, and the designated bidder system, in which only designated contractors are invited to bid by the contracting party. But although the laws governing accounting and local governments stipulate that bidding for public works must be conducted by open bid, most projects, especially large ones, adopt the system of designated bidder. Indeed, it is no big secret that except for a handful of projects, the successful bidder has been selected even before the bidding process begins for a particular public works project.

If the designated bidder system encourages collusion, then why is it allowed to continue? The bureaucrats give the following reasons why the system is better than an open bid: open bidding makes the selection process cumbersome because there are more bidders; it becomes difficult to eliminate dishonest contractors; and small- and medium-sized companies have less opportunity to make successful bids.

Even if the designated bidder system works to narrow down the number of potential contractors, I doubt whether government agencies are capable of screening contractors for every single project that makes up the 40 trillion yen public works market. Still less can they eliminate dishonest contractors who try to cut corners.

If I am correct, then the only rational explanation for maintaining the designated bidder system is to give small- and medium-sized contractors a chance to get contracts. It is as if the bureaucrats are saying that contractors must collude to give smaller companies with less financial as well as technical capabilities an opportunity to get work. By letting the designated bidder system continue to operate, the bureaucrats can find postretirement positions not only with the big contractors but also with smaller companies, and they can sell favors to the construction *zoku,* or politicians who have strong ties with the industry.

The construction market in Japan is very crowded, with more than 500,000 contractors. Thus one would expect prices to fall because of excess competition. But because the participants collude to keep contract prices high, it is said that public works projects are 30 percent more expensive than in the United States. Because the total market is worth 40 trillion yen, then by American standards, 10 trillion yen of taxpayers' money is going to waste.

Perhaps as a result of the many incidences of collusion that have been exposed in the last few years, there is talk about introducing a limited open bid system. But very few people mention the possibility of prices coming down as a result. Because the contracting government agency sets a "minimum price," any bidder who quotes a lower price is eliminated from consideration. The minimum price is set to make sure that the contractor duly executes the project and to avoid dumping. This price, however, is usually "inflated." Even if a contractor were to quote a lower price in an open bid, that company would most likely be disqualified for going below the minimum price. I have heard people say that for a certain project, all bidders were eliminated for this very reason.

Major steps could be taken to deregulate the market, such as introducing "a bid bond system" in which the Ministry of Construction or local governments entrust private insurance companies with the job of screening bidders and overseeing the execution of projects. If something like this is not done, the current system will only unnecessarily increase the number of bureaucrats involved in these projects and continue to squander the money of Japanese buyers.

Job Placement Agencies

We often hear the term "Heisei deflation" used to describe the recent state of the Japanese economy. Corporate restructuring is affecting an increasing number of middle-aged and senior employees; new university graduates are finding the job market extremely tight. Women who have completed four years of college education are facing a most difficult situation; only one out of every two female graduates has successfully landed a job. Their predicament is likened to "the Ice Age" as far as finding employment is concerned.

At the same time, the Japanese seem to be taking a different attitude toward work itself. Nowadays, people want more freedom. They seem no longer willing to devote themselves selflessly to the company that they work for. An increasing number of people are attracted to the way Europeans and Americans view their jobs; they switch jobs for a variety of reasons—one often-cited reason being to take advantage of an opportunity that will allow them to move up in their careers. This attitude not only can be observed among young Japanese but is also becoming more prevalent with the older generation as well.

Here is where job placement agencies come into the picture. This business grew rapidly in the 1970s, as something quite different from the traditional pattern of work in Japan. At the beginning, many job placement agencies were accused of not clearly stipulating either the terms of a contract or working conditions. These agencies, however, and the services they provide were given legal recognition when the Job Placement Agency Law (*Rodosha Haken Ho*) came into force in 1986.

This law classifies job placement agencies in two categories. The first category of service is called special placement services. In this situation, people are hired on a permanent basis by the agency and sent out on a temporary basis to specific assignments. The second category is called general placement services, in which temporary people are hired when needed. The law stipulates that agencies offering special placement services must notify the Ministry of Labor before engaging in this line of business, while those agencies dealing with general placement services must be licensed. The law is quite restrictive. It regulates the types of jobs these agencies can deal in; for example, such agencies cannot hire people to engage in sales or management-type activities.

These restrictions have been somewhat relaxed as a result of the revision in 1994 of the Law for the Steady Employment of Older Workers. In principle, with the enactment of "Special Measures for the Placement of Older Workers," people over the age of sixty could work through placement agencies and accept any kind of job, except for the following four types of employment: port and transportation; construction; security; and manufacturing. One would think that the government should deregulate so that all people, not only older workers, could engage in different kinds of temporary employment. Yet the Ministry of Labor does not show any interest in deregulation.

The ministry still believes that only traditional types of employment are normal. As one official from the ministry's Employment Security Bureau said, "We have to make sure that this new phenomenon, the job placement agency, does not take jobs away from people who work full time in the traditional sense. This is true especially because work offered through placement agencies tends to disrupt the balance of supply and demand in the labor market."[4] The ministry acts as if placement agencies were responsible for the current state of the Japanese market.

Critics have pointed out that the ministry may see placement agencies in this light because the government-run unemployment offices are looked on with great distaste. The services offered by the government are growing increasingly unpopular, as the private sector tends to offer more useful information to people in search of employment. In this sense, the government is in competition with placement agencies.

According to a senior officer of the *Keidanren* (Federation of Economic Organizations), "It is true that the Labor Ministry's mission in the past was to ensure that people would continue being employed. But today, whatever the Ministry does seems to make matters worse. It doesn't realize that people no longer expect it to take the initiative in improving working conditions, especially because people have opted for different types of employment and value their jobs differently than in the past. It has been quite some time since critics began saying that the unemployment offices have outlived their usefulness. Less than 20 percent of people seeking employment in large cities avail themselves of the services provided by these offices. So it is quite natural that people are saying that they are no longer necessary."[5]

Some attribute the ministry's stubbornness to the fact that it is simply behind the times. They also point out the fear of the bureaucrats that its vested interests are at stake. Those people who work for the commerce and labor sections of prefectural government offices are, technically speaking, employed by the national, and not local, governments. They are in an awkward position in that they provide local government services under the direction of the prefectural governor, yet in matters relating to personnel they are controlled by the Ministry of Labor. About 2,300 people are employed by these sections nationwide. Obviously, these sections are headed by people from the Ministry of Labor. The ministry, desperately trying to keep these managerial positions, feels threatened by job placement agencies.

The ministry typically answers such criticism by referring to treaties and regulations set by the International Labor Organization (ILO). The ministry claims that without government supervision, it is not possible to keep people employed or to prevent private job placement agencies from sending people into questionable sex-related businesses or into harsh working conditions.

Nowhere, however, do labor treaties or agreements stipulate that it is the responsibility of the government to oversee the labor market. The ILO treaties were concluded with the objective of improving working conditions in developing countries in order to bring them up to par with industrialized nations. Japan is one of the greatest economic powers in the world today. It is one of the leading countries in terms of low rates of unemployment and a stable labor market. Unfortunately the mentality of the Ministry of Labor is still in an "underdeveloped" state.

The Telecommunications Industry

NTT (Nippon Telegraph and Telephone Corporation) was created as a result of the privatization of the industry in 1985. Shortly after that, three NCCs or new common carriers—DDI Corporation (DDI), Japan Telecom (JT), and Teleway Japan (TWJ)—entered the domestic telecommunications market, while International Digital Communications (IDC) and International Telecom Japan (ITJ) joined *Kokusai Denshin Denwa* Co., Ltd. (KDD) in providing international telecommunications services.

In this way, the government monopoly over the telecommunications market was dismantled. The newly privatized service providers began competing over price and service quality. Privatization was welcomed. Rates were cut by more than 50 percent in some service areas. Understandably, consumers also began to question why rates were so high before the breakup of NTT.

In Japan, the Telecommunications Law stipulates that only certified service providers designated as either a type I or type II telecommunications carrier can enter the market. A type I carrier services customers by using its own hardware; for example, it can install telecommunication lines. But a type II carrier essentially offers software services to its customers, while leasing lines from type I carriers in order to deliver its services.

To be more specific, type I carriers include the following—NTT, which services the domestic telecommunications market; the NCCs, which offer long-distance services; KDD, and others which offer international services; local telecommunications service providers such as cable TV (for example, Tokyo Telecommunications Network); satellite telecommunication service providers (such as Nippon Satellite System); and mobile telecommunication service companies. Information network service providers belong to the type II category; companies such as Nifty Serve and PC-based VAN services (value-added networks) are seeing their popularity boom.

Despite the rapid development of the telecommunications business and a flurry of new business activity, the Ministry of Posts and Telecommunications still retains considerable control over the industry because of its ability to license and certify.

It is true that type II carriers are simply required to register or notify the ministry of their intention to enter the market. But type I carriers need to be licensed by the minister for posts and telecommunications not only to gain entry into the market—or retreat from it. They must have the provisions of all contracts approved by the ministry as well. In other words, service providers do business at the pleasure of the ministry, because they can be penalized for behavior that the ministry does not approve.

Why does the ministry desperately want to maintain the authority to license and certify telecommunication service providers? The reason is simple: the ministry wants to fulfill its long-awaited desire to become a "first-class" ministry. The Ministry of Posts and Telecommunications has always been viewed as a "third-class" ministry, merely responsible for mail services and the postal savings system. Now that Japan is quickly becoming a highly information-based society, the ministry wants to seize this opportunity to achieve its goal. By taking advantage of its licensing authority, and by using the carrot-and-stick approach, the ministry can find a large number of positions so that senior bureaucrats can "descend from heaven" *(amakudari)* upon retiring. Not only is it looking to NTT, but also to the many new service providers that have been "sprouting up like mushrooms after the rain" (in other words, after privatization), and even further to hardware manufacturers that belong to the "NTT family."

An incident that occurred in May 1994 bore testimony that this is indeed its strategy. The ministry tried to force the appointment of Vice President Shigeo Sawada, former vice minister, as the next president of NTT. NTT fought back hard on this occasion, and President Hitoshi Kojima was appointed for a second term. In the course of these negotiations, the ministry reportedly threatened to break up NTT.

According to one observer, "The ministry agreed to the privatization of NTT because it figured that as long as it could maintain control over NTT, which had a more-than-dominant share of the telecommunications market, it could continue to exercise discretion over the industry through its licensing authority. However, NTT employees were not pleased to find arrogant former bureaucrats in their organization. As a result NTT, including its union, was not very compliant. So the next tactic was to break up NTT, weaken it, and make it easier to control."[6]

Although it has been privatized, NTT has yet to shed its bureaucratic mentality. Perhaps breaking it up may serve as a sort of shock therapy to revamp the organization. But this should not be accepted if it ends up only expanding the interests of the ministry. Japan is said to be twenty or even thirty years behind the United States in the area of advanced information technology. The ministry's insistence on maintaining licensing authority is a principal cause of this great delay.

The High Price of Gasoline

According to a survey conducted by the Agency of Natural Resources and Energy, the average price in Japan for a liter of regular gasoline in

July 1995 was 115 yen. The price of gasoline had fallen by about 10 yen over a span of one year, to its lowest level since 1976. Consumers were surprised when a gasoline station in Komaki, Aichi Prefecture, began selling gasoline at 100 yen in May 1994. It is not hard to find gasoline selling at less than 90 yen a liter along the highway in Saitama Prefecture, where prices have collapsed.

It appears as if gasoline has really become cheaper, as if the now popular expression "price destruction" applies to this case. One cannot ignore the fact, however, that during a period of time when the yen appreciated by 20 percent, gasoline prices only came down by 8 percent. In fact, in comparison to other countries, gasoline is incredibly costly in Japan.

According to data collected by *Nikkeiren* (Japan Federation of Employers' Associations), the price differential for regular gasoline in 1993 was large. When compared with the United States, a liter of gasoline cost 91 yen higher in Japan; when compared with the average price in Britain, France, and Germany, it was 29 yen higher. Furthermore, the gains made as a result of the stronger yen were not passed on to the consumer at all; thus, the price differential between the United States and Japan rose to 92 yen in a subsequent survey.[7] Put simply, Japanese consumers pay five times as much as American consumers for a liter of gasoline, 115 yen versus 23 yen.

Why this unreasonable difference in price? It is caused by taxes; the cost structure of the petroleum industry; and the infamous Provisional Law Concerning the Importation of Designated Petroleum Products.

To begin with, gasoline is subject to four types of taxes—the tariff on crude oil, the petroleum tax, the gasoline tax, and the consumption tax. Except for the consumption tax, the other three are specific taxes, meaning that the burden of paying the tax does not change even if the retail price changes. One must also not forget that the gasoline tax is a very hefty one. For gasoline retailing at 115 yen, the tax portion totals 59.60 yen, of which 53.80 is the gasoline tax. Japanese consumers, if they want to pay less at the pump, must first make strong demands that the gasoline tax be lowered.

The next problem lies in the cost structure. The cost of refining and distributing a liter of gasoline in Japan is 25 yen, compared with 9 yen in the United States, making it 2.5 times as expensive.

Japanese oil companies explain the discrepancy this way. Unlike the major oil companies in the United States and Europe, which have both upstream operations (involving exploration and development) and downstream operations (including refining and distribution), they are forced to make their downstream business profitable. Is this an acceptable explanation? The industry as a whole is keeping cost up and making the consumer bear the brunt of it. Witness the complex distribution system involving first- and second-tier wholesalers, high transportation costs including coastal shipping and tankers, the cost of paying an average of six to seven people working at each gasoline station, and the various facilities to meet the safety standards imposed by stringent fire regulations.

The operation of self-service stations would go a long way toward cutting distribution costs, but this prospect does not look too promising. A study group has been set up under the Fire Defense Agency to look into the regulations for safety considerations. The group is expected to put a recommendation together in late 1997. Even if the group comes out in support of self-service gasoline stations, new regulations will likely be put in place when the law is introduced approving such businesses, in order to help keep the jobs of approximately 400,000 people who are said to be employed by the petroleum industry.

The final obstacle is the law concerning petroleum imports. This law was introduced in 1986, as a temporary measure designed to restrict the importation of petroleum products to domestic refiners. This effectively prevents distributors from buying cheap foreign products. The law was only effective until April 1996, so after that, companies that are not in the refining business should be eligible to import. It is almost certain that gasoline from countries with lower refining costs, for example, South Korea, will enter the market. Cheaper gasoline, a trend that has been continuing for some time, may be seen as a sign that the industry is preparing for what will happen after the law is repealed. It is hoped that further "price destruction" will result following importation of larger quantities of cheaper gasoline from countries that are geographically close, such as South Korea—especially when this supply is directed toward the Japan Sea coast, where the cost of gasoline is higher than the national average.

Many, however, who were initially eager to import began to waver. This included major participants in the market with exclusive contracts to handle gasoline, trading firms, and supermarkets. I interviewed these people to find out what lay behind their indecisiveness. It developed that new entrants were required to demonstrate that they met the following criteria—the ability to supply in a consistent manner; stockpile; and ensure quality. They found the requirement to stockpile especially problematic.

It is said that gasoline prices will generally fall by 10 yen when the law is abolished. The average price nationwide, however, has already fallen by that much during the past year. Potential new entrants think twice because they fear that they will not be able to make a profit with such depressed prices—especially if they are hit with an increase in the cost of stockpiling. Even if the temporary law is repealed, there will, without doubt, be a new barrier to entry.

When one takes into account the tax burden, the high cost of distribution, and measures taken to keep people in the industry employed, then it is not an exaggeration to say that it will be virtually impossible for Japanese consumers to enjoy gasoline at prices comparable to those in the United States.

Conclusion

It is safe to say that the "new party" boom, which took place in the Lower House elections of 1993, was a manifestation of populist anger at industry-biased politics. The Hosokawa administration lasted only eight months, but public opinion polls regularly showed support ratings in the seventies. Japan still has the Large-Scale Retail Store Law that limits supermarkets, department stores, and other large retailers, and a system that supports retail prices by allowing cartels in cosmetics and pharmaceuticals. It is the owners of small shops, the cosmetics shops, drugstores, and so on, who are the mainstay of the LDP. The New Frontier Party that raised its flag at the end of 1994 is also a party that pledges to throw its weight behind consumers and householders. Even Hashimoto's LDP regime has made gestures in the direction of deregulation.

With ten million people a year now able to travel abroad, the Japanese have come to know for themselves how adversely the domestic-overseas price gap is affecting their livelihood. Indeed, the popularity of overseas travel stems from the reality that it is cheaper than domestic travel. Ultimately, Japanese politics will have to focus on the consumer. Slowly, Japan is divesting itself of postwar politics. We can only hope for a period of reform.

Notes

1. Economic Planning Agency of Japan, *Commodity Prices White Paper* (Tokyo: Ministry of Finance Printing Bureau, 1994). In this chapter, yen figures have been converted at 100 to the U.S. dollar.

2. *The Report of the Advisory Group on Economic Structural Adjustment for International Harmony*, submitted to Prime Minister Yasuhiro Nakasone, April 7, 1986.

3. *The Report of the Research Committee on Economic Reform,* submitted to Prime Minister Morihiro Hosokawa, December 16, 1993.

4. Conversation with author.

5. Conversation with author.

6. Conversation with author.

7. These data are as of July 1995.

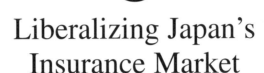

CHAPTER EIGHT

Liberalizing Japan's Insurance Market

Charles D. Lake II

DURING A government-to-government meeting on insurance in 1994, a senior Japanese Finance Ministry official greeted with laughter a U.S. proposal to liberalize automobile insurance. The official was responding to the U.S. negotiators' informal proposal that the Japanese government undertake a commitment to deregulate certain automobile insurance products to demonstrate that Japan was serious about liberalizing its insurance market. After regaining his composure, the official dismissed even the possibility of considering such a proposal to deregulate the automobile insurance. He noted that such measures would never be taken by the Ministry of Finance (MOF), at least for another decade. This exchange, which took place as part of the negotiation on insurance under the U.S–Japan Framework Talks, was typical of MOF's strong resistance to proposed U.S. market-opening measures.[1]

Only two years later, however, on December 15, 1996, MOF agreed to take a series of steps that would significantly liberalize a segment of Japan's automotive insurance. This radical shift in MOF's posture occurred in large part because of efforts by the Office of the U.S. Trade Representative to ensure compliance with, and to negotiate supplementary measures which enhanced, the 1994 U.S.–Japan Insurance Agreement.[2] U.S. Trade Representative Charlene Barshefsky and her team received applause for their accomplishment in the United States[3] and resentment from Japanese insurance industry leaders who were desperately fighting to protect their "sacred cow," automobile insurance.[4] How was this significant concession achieved? What were the barriers to insurance deregulation in the first place? Does this most recent agreement signify the end of trade disputes between the United States and Japan at least on insurance? This chapter is a brief study of these and other issues that affect the international trade and regulation of the very lucrative insurance market in Japan.[5] It is intended to provide additional background to observers with a general interest in the Japanese barriers that confront foreign insurance providers and to show how the domestic constituents of the regulatory system known in Japan as the *Goso Sendan* system impeded, and continue to limit, market access and deregulation in the Japanese insurance market.

The phrase "*Goso Sendan* system" is a metaphor used to explain MOF's regulatory policy of micromanaging competition in the financial sector, which emphasizes uniformity and cooperative arrangements among competitors.[6] Under the *Goso Sendan* system, even the weakest financial institutions in Japan, which include some insurance firms, are permitted to survive as participants in the "convoy."

At the center of the U.S.-Japan dispute on insurance was a policy debate that revealed a clash of two fundamentally different regulatory philosophies: one emphasizing "strict regulation" and the other "liberal market regulation." In this regard, strict regulation emphasizes order and uniformity based on the micromanagement of the insurance market and protection of insurance companies. Many observers conclude that Japan has taken the strict regulation approach in the past. The liberal market regulation advocated by the U.S. attempts to stimulate greater competition through entrepreneurial freedom for companies that are driven by their desire to meet consumer needs. Using solvency and financial soundness of the companies as the basis, the regulations are applied only as prudential measures under this approach.[7] The central question that was posed to MOF throughout the negotiation and during the implementation of the agreement was whether the ministry should move away from the strict regulation approach, and if so, how to effectively make that transition while balancing the interests of the various parties involved, including large and small domestic firms, foreign firms, and most importantly, the policyholders or consumers. This chapter provides a general discussion of these issues.

"Excessive Competition": The Principle behind the *Goso Sendan* System

An important historical context behind MOF's regulatory philosophy is its distrust of the value of market-oriented competition. According to Yukio Noguchi of Hitotsubashi University, under the economic regime developed during and after World War II, a wide range of Japanese institutions engaged in the "rejection of competition."[8] He states, "As the phrase "excessive competition" indicates, the notion that "competition is evil" became generally accepted. This notion holds that "competition" ignores the weak and serves the unilateral interests of the strong; hence, it must be restricted from the point of view of social fairness."[9]

Noguchi then concludes that "the *Goso Sendan* system associated with" the regulation of financial services is based on the principle of "rejection of competition" and its implementation "makes possible the survival of borderline financial institutions."[10] MOF's traditional regulatory approach to insurance clearly shows that it viewed "excessive competition" as a threat to the development of the Japanese insurance industry. Indeed, an illustration of MOF's difficulty in fully accepting competition and its allergic reaction to "confusion in the marketplace" can be found in the historical perspective provided by key MOF regulators themselves with respect to Japan's past market developments and regulatory experiences.[11] For example, in explaining why the national government increased its supervisory authority by enacting the first insurance business law in 1900,[12] an MOF official explains that as a number of companies experienced management problems owing to "non-modern accounting methods and *intensified competition*, the need for government supervision of insurance companies was enhanced."[13]

Similarly, in explaining Japan's experience after World War II, MOF officials expressed their distrust of competition. Following World War II, various laws were enacted to supplement the old insurance business law, including the 1948 Law Concerning the Control of Insurance Solicitation. The officials note that these laws were introduced in part to address the concern that the difficult economic circumstances Japan faced after the war would lead to "competition to win contracts and confusion in the solicitation practices."[14] One MOF official explained that after World War II because "the order associated with the solicitation of life insurance products was seriously disturbed and unjust solicitation practices became rampant, and because this situation could not be left alone from the point of view of policy holder protection and proper development of the industry, the Insurance Solicitation Law was enacted."[15]

Thus, competition was viewed negatively and as having contributed to past disturbance in the market "order." To MOF officials, it was entirely reasonable to regulate the market strictly because if "intensified competition" to "win contracts" were allowed, "confusion in the market order" would result and the government would ultimately be forced to rescue the industry. The *Goso Sendan* system provided a practical solution that accorded harmony and stability among all parties.

The Elements of MOF's Insurance *Goso Sendan* Regulatory Regime

Having rejected a regulatory approach that maximized the use of market mechanisms, MOF established a regulatory regime that emphasized micromanagement by government and self-regulation by the domestic industry. MOF has been able to sustain the *Goso Sendan* system because of its strong regulatory power, a nontransparent administration of that power, the existence of a highly concentrated industry structure, and tolerance of exclusionary business practices fostered by restrictions on distribution.

MOF's Strong Regulatory Authority

Regulation of insurance in Japan is the sole responsibility of MOF, particularly the Insurance Department of MOF's Banking Bureau.[16] The old Insurance Business Law required that all insurance companies in Japan be licensed and take the corporate form of either a joint-stock or a mutual company with capital or an initial fund of a specified amount.[17] The law also prohibited insurance companies from engaging in other types of services and from concurrently doing business in the life and nonlife sectors.[18] In addition, MOF was accorded the authority to demand reports from companies, conduct on-site inspections, remove officers, and apply sanctions to the insurance companies for violations of the laws or rules.[19] More importantly, the comprehensive legal authority accorded to MOF provided the backdrop for MOF to have the power informally to utilize "administrative guidance." Although companies were technically not required to follow "administrative guidance," the fear of retaliation in an unrelated matter compelled companies to abide by MOF's directives.[20] This strong regulatory authority in turn was to control competition to avoid "confusion in the market place." Many observers believe that the restrictive approach taken by MOF stifles product innovation and competition based on rates. One Japanese industry observer noted, "[MOF's] procedure from application to actual approval is so complicated . . . it cannot be denied that MOF's [product] review process is obstructing the diversification of product development."[21]

Other observers also believe that through extensive review of new products and emphasis on intercompany cooperation, MOF greatly restricted product and price differentiation.[22] The length and scope of the review process ensures that prices remain constant and that new products are introduced to ready competition.[23] According to the U.S. industry, these practices reinforce the dominant position of the large domestic companies in Japan because of "MOF's historical tendency to enforce uniformity of product design and pricing for most life and nonlife products, which has limited the ability of small/foreign companies to use product innovation as a way to gain market share."[24]

The Nontransparent Regime

MOF's ability to manage competition was also enhanced by the "opaque" nature of the old Insurance Law. This issue was recognized as a problem by competition policy experts in Japan. Indeed, as early as 1989 a Fair Trade Commission (FTC) study group was attacking MOF's regulatory approach to insurance with its published report noting the lack of transparency and extensive use of administrative guidance by MOF.[25] In the report, the FTC study group stated that "because the licensing standards are not established by law and left to the discretion of the regulatory agency, they have become nontransparent . . . [hence,] there is a need to ensure transparency related to the licensing standards."[26]

The same FTC report noted that in order to enhance competition in the market the Japanese government should take steps to liberalize the nonlife rating system by using more flexible rates such as banded rates (in which individual companies are permitted to choose a rate within a "band" of rates, for example, 10 percent to 30 percent).[27] The study group also called on MOF to allow the approval of new products on a more flexible basis and recommend that trade associations limit their interventions in the marketplace. The Life Insurance Association was specifically named to "abolish its regulation concerning the registration of solicitation materials and related standards."[28]

The role of trade associations in Japan is quite significant, and they are used by domestic companies to effectively influence the administration of regulations. In fact, a Japanese professor remarked that MOF's regulation of the life insurance industry "is in most cases guided by large life insurers."[29] Because MOF has a relatively small staff, it relies heavily on the support of trade associations—which have traditionally restricted foreign membership—to regulate their member companies.[30] MOF's Insurance Department ordinarily consists of approximately forty officials. Under the Japanese system, these forty officials in effect have the sole responsibility to regulate the world's second largest insurance market with approximately $320 billion in premiums. In stark contrast, even a single state like New York has more than 1,000 insurance regulators.[31] Consequently, MOF heavily relies on the industry to "self-regulate." The problem with self-regulation is that entrenched, large domestic firms in leadership positions at the trade associations obtain a quasi-government authority to bring "order" into the industry as MOF's deputy. This "official" role provides large domestic firms with an additional competitive edge over foreign firms.

The shortcomings of the old Insurance Law were further complicated by the interrelationship of the law to other laws, such as the Commercial Code, which in turn further made the regulatory system nontransparent.[32] Courageous efforts by Japanese insurance experts to explain in English the relevance of the Commercial Code, for instance, only show how complicated the problem of legal interpretation has been in the past.[33] In fact, MOF officials would probably be the first to admit that the old law lacked clarity.[34] Moreover, as it is well known, legal theories are not extensively tested through litigation in the judicial system and recorded as precedents. Thus MOF's nontransparent interpretations of such "theories" take on an added influence by enhancing MOF's regulatory discretion.

One consequence of the law's vagueness was the emergence of the so-called *Daisan Bunya* ("the third sector"), which is a phenomenon unique to Japan.[35] Because the old Insurance Law lacked precise definitions for even terms as basic as "life" or "insurance against loss," MOF, through its discretionary authority, developed the third sector to license products that did not clearly fall within the definitions provided by the old law.[36] Consequently, the third-sector products, which can be categorized broadly as personal accident, sickness, nursing care, and hospitalization covers, were licensed to life companies and nonlife companies beginning in the 1960s.[37] In 1992 the total third-sector market premiums were about ¥1.5 trillion (approximately $12.0 billion) and the foreign share in this niche sector was about 38 percent that year.[38] Given that foreign market share in Japan has been limited perennially to less than 3 percent of the total insurance market,[39] the third-sector market share shows foreign firms' disproportionate dependence on that market.

Distribution Barriers and Exclusionary Business Practices

Compounding the problems created by the regulatory regime is the fact that product uniformity and limited competition enhance the role *keiretsu* affiliation plays in purchases of insurance products. According to a 1987 survey report published by the FTC, "Group ties and fostering financial links were the primary factors determining the choice of . . . insurance suppliers, with . . . 75.3 percent identifying [one of these] as the primary factor in choosing their current insurance company."[40] One American analyst concluded in 1992 about the FTC findings:

> For smaller Japanese firms as well as foreign companies trying to sell insurance in Japan, the implications would appear to be obvious: the lack of competition in both types of insurance provides buyers [with] an excuse to apply noncompetitive criteria in choosing their insurers . . . *In short, the argument that* keiretsu *act as an impediment to market access to U.S. firms may be stronger with respect to the insurance industry than it is for other industries.*[41]

In 1993 the American Chamber of Commerce in Japan (ACCJ) reached a similar conclusion. In a report entitled the "Study of Japanese Insurance Procurement Practices within *Keiretsu* Groups," the ACCJ Financial Services Committee found the following:[42]

> [Eleven] *keiretsu* member companies account for more than 80 percent of the total nonlife insurance market in Japan. With respect to the purchasing practices of the . . . groups studied, on average over 70 percent of the nonlife insurance business of these *keiretsu* groups is given to the respec-

tive member insurance companies of the groups. Moreover, at least 92 percent of the insurance business of such groups is handled by financially related insurers.[43]

An important issue relating to *keiretsu* and the distribution of insurance products has been the traditional prohibition against independent insurance brokers. In Japan, most corporations have created wholly owned, in-house insurance agents known as "case agents."[44] The case agents system reinforces *keiretsu* purchasing practices because it makes it extremely difficult for professional, independent intermediaries to compete since they are in competition with the "case agents" of corporations whose business the independent intermediaries are trying to solicit.[45] However, resolving this problem is not simple because the introduction of a broker's system, in and of itself, will not lead to a meaningful deregulation unless it is accompanied by other liberalization measures affecting the approval of insurance products and rates. When all products are uniform, risk management consultants are simply unable to operate effectively.[46]

Another issue related to distribution is the Japanese insurance market's concentrated structure. Japan's insurance industry is dominated by a small number of enormous companies—some of the world's largest companies.[47] The top ten Japanese insurers control 82 percent of the life insurance market and 79 percent of the nonlife market.[48] By comparison, the top ten U.S. companies control 35 percent and 30 percent respectively.[49] Additionally, while the United States has several thousand life and nonlife insurance companies, Japan has very few companies: thirty life and fifty-nine nonlife.[50] The dominance of these companies is also self-perpetuating because it promotes the lack of competition, while at the same time increasing the interdependence of these companies and the MOF. Moreover, these large domestic companies are the major beneficiaries of the *Goso Sendan* system and the self-regulation approach.

U.S.–Japan Framework Talks and the Insurance Agreement

Although market access to Japan's lucrative insurance market has been a trade issue for over two decades, the long-standing problems arising from the *Goso Sendan* system took on an added dimension when it became clear that the Japanese government was considering plans to target the third sector for deregulation of entry restrictions without reforming other more significant aspects of the system that impeded meaningful foreign access in Japan.[51] These developments brought insurance to the center stage of U.S.–Japan trade relations in 1993.[52] The Clinton administration responded by including insurance as one of the four priority areas for negotiations under the new U.S.–Japan Framework Talks.[53]

The principal U.S. objective during the negotiation was promotion of deregulation, particularly in the primary areas of life and nonlife insurance sectors, while ensuring fairness in the treatment of foreign firms in Japan. The U.S. government also needed to ensure that the interests of foreign firms—particularly in the third sector—were not unfairly targeted in the name of "deregulation" only to provide domestic firms with yet another MOF-created competitive advantage.

The American and Japanese negotiators held extensive negotiations on insurance under the U.S.–Japan Framework Talks and concluded an agreement on October 1, 1994.[54] The Insurance Agreement, which contained the "goal of achieving significant improvement in market access for competitive foreign insurance providers and intermediaries in Japan," was signed officially on October 11, 1994.[55] The agreement was one of the many "results-oriented" agreements negotiated by the Clinton administration and contained a commitment by the two governments to assess compliance based on "objective criteria."[56] Under the agreement, MOF undertook a number of commitments designed to enhance transparency, procedural protection, liberalization, and competition policy in the Japanese insurance market. The agreement was hailed by U.S. industry leaders at the time as "comprehensive, fair, and verifiable and [one] that should produce concrete and measurable progress."[57]

As a general approach, the Insurance Agreement was crafted to provide the U.S. government and industry with the means—or what the U.S. negotiators often referred to informally as "hooks to hang our arguments"—constantly to revisit key regulatory issues with the Japanese government. In other words, it was designed to establish a basic framework and standards for the United States to press MOF constantly for deregulatory measures while ensuring fairness in the reform process. A somewhat unique circumstance affecting the insurance reform process demanded this approach. At the time of the signing of the agreement, the Government of Japan was still working on legislation to restructure fundamentally the old Insurance Law. Unlike the banking and securities sectors, the Japanese parliament had yet to complete such an overhaul of the basic law that regulated the insurance sector. The negotiators were also quite cognizant that once the law was passed, MOF, particularly the Insurance Department, would likely be "creative" in using its implementing regulation to maintain its strong control over the industry.

Besides general principles, the agreement contained Japanese government commitments designed to address the issues discussed above. In the area of transparency, for instance, the agreement called for MOF to compile, publish, and make publicly available standards for approval of licenses and new products, and to put administrative guidance in writing upon request. MOF also agreed to review applications without delay as well as to avoid using administrative guidance to require insurance providers to coordinate or consult with other insurance providers on license, product, and rate applications. In addition, MOF confirmed that no limits would be imposed on the number of applications for new products and rates, and committed to treat business-sensitive information in license, product, and rate applications as protected confidential information. Moreover, to ensure that foreign firms have meaningful and fair opportunities to be informed of, comment on, and exchange views with regulators regarding insurance, MOF made the commitment to take specific steps to increase such exchanges.

The Government of Japan also agreed to liberalize the regulation of specific insurance products in order to increase the ability of insurance companies to innovate product and price by implementing a three-stage deregulation plan.[58] These commitments included increased flexibility in the rates that may be applied to certain large commercial risks, as well as the introduction of a "file and use" approval system for certain products;[59] a notification system for product approvals of large commercial risks with eventual expansion of the notification system to other lines;[60] a broker system to diversify and promote competition in insurance distribution channels; and free rates for certain specified products.[61]

To address issues arising from *keiretsu* and exclusionary business practices, the Government of Japan committed to "strictly enforce" the Antimonopoly Law in the insurance sector and review Antimonopoly Law exemptions applied to the insurance sector.[62] The Japanese government also committed to work with domestic and foreign insurance companies to select an independent research firm to conduct a study of the extent and effects of intra-*keiretsu* transactions and case agents in the Japanese insurance market.[63] Furthermore, the Japanese government made the commitment that the FTC would later examine the Japanese insurance market concerning *keiretsu* and other related issues.[64]

The solution to the third-sector targeting issue was a commitment made by the Japanese government to "avoid any radical change" in the business environment in the third sector until foreign firms were first accorded sufficient opportunities (that is, "a reasonable time") to compete on equal terms on the basis of product and rate in the major product categories in the life and nonlife sectors, and not to allow "mutual entry" into the "third sector" as long as any substantial portion of the life and nonlife sector is not deregulated.[65]

U.S. Challenge to Ensure Compliance

Following the signing of the agreement, the long-awaited new Insurance Business Law was passed in May 1995.[66] The new law, which consists of nearly 500 provisions,[67] was drafted by MOF officials based on a June 1994 paper submitted to the regulators by the special legal committee of the Insurance Council.[68] The new Insurance Business Law provides the basic legal framework to transform Japan's insurance system for the first time in half a century. However, as of this writing, the new law has yet to provide actual significant improvements in the marketplace with respect to transparency, deregulation, and fair competition because of the way the law has been implemented.

1995 Insurance Business Law

Although a comprehensive review of the new law is beyond the scope of this chapter, the major elements of the new Insurance Business Law include, among other things, provisions enabling the mutual entry of life and nonlife companies through subsidiaries; the introduction of the "notification system" for certain products and rates specified by MOF; deregulation of exclusive agency arrangements in the life sector; introduction of the broker system; and significant revisions to the nonlife rating association system.[69] With respect to licensing requirements, in comparison to the old system, the new law clarifies the applicable conditions by specifying requirements concerning basic documents, financial base, and management qualifications.[70] The new Insurance Business Law also introduces solvency margin requirements, policyholder protection funds, and enhanced disclosure requirements.[71]

The new law also narrows the scope of the Antimonopoly Law exemption applied to the insurance sector.[72] Under the new law, even in areas in which a particular joint activity has been exempted from the antitrust law enforcement, the FTC can now seek from MOF suspensions or changes to the activities in question.[73] If MOF fails to act on the FTC request within a month, the FTC is then authorized to take enforcement actions against the companies.[74] Although the rating associations continue to be exempted from the Antimonopoly Law, they do not obtain a blanket exemption.[75] For example, for products in which the rating association formulates a banded rate, the companies are free to determine their own rates within that band or range. Regardless of the fact that such a band may have been established by an exempted rating association, if the competitors enter into an agreement to fix the actual rate in use, such an agreement can be in violation of the Antimonopoly Law.[76] These developments, therefore, constitute an improvement from the old law, although some experts were already arguing in 1995 that further review of the insurance Antimonopoly Law exemption system would be appropriate.[77]

In relation to the third-sector issue, the new law provides a specific provision to address the concerns of domestic and foreign firms. Article 121 states, "The Finance Minister may, for the time being, attach necessary conditions to the licenses . . . so as to avoid drastic change in the management environment relating to the [third sector] business . . . whose management relies to a greater degree on the [third sector].[78]

Negotiation of the Supplemental Measures

The passage of the new Insurance Business Law required MOF officials to work on implementing regulations. The new Insurance Business Law, like the old law, still delegates significant authority to MOF to establish specificity through its ministerial regulations and ordinances, for example, provisions dealing with the notification system and the registration of brokers. This delegation of authority makes MOF susceptible to pressure from the domestic insurance industry, and consequently, the proposed regulations and directives announced by MOF in 1995 heavily reflected domestic industry views and led to a new dispute over the interpretation of the Insurance Agreement.

A new U.S.–Japan dispute that erupted in late 1995 focused on the interpretation of one of the key provisions of the Insurance Agreement relating to the third sector. Despite the commitment made in the agreement, it became clear to the U.S. industry and the U.S. government that the domestic insurance industry in Japan expected to be able to aggressively enter the third sector without the required deregulation in the primary sector. In the *1996 National Trade Estimate Report*, the U.S. government noted, "The U.S. is gravely concerned about MOF's intentions to permit certain activities of Japanese insurance subsidiaries in the third sector, without first fulfilling the conditions established in the agreement with respect to deregulation in the primary life and nonlife sectors."[79]

To the U.S. government, "This linkage, i.e., the implementation of meaningful broad-based deregulation of the primary sectors prior to allowing expanded entry into the third sector by the Japanese insurance subsidiaries, [constituted] a fundamental aspect of the insurance agreement."[80] The USTR further affirmed that "this linkage was agreed to by both governments to prevent immediate, discriminatory and selective deregulation of the third sector, while retaining protection for large Japanese insurance firms in the primary life and nonlife sectors, which constitute roughly 90 percent of Japan's insurance market."[81]

The Insurance Agreement provided for follow-up consultations, and the consultations quickly turned into "negotiations" to confirm the agreed-upon interpretation of the Insurance Agreement as well as to spell out specific measures to "clarify" the original agreement. Such measures would have to ensure MOF compliance with the third sector provision but also promote "much needed competition [in the Japanese market], [so as to] result in a cost savings and greater product choice for Japanese business and consumers."[82] Accordingly, during talks in late 1995 and early 1996:

> The U.S. Government spelled out in concrete terms a detailed vision, to be implemented in phases, of substantial deregulation of the Japan's primary life and nonlife sectors. Specifically, the U.S. called on MOF to initially implement meaningful deregulation of Japan's large and sophisticated commercial fire market, and to allow for innovation in the marketing of automobile insurance. Later deregulation would eventually result in broad application of a notification system.[83]

However, these efforts did not result in a resolution, and it appeared in early mid-1996 that the United States and Japan would have a showdown over compliance with the Framework trade agreement that had just been concluded only a little over a year earlier. In fact, the Japanese industry began preparing for operations of their new subsidiaries to begin on October 1, 1996, with new licenses to be issued the day before.[84] Although the initial pressure led to a tentative agreement between USTR and MOF to "freeze" these activities, a new deadline was set for December 15, 1996, to complete the negotiations.[85]

After a number of negotiating sessions (which also involved U.S. Trade Representative Charlene Barshefsky and then-Finance Minister Hiroshi Mitsuzuka), the United States and Japan agreed to the Supplementary Measures by the Government of the United States and the Government of Japan Regarding Insurance ("Supplementary Measures"), which was signed on December 24, 1996. The two governments agreed to implement these Supplementary Measures "as an integral part" of the Insurance Agreement.

In the Supplementary Measures, the Government of Japan committed to deregulate its primary insurance markets by early 1998 and to enact legislation and promulgate regulations implementing four key insurance market deregulation measures by the end of 1997 and the beginning of 1998. The four key areas include deregulation of the primary sectors of Japan's insurance markets, in particular the nonlife areas of life, automobile, fire, and some forms of casualty insurance.[86] More specifically in the area of automobile insurance, for example, the Government of Japan agreed to allow the introduction, in September 1997, of automobile insurance with variable premium rates so as to be able to differentiate on the basis of age, sex, geography, auto usage rates, driving history, or vehicle characteristics.[87] The Japanese government also committed to the "elimination of obligations for members of a rating organization to use rates calculated by the rating organization,"[88] an organization which U.S. Trade Representative Barshefsky referred to as "a euphemism for a cartel."[89]

With respect to the third sector, the Government of Japan reinforced commitments that provide further limitations against large Japanese insurance companies entering the third sector until primary sector deregulation has taken full hold in Japan, as defined in the Supplementary Measures.[90] In return, the U.S. government agreed to allow certain limited entry by the Japanese firms. However, the U.S. Trade Representative noted that "the changes the United States has agreed to represent 'less entry than non-radical change' and affect only about 15 percent of the sector, which itself makes up no more than 5 percent of Japan's overall insurance market . . . . The changes permit very, very limited and controlled entry by Japanese companies."[91]

Conclusion: The Breakdown of the *Goso Sendan* System Begins

The Government of Japan reaffirmed in the Insurance Agreement and the Supplementary Measures that it will "undertake fundamental reform and deregulation"[92] in the Japanese insurance system, among other things, through liberalization of the approval process for insurance products and rates based on the principle that liberalization can promote competition and enhance efficiency among insurance companies for the benefit of Japanese consumers.[93] Under this principle, it is clear that the *Goso Sendan* system cannot be allowed to survive or the true intent and spirit of reform and deregulation will have been ignored.

In essence, the Government of Japan committed to embrace competition instead of government limitations to avoid "excessive competition" and to use solvency and financial soundness as the basis for prudential regulation. Cozy relationships with trade associations and companies will no longer provide the basis to regulate the market. The benefits of these changes are apparent. By allowing product differentiation and distribution based on the needs and demands of the policyholders, the insurance companies will be forced to innovate and satisfy consumer needs. For consumers, this means better service and lower costs. These changes, however, will also force large companies to make tough choices, and some companies will ultimately not survive the real competition.

However, it is important to recognize that the deregulation and reform of the *Goso Sendan* system is at its early stage. Because painful changes are expected, the process of effectively dismantling the *Goso Sendan* system will not be easy and will not occur overnight. Indeed, given that the new insurance law provides MOF with enormous discretionary power to determine the specifics of such changes, the ministry will be under continuous political pressure to protect the domestic industry. Despite its recent problems with scandals, MOF remains one of the most powerful ministries in Japan with close relations to political and industry leaders. In exercising its discretionary power, MOF would have to balance its bureaucratic and political interests with the interests of large and small domestic and foreign firms, and consumers.

A meaningful and lasting reform of the *Goso Sendan* system also requires changes that go beyond the issues currently under discussion in *Kasumigaseki*. For instance, MOF must take steps to ensure that exclusionary business practices are not used to replace the "managed competition" it helped administer under the old system. Regulatory powers cannot be, in effect, delegated to trade associations dominated by large domestic companies or to industry groupings. Deregulation does not mean "privatization" of regulation to such groups or a simple change of leadership of the *Goso Sendan* from government to leaders of *keiretsu* groups. Ultimately, although private exclusionary business practices have been conveniently ignored in the past as a "private sector matter," the Government of Japan bears the responsibility to address problems arising from the market structure it helped establish. In this regard, the FTC must be aggressive in its efforts to enforce the Antimonopoly Law in order to silence the critics who contend that it rarely touches industries under the jurisdiction of MOF. Additionally, as competition intensifies in the future, the Government of Japan may be forced to consider whether the government itself should be competing with private insurance businesses through the Postal Life Insurance system, the largest life insurance institution in the world.

Whether it is the implementation of deregulation measures or actions against private anticompetitive practices in the Japanese insurance sector, it would be essential for the U.S. government, particularly the Office of the U.S. Trade Representative, to be fully engaged. The most recent dispute over insurance demonstrates the validity of this point. A trade agreement becomes a meaningful instrument to promote deregulation and market access—instead of a meaningless piece of paper—only when the agreement is actually enforced, an obvious point often forgotten by some U.S. officials who prefer things to be quiet. However, the history of U.S.–Japan trade relations is unfortunately filled with numerous examples demonstrating that bilateral trade agreements are not "self-executing," and are only fully enforced when the U.S. government takes the necessary steps to ensure that they are enforced. The Insurance Agreement effectively provided the "hooks" to ensure compliance and a basis to press for additional deregulation commitments in the Supplementary Measures. Yet the text of the agreement merely provided the negotiating framework to seek concrete actions by the Japanese government, and such actions were taken because of the dedication and hard work of the officials at the Office of the U.S. Trade Representative to press for appropriate actions. Like other trade agreements, the Insurance Agreement will require continuous monitoring measures by the U.S. government to ensure compliance. Such U.S. government efforts will complement the activities of those reform-minded leaders in the Japanese government and industry truly to transform Japan's insurance regime into a system that serves the interest of consumers.

Notes

1. Joint Statement on the United States–Japan Framework for a New Economic Partnership, July 10, 1993. The insurance negotiations took place in the Regulatory Reform and Competitiveness Group. See Charles Lake and James Southwick, "Japan–United States: Measures Regarding Insurance," *International Legal Materials,* vol. 34 (1995), pp. 661–75, for a brief discussion and the full text of "Measures by the Government of the United States and the Government of Japan Regarding Insurance." (Hereafter Insurance Agreement.)

2. There are certain other considerations that forced MOF to be forthcoming, such as the impact of Prime Minister Ryutaro Hashimoto's announcement of his Big Bang package to restructure Japan's financial markets by 2001 and domestic political pressure to reorganize MOF as part of administrative reform measures. U.S. Trade Representative Barshefsky noted the positive influence of the Big Bang plan during a press briefing: "It is the advent of this Big Bang that helped provide MOF with the basis for genuinely moving forward on the deregulation as envisioned in the 1994 agreement." Mark Felsenthal, "Barshefsky, Pleased with Insurance Pact, Views Japan's Time Line Pledge as Key," *BNA International Trade Reporter*, December 17, 1996, p. A-23.

3. Brian Bremner, Amy Borrus, and Nicole Harris,"One Big Bang for Insurers in Japan," *Business Week*, December 30, 1996, p. 56. The article noted that "[unlike] the recent run of vague bilateral trade pacts, Clinton's team might justifiably put this one in the win column."

4. Editor's interview, "Extremely Disappointed with the U.S.-Japan Agreement on Insurance Says President of Tokyo Fire and Marine," *Shukan Toyo Keizai*, January 11, 1997, p. 80.

5. According to Office of the U.S. Trade Representative, *1995 National Trade Estimate Report on Foreign Trade Barriers* (Washington, 1995): "Japan has the second largest insurance market in the world . . . . Total Japanese insurance premium income in 1992 was ¥39.9 trillion (approximately $320.1 billion) of which the total life premium income that year was ¥29.5 trillion (approximately

$236.7 billion); and the total nonlife net written premium income was ¥10.4 trillion ($83.4 billion). The foreign share of the Japanese insurance market in 1992 was about 2.7 percent of life premiums and 3.5 percent of nonlife premiums . . . . These commercial market figures do not include the huge amount of insurance that the Ministry of Posts and Telecommunications sells. If the life premiums collected by Japan's postal service are included, the foreign market share of Japan's market would be even lower" p. 187). It should be noted that the foreign share would be significantly lower if premiums collected by the National Mutual Insurance Federation of Agricultural Cooperatives (*Zenrenkyo*) were added to the total.

6. The phrase *Goso Sendan* literally means "convoy," and it is used to explain how MOF protects large and small companies by allowing them to cooperate and, in some instances, to collude with each other for mutual survival just as large and small ships in a convoy may cluster in a storm.

7. The International Insurance Council (IIC), "Aide Memoire: Japan Insurance Issues 1" (Washington, December 4, 1992). See also IIC, "Statement on Japan Insurance Liberalization Submitted to USTR in Support of Negotiations under the United States/Japan Framework Agreement 1" (Washington, November 3, 1993).

8. Yukio Noguchi, *1940 Nen Taisei: Saraba "Senji Keizai"* (The 1940 system: Farewell to the "wartime economy") (Tokyo: Toyokeizai Shinposha, 1995), p. 140. Noguchi is a former MOF official. He uses the phrase *"kyoso hitei,"* which has been translated here as "rejection of competition."

9. Ibid., p. 141.

10. Ibid., p. 142.

11. Toyomi Takimoto, director for Second Insurance Division, Insurance Department, Banking Bureau, MOF, *Zusetsu Nippon No Songai Hoken* (Japan's Nonlife Insurance Illustrated) (Tokyo: Zaikei Shohosha, 1994) (hereafter, Takimoto, *Zusetsu Nippon.*); Satoshi Nishikawa, director for First Insurance Division, Insurance Department, Banking Bureau, MOF, *Zusetsu Nippon No Seimei Hoken* (Japan's Life Insurance Illustrated) (Tokyo: Zaikei Shohosha, 1994). According to Nishikawa, the book was prepared by the staff in the MOF Insurance Department (see Nishikawa's preface to *Zusetsu Nippon*). Takimoto and Nishikawa participated in the insurance negotiations under the U.S.–Japan Framework Talks. Although Nishikawa only attended one meeting, Takimoto represented the Insurance Department throughout the negotiations and was viewed by many U.S. negotiators as a formidable presence on the Japanese delegation.

12. Takimoto, *Zusetsu Nippon No*, p. 4. Although modern insurance was not

introduced in Japan until the founder of Keio University, Yukichi Fukuzawa, popularized the term *hoken* (insurance) in the late 1800s. By the year 1900, a significant number of domestic companies had been established. The insurance products were first introduced into Japan by foreign nonlife insurance companies providing coverage to other foreign firms storing goods in the port city of Yokohama (Ibid., p. 3). The first Japanese marine insurance company was established in 1878, and the first fire insurance company in 1887, increasing the number of nonlife (property and casualty) companies to twenty-five by the year 1900. The first Japanese life insurance company was established in 1881. Nishikawa, *Zusetu Nippon No Seimei Hoken*, p. 16.

Until the national government established its regulatory authority in 1890, the local governors regulated the establishment of insurance companies. Nishikawa, *Zusetu Nippon*, p. 182. At the national government level, until the authority was transferred to MOF in 1941, the Ministry of Commerce and Agriculture, and later the Ministry of Commerce (forerunner to the current Ministry of International Trade and Industry (MITI)), held the supervisory authority. Takimoto, *Zusetu Nippon*, p. 4.

13. Takimoto, *Zusetsu Nippon No Songai Hoken,* p. 6. Emphasis added.

14. Ibid., p. 10. The author uses the phrases "*keiyaku kakutoku kyoso*" and "*boshu chitsujo konran.*"

15. Nishikawa, *Zusetsu Nippon*, p. 194. The author uses the phrase "*boshu chitsujo ga ooini midare.*"

16. MOF derives its regulatory authority from, among other things, its Establishment Law and the Insurance Business Law. Until the enactment of the new Insurance Business Law in 1995, the Insurance Business Law of 1939, as amended, played a central role in the regulation of insurance in Japan. In addition to this law, various laws such as the Commercial Code, the Law Concerning Foreign Insurers of 1949, the Law Concerning the Control of Insurance Soliciting, and the Law Concerning Nonlife Insurance Rating Organizations, among other things, controlled the regulation of insurance.

17. Takimoto, *Zusetsu Nippon No Songai Hoken,* p. 204. See also Nishikawa, *Zusetsu Nippon No Seimei Hoken*, p. 184. Although the Insurance Business Law sets forth requirements for the conduct of insurance business, the Commercial Code governs insurance contracts. The Civil Code applies where no specific provision of the Commercial Code is applicable.

18. Takimoto, *Zusetsu Nippon No Songai Hoken*, p. 203. It should be noted, however, that private insurance is not the only insurance available in the life sector. In addition to private insurance underwriters, the Post Office Life Insurance Bureau and the National Mutual Insurance Federation of Agricultural

Cooperatives (*Zenkyoren*) provide life insurance products. The Post Office Life Insurance Bureau was established in 1916. The agricultural cooperatives began selling life insurance products in the postwar period and formed the National Mutual Insurance Federation of Agricultural Cooperatives (*Zenrenkyo*) in 1951. Nishikawa, *Zusetsu Nippon No Seimei Hoken,* pp. 8–25.

19. Katsuro Kanzaki, *Kinyu Shoken Hoken Housei* (Finance, securities, insurance, [their] legal systems), *Juristo,* no. 1073 (August 1, 1995), p. 260. The Banking Bureau's Inspection Department conducts the inspection of the company books.

20. MOF is sometimes asked to issue administrative guidance to resolve a conflict among competitors. Thus administrative guidance should not be viewed simply as unilateral directives from the government. Although the new governmentwide Administrative Procedure Law went into effect in October 1994, the law has not effectively curtailed MOF's ability to use administrative guidance. For background on administrative guidance, see Katsuya Uga, *Gyosei Tetsuzuki Ho No Kaisetsu* (Commentary on the administrative procedure law) (Tokyo: Gakuyo Shobo, 1994), pp. 137–48. For a comprehensive discussion of administrative guidance, see also Kazuo Yamanouchi, *Komuin No Tameno Gyosei Shido Ron* (Theories on administrative guidance for public officials) (Tokyo: Finance Ministry Printing Bureau ed., 1986).

21. Gouhei Nishina, *Sannen Go No Seiho Gyokai Fuchin No Kozu* 109 (The composition of life insurance three years from now) (Tokyo: KK Besto Book, 1992).

22. IIC, "Aide Memoire," pp. 4–5.

23. Ibid. See also James Bedore, *United States International Trade Commission, Industry and Trade Summary: Insurance* (Washington: U.S. International Trade Commission, 1991), p. 16.

24. U.S.-Japan Business Council, *Japan's Financial Services Market: The Case for Expanded Access* 5 (Washington, June 3, 1993).

25. *Kyoso Seisaku No Kantenkara No Seifu Kisei No Minaoshi* (Review of government regulation from the point of view of competition policy) (Fair Trade Commission, 1989), reprinted in Tsuruta, ed., *Seifukisei No Kanwa To Kyoso Seisaku* 3-44 (Deregulation of government regulation and competition policy) (Tokyo: Gyosei, 1989).

26. Ibid., p. 34. The study group also noted in the same paragraph that "for several decades, excluding the entry of foreign-capital affiliated domestic companies or branch offices of foreign companies, there has not been any new entry into the insurance sector." In other words, at the time the report was issued, no new domestic insurance company had been licensed to enter the insurance market in Japan for several decades.

27. Ibid., p. 35. The term *"han i ryoritsu"* is used for banded rates. The study group also noted that even when banded rates are permitted, the companies engaged in horizontal pricing; thus, "there is a need to take steps to ensure that, at a minimum, free competition takes place within the banded rates."

28. Ibid.

29. Yoshio Maya, *"Riyosha Fuzai No Sogokinyukikanka Ron* (Formation of general financial organizations without consideration to users), *Ekonomisuto,* March 23, 1993, p.21.

30. IIC, "Aide Memoire," pp. 3, 11. The limited staffing at MOF also acts as a barrier in that it greatly slows down the process of licensing for new companies and new products (p. 3). During the negotiations of the Insurance Agreement, the Japanese trade associations changed their rules to allow foreign participation. The Marine and Fire Insurance Association of Japan now has foreign members on its roster.

31. National Association of Insurance Commissioners (NAIC), *Insurance Department Resources Book* (Kansas City, 1994) table 2. In 1993 New York had 929 full time officials and a significant number of contractual employees.

32. As noted earlier, although insurance providers were regulated by the Insurance Business Law, insurance contracts were governed by certain provisions of the Commercial Code.

33. Zentaro Kitagawa, *Doing Business in Japan*, vol. 3 (Matthew Bender and Co., 1995), § 12.01[3][a] (1995). The author of the chapter on nonlife insurance explains: "Articles 629 through 668 of the Commercial Code apply to nonlife insurance stock companies that underwrite non-marine insurance. These articles do not directly apply to the legal relationship between the policyholder and the insurer in a mutual company (mutual insurance) because such a relationship does not fall under insurance performed as a business as defined in the Commercial Code, article 502, item 9. However, article 664 of the Commercial Codes makes these articles applicable *mutatis mutandis* to mutual insurance 'unless the nature of such insurance does not permit such application.'

34. Government of Japan, *Report Prepared for the Insurance Committee of the OECD*, April 1986, p. 3. The Japanese government report goes on to say that the Japanese legal theories "of which the most generally accepted is that insurance business, in order to be so called, must cover a specified category of events, the occurrence of which is fortuitous; meet the monetary demand of the beneficiary; be based on an association of a large number of people exposed to analogous risks; be supported by contributions, the amounts of which are determined by a rational calculation; be an economic institution; and be organized

as an independent undertaking and not as an integral part of any concern undertaking business other than insurance, and managed on a planned, continuing,
and non-exclusive basis." For example, in a report submitted to the Organization for Economic Cooperation and Development (OECD), a MOF representative noted, "The Japanese Insurance Business Law gives no clear definition of
'insurance business'; the only source to be looked to for a definition is, therefore, the various theories underlying Japanese laws ."

35. Foreign Nonlife Insurance Association (FNLIA), *Position Paper* (Tokyo,
September 3, 1992), p. 3.

36. Ibid. It should be noted, however, that the third-sector products were still
licensed either as life or nonlife products. In other words, they were licensed as
"life third sector" or "nonlife third sector" products. The third-sector products
also take the form of "riders" attached to other primary life and nonlife products.

37. Ibid. See also Nishikawa, *Zusetsu Nippon*, p. 10.

38. Office of the U.S. Trade Representative, *1995 NTE Report,* p. 187.

39. Ibid.

40. The Study Group on Trade Friction and Market Structure, *Long-Term
Relationship among Japanese Companies* (Tokyo, 1987), pp. 6–7.

41. Douglas Ostrom, *Japan's Sleeping Insurance Giants: Roused and
Ready?* in Japan Economic Institute (JEI) Report 14, no. 17a (Washington:
Japan Economic Institute of America, 1992). Emphasis added. The author
noted, for example, "Of the seven largest Japanese life insurance companies,
all but Dai-Ichi Mutual Life are members of the president's club of the six
major keiretsu" (p. 12).

42. ACCJ Financial Services Committee, *Study of Japanese Insurance Procurement Practices within Keiretsu Groups* (Tokyo, 1993), overview. The research for the report was completed "by a number of independent marketing
and research consultants" and "all eight major horizontally connected *keiretsu*
groups and six randomly selected vertically integrated *keiretsu* groups [were]
included" (overview).

43. The Marine and Fire Insurance Association of Japan rejected the ACCJ
report with the classic response: "What matters in selecting insurance companies is sales effort and the quality of services . . . '*keiretsu*' and cross-shareholding
have never been entrance barriers to the Japanese market." Letter from the Chairman, Planning Committee, Marine and Fire Insurance Association of Japan, to
the Chairman, Financial Services Committee, ACCJ (September 17, 1993).

44. National Association of Insurance Brokers (NAIB), *Position Paper,* presented to Ministry of Finance (Washington, April 15, 1993).

45. Ibid.

46. Office of the U.S. Trade Representative, *1994 National Trade Estimate Report on Foreign Barriers* (Washington, 1993), p. 164.

47. Office of the U.S. Trade Representative, *1993 National Trade Estimate Report on Foreign Barriers* (Washington, 1993), p. 158. For example, Japan's largest life insurance company, Nippon Life, owns 3 percent of the outstanding shares of the Tokyo Stock Exchange. See Bedore, *United States International Trade Commission*, p. 16.

48. IIC, "Aide Memoire," p. 1.

49. Ibid.

50. Ibid., p. 5.

51. See *United States–Japan Trade Negotiations,* testimony of H. Edward Hanway, chairman, International Insurance Council, Hearings before the Subcommittee on International Trade of the Senate Committee on Finance, 103d Cong. 1 sess. (Government Printing Office, 1993), p. 89. Indeed, the USTR's annual report on trade and market access barriers has cited Japan's insurance sector every year since the report began in 1986. See Office of the U.S. Trade Representative, *1986–1995 National Trade Estimate Report on Foreign Trade Barriers* (Washington, various annual issues).

52. According to the U.S. Trade Representative, *1993 NTE Report*, the U.S. government "has been pressing Japan in the Uruguay Round services negotiations to liberalize multilaterally the insurance market . . . . The USTR has also proposed bilateral consultations with the Government of Japan regarding the liberalization and deregulation of the Japanese insurance market in general" (p. 159). It is noteworthy that the report also states: "Given that Japan lacks meaningful administrative processes that will permit foreign firms to comment on the reform process and participate in the MOF rulemaking procedures, the establishment of an on-going government-to-government process is essential in ensuring that the U.S. insurance companies are provided with fair and nondiscriminatory treatment in the reform process" (p. 159).

53. According to Office of the U.S. Trade Representative, *1995 NTE Report*, "The United States Government selected insurance in 1993 as one of the priority sectors under the U.S.–Japan Framework Talks because the Japanese government was in the process of implementing a major reform—first in 50 years—of its insurance system in Japan. In addition, increasing foreign access in financial markets like the insurance market in Japan may indirectly have additional benefits in the long run in changing how Japan has traditionally done its business" (p. 187).

54. Kanzaki, *Kinyu*, p. 20.

55. U.S. Trade Representative, *1995 NTE Report*, p. 187.

56. The two governments agreed that the assessment of the implementation of the "Agreement, as well as the evaluation of progress achieved, will be based on the overall consideration of objective criteria, both quantitative and qualitative." Examples of quantitative indicators include the number and ratio of approvals for new or modified products and rates; the value of premiums by foreign insurance providers in Japan, in the aggregate and in market subsectors as appropriate; and the market share of total insurance premiums for foreign insurance providers, in the aggregate and in market subsectors. Examples of qualitative indicators include how MOF reviews applications and notifications, as well as meaningful and fair opportunities for foreign insurance providers in Japan to be informed of, comment on, and exchange views with MOF officials. An important criterion regarding competition policy was also included with reference to "aspects of market conditions and business practices" (that is, *keiretsu* practices).

57. Statement by the chairman of the International Insurance Council (Washington, October 1, 1994).

58. Lake and Southwick, "Japan–United States," p. 663.

59. Such products include boiler and machinery, credit card theft and burglary, computer comprehensive, moveable comprehensive, and directors' and officers' liability insurance.

60. Such risks include hull, cargo, and aviation insurance.

61. Lake and Southwick, "Japan–United States," p. 663.

62. Insurance Agreement, pp. 15–16.

63. Ibid.

64. Ibid.

65. Ibid., p. 11.

66. Insurance Business Law, P.L. 105 (1995). For an overview of the new law see Yoshihiro Tamura, *Hokengyoho Kaisei No Gaiyo* 20 (Summary on the Revision of the Insurance Business Law), NBL No. 572 (1995). Mr. Tamura was a deputy director in the Insurance Department of the MOF.

67. The number 500 includes the supplementary provisions.

68. The Insurance Council (*Hoken Shingikai*) provides the minister of finance with official advice and recommendations, among other things, on "important issues affecting the administration of the insurance regulatory system and matters related to its reform." Management and Coordination Agency, *Shingikai Soran* 149 (Overview on advisory councils) (Finance Ministry Printing Office, 1990). Following a typical Japanese government advisory committee make-up, the twenty-member Insurance Council consists of representatives of the Japanese insurance industry, academia, former government officials, jour-

nalists, and consumer groups. Although under article 8 of *Kokka Gyosei Soshiki Ho* (the National Government Organization Law), the advisory committees are technically "independent," MOF officials heavily influence the proceedings by setting the agenda and providing background materials they deem appropriate.

69. Tamura, *Hokengyoho*, pp. 21–22. With regard to mutual entry, the law provides a "fire-wall" between the parent and subsidiary to ensure arms-length transactions, according to Tamura. The term "notification system" is a translation of "*todokede seido*."

70. Masaru Oogo, *Hokenseido Kaikaku to Dokusen Kinshi Ho* (Antimonopoly Law and the insurance system reform), *Kosei Torihiki*, no. 537 (1995), p. 32. Oogo is an official of the FTC.

71. Ibid., pp. 22–23.

72. Ibid., p. 33.

73. Ibid., p. 35. See articles 102 and 105.

74. Ibid.

75. The rating association will undergo major changes pursuant to the agreement reached in December 1996 between the governments of the United States and Japan.

76. Oogo, *Hokenseido Kaikaku tu Dokusen Kinshi Ho*, p. 37. The standards required for enforcement actions under the Antimonopoly Law must obviously be met.

77. Ibid. Oogo noted that Japan's insurance exemption system "operates quite differently" than the U.S. and European systems and should be reviewed further.

78. The term "drastic" is a translation of the Japanese word "*kyugeki*," which in some circumstances can be translated as "radical." It is noteworthy that Japanese government officials recognize in their writings that the commitment made pursuant to the Insurance Agreement regarding the third sector was specifically addressed in this provision. For example, Oogo, *Hokenseido*, of the FTC comments, "The supplementary article [121] addressed the substance of the agreement reached in October 1994 under the Japan-U.S. Framework that . . . the liberalization in [the third sector] will not be implemented unless significant portion of life and nonlife sectors are deregulated (p. 33). See also Tamura, *Hokengyoho*, p. 21. Tamura specifically references the Insurance Agreement as well as the Insurance Council report.

79. Office of the U.S. Trade Representative, *1996 National Trade Estimate Report on Foreign Trade Barriers* (Washington, 1996), p. 193.

80. Ibid.

81. Ibid.

82. Ibid.

83. Ibid.

84. *Asahi Shimbun*, January 15, 1997, p. 12.

85. Ibid.

86. Supplementary Measures, pp. 2-5. For instance, MOF agreed to add, effective April 1, 1997, the following ten products to the list of products to which the notification system applies with respect to rates and riders: medical malpractice liability insurance; advanced loss of machinery profit insurance; delayed start of construction insurance; civil engineering completed risks insurance; nuclear energy insurance; umbrella liability insurance; environment liability insurance; erection insurance; moveable comprehensive insurance; and computer comprehensive insurance.

87. Ibid., p. 5.

88. Ibid., p. 3.

89. *BNA International Trade Reporter*, December 17, 1996, p. A-22.

90. Supplementary Measures, pp. 5–7.

91. *BNA International Trade Reporter*, December 17, 1996, p. A-22.

92. Supplementary Measures, cover note.

93. Insurance Agreement, p. 8.

CHAPTER NINE

Between Bureaucrat and Buyer: Japan's Nonprofit Industry Groups

John P. Stern

DEREGULATION OF THE domestic market is again being discussed in Japan. From the American perspective, deregulation in Japan will not achieve its objective until less attention is paid to pruning specific regulations and more attention is paid to the mechanisms of Japanese government that hamper fair competition. Indeed, were the U.S. government and media truly to understand the tangled mass of anticompetitive practices that grow on the tree of the Japanese economy and consider how to remove them with the fewest strokes of the ax, they would focus more attention on the market gatekeeper role of Japanese nonprofits.[1]

The proliferation of nonprofits poses a formidable challenge to the larger cause of deregulation as well as the efforts of foreign companies to gain entry to the Japanese market. The Fair Trade Commission of Japan counted 14, 1966 industry associations in Japan as of March 31, 1993—the roster of nonprofits under the jurisdiction of the Ministry of International Trade and Industry (MITI) alone is more than an inch thick.[2] In most states of the United States, one can incorporate a nonprofit industry group in the same fashion as one incorporates a for-profit corporation, with the local government inquiring only whether the articles of incorporation are in the proper form, the corporate name is available, and the filing fee has been paid. If one wishes the incorporated entity to be exempt from corporate income tax, one must satisfy the state and national tax authorities that the activities of the entity conform to a statutory list of approved tax-exempt activities.[3] Registration authorities in the United States do not inquire as to whether there are competing non-profit groups in the same jurisdiction, nor do they try to dictate the personnel of the new organization.[4]

In Japan, article 34 of the Civil Code provides that nonprofits can only be incorporated after receiving permission from the ministry with jurisdiction over the activities proposed for the new organization.[5] The reasoning behind the Civil Code provision is that ministries should be good judges of whether the public interest would be served by granting the new entity relief from corporate taxes and would be honest auditors of the new organization's finances.

Article 34 of a nearly century-old legal code is also the source of increasing friction among ministries, as technology makes it more difficult to define the boundaries between nonprofit organizations. For example, because the Japanese version of the so-called information highway is expected to become a larger industry than automobiles and consumer electronics combined, control of the information highway is a major goal of many ministries.[6] As a result, the formerly clear distinctions between computers (under MITI jurisdiction) and telecommunications (under Ministry of Posts and Telecommunications jurisdiction) have become blurred, and nonprofit organizations with overlapping interests exist.[7] The formation of new nonprofit organizations by any ministry must be approved by the Cabinet, so that competing ministries can and do veto proposals from rival ministries.[8] Nevertheless, activities that seemed to be separate at the time the formation of two nonprofit organizations under two ministries was approved can, over time, bump up against one another.[9] Conversely, ministerial attempts to pigeonhole broad technologies, such as software, into the jurisdiction of one nonprofit group can hamper the ability of Japanese industry to deal with evolving issues.[10]

The Civil Code provides bureaucrats with the spark of life for nonprofit industry groups and the power to supervise their finances.[11] It is virtually impossible to form an incorporated nonprofit without active promotion by the career civil service. As one observer commented:

> It would be a huge burden to try to form a nonprofit corporation without bureaucratic backing. One must submit scores of documents, starting with the proposed articles of incorporation, the business plan, the dues structure, the identity of the membership, the scope of activity, relations with other such organizations, etc. The amount of labor required of the appli-

cant is huge. Even after all this, permission will not be given. There are plenty of cases in which groups of companies abandoned the idea of incorporating.[12]

Indeed, an organization of Japanese importers of American high-technology products has pleaded with MITI for years for nonprofit status to date without success.[13] None of the foreign nonprofit manufacturing associations in Japan has been afforded nonprofit status under Japanese law, owing to their unwillingness to have their trade activities and financial status controlled by the Japanese government.[14]

Japan's Civil Servants Law provides the motive for injecting the personal interest of the bureaucrat into the establishment of new nonprofit industry groups. Contrary to popular opinion in the United States, Japanese civil servants do not enjoy unrestricted license to retire to the private sector. The Civil Servants Law provides that a public servant may not become employed, for a period of two years after leaving public office, without a waiver by the National Personnel Agency,[15] by a *for-profit* organization that was under the jurisdiction of the public servant during a period up to five years prior to termination of public service.[16] This leaves a public servant with two choices while waiting out the statutory two-year ban on starting a second career with a corporation that would be most likely to value the bureaucrat's connections: pursue a post with a for-profit corporation not directly under the jurisdiction of the public servant prior to the termination of public service[17] or pursue a post with a nonprofit organization.

The Japanese on the average live longer than people in most other countries, but they retire from salaried white-collar occupations earlier. Providing for the material needs of nearly one-quarter of one's life without a job is a sobering thought: the fear of an impoverished retirement gnaws at the average salaried Japanese and is a major reason for Japan's high personal savings rate. Public servants in central ministries, however, have an opportunity to create *amakudari saki* ("a place to which one may descend from heaven"), nonprofit organizations to which they can retire for a second career. Indeed, for many bureaucrats it is "a badge of honor to create new industry foundations while employed as a public servant."[18] Ministries are often on the lookout for opportunities to create new *amakudari saki,* even out of adversity: in negotiating the first U.S.-Japan Semiconductor Agreement, MITI allowed the United States to pressure Japan to accept the agreement with a provision creating a nonprofit organization related to semiconductor market access.[19] The agreement was initialed in July 1986, but it was well into October 1986 before there was a clear idea inside MITI concerning the organization's structure and purposes.[20] The first executive director of the new semiconductor-related organization was an ex-MITI official who had directed the major research project creating the competitive semiconductor industry in Japan that nearly wiped out American competition: not the first person who would come to mind for the job of promoting foreign-brand semiconductors in Japan.[21] MITI reportedly promises its ex-officials above a certain level three jobs after they leave the ministry, and this principle often seems to override considerations of effectiveness in the post.

A mere unfunded nonprofit industry group is of no use in providing a salary or pension to a retired government official.[22] Thus ministries must consider the financial stability of nonprofit industry groups. The ideal source of financial stability, of course, is a well-conceived organization addressing a clear need of a wide variety of potential financial contributors. In the telecommunications standards area, for example, the principal Japanese network standards organization, the TTC, receives dues contributions from hundreds of Japanese and foreign-capital organizations because there is widespread interest in the success of private sector consensus on telecommunications networks. Although the organization was chartered by the Ministry of Posts and Telecommunications, membership is not a prerequisite for telecommunications market access. This, therefore, is an example of a Japanese nonprofit supported by private industry without negative effects on market access.

Unfortunately, the ideas of bureaucrats for postretirement careers sometimes exceed the interest of industry in paying for them. The *Keidanren*, for example, has reportedly refused at least nine times, since 1991, to fund ministerial ideas for new nonprofit organizations.[23] Some of the ideas, such as a sports promotion foundation to which industry was asked by the Ministry of Education to contribute ¥10 billion (over $80 million) seem totally unnecessary. Others, such as an organization proposed by the Ministry of Transport to place facilities for the handicapped in railroad stations, would have performed functions that arguably should be funded by government, not by a ¥2 billion industry contribution.[24] In addition, none of the requests for funding new organizations were accompanied by promises to sunset organizations that had outlived their usefulness. As Tadahiro Sekimoto, then president of NEC Corporation and a *Keidanren* vice chairman, reportedly said:

The executive director of the industrial products recycling foundation to which I belong is a ministry alumnus. It is acceptable to welcome a retired civil servant as a method of promoting communications with the ministry in charge. If there are good people in government, I think it is just fine that government and the private sector can work together. And in this case, the private sector asked the government to form a foundation for this purpose, which also has important social consequences. However, although foundations and the like should be created if necessary, they should also be eliminated as necessary. One must promote a "scrap and build" mentality. After periodic general inspection, those organizations that are behind the times, or are not important, should be eliminated. I believe that the ministry does not sufficiently understand this. Goals should be set, and reductions should be effected where necessary.[25]

A less-studied consequence of *amakudari saki* that are insufficiently desired by industry, however, is an increase in regulations impeding market entry. This occurs because ministries will often give favored nonprofit groups a monopoly on quasi-government functions such as certifications, standards, and approvals. The income that the nonprofit group obtains from certification and approval fees, or from member companies that join to obtain closely guarded information about standards, funds the personnel costs of the organization.

Nonprofit industry groups with quasi-governmental monopolies are common in U.S-Japan trade disputes. For example, in 1991–92, a U.S. manufacturer of slot machines reportedly complained to the Office of the U.S. Trade Representative that of more than 700,000 *pachislo* slot machines in gambling parlors in Japan, not a single one was foreign made.[26] Industry sources reported that every Japanese manufacturer of slot machines priced its product at around ¥400,000, with no discount for quantity purchases.[27] The Japanese press traced the problem to the Japan Electric Amusement Machine Association,[28] a nonprofit industry group peopled with ex-National Police Agency officials, which issued a set of unpublished guidelines for slot machines determining the sole machines approved for use in Japan by the National Police Agency.[29]

Testing agencies have been cited as market barriers by American telecommunications and computer equipment companies for more than a decade. In Japan, as in the United States, equipment connected to the public telephone network must be certified as not causing harm to that network. In the United States, companies selling equipment that connects to the public telephone network, such as modems used to send computer data down telephone lines, have several options for complying with certification requirements. They may conduct their own tests of compliance with published standards and affix a statement of compliance. Or they may employ independent testing laboratories to certify their compliance. One of the largest testing laboratories in the United States, Underwriters Laboratories, has substantial operations in Japan to make it easier for Japanese exporters to meet U.S. certification requirements of various sorts.

In contrast, in Japan, every modem, circuit switch, voicemail system, computer card, telephone, headset, terminal or other type of equipment that connects to the public telephone network must be tested by a single nonprofit organization established in 1984, commonly called "the JATE."[30] The JATE (Japan Approvals Institute for Telecommunications Equipment) was given a testing monopoly by key telecommunications liberalization enabling legislation[31] passed by the Diet. The JATE's senior personnel come from positions connected with its supervisory ministry. This situation has been the source of periodic protests by the U.S. government. In 1984–85, the U.S. government required the JATE to publish its certification procedures and process applications from foreign-capital companies without discrimination. Subsequent protests have led to lower JATE fees, shortened processing times, and better documentation in English of requirements.[32] Nevertheless, the lack of an overseas presence by the JATE means that most U.S. exporters are unaware of its existence and unable to satisfy its requirements. Two Fortune 500 computer companies, a famous Silicon Valley firm and a leading Texas-based firm, found that they had released products in the Japanese market that did no harm to the public network but that had not been certified by the JATE. These companies hastily arranged compliance, but the episodes prove that even companies with large Japan operations find JATE procedures arcane. More than ten years after the JATE's establishment, its procedures continue to draw criticism from the American Chamber of Commerce in Japan.[33] The most recent bone of contention is the JATE's practice of certifying the applicant, not the product. In other words, if U.S. company X has its modem certified by the JATE, and U.S. company X is acquired by U.S. company Y (a very common occurrence in the U.S. telecommunications market), even if the modem is the same one as sold prior to the merger, the JATE requires that the modem be resubmitted for certification because the original applicant was absorbed by a new company. Also common is the situation in which U.S. company A names Japanese distributor B to distribute a product in Japan that requires JATE certification. Distributor B applies for and obtains a JATE seal of approval. Some time later, U.S. company A, dissatisfied with the performance of distributor B, decides to market the same product via distributor C. Once again, since the original applicant B is no longer selling the product, sales must stop while the new distributor applies for certification of the same product that was found harmless the last time around. Since product cycles in the U.S. computer industry are typically less than six months, the wait for JATE recertification is a significant impediment to U.S. exporters' ability to offer the latest technology to Japanese customers.

Despite the JATE's arguably negative effect on the variety of products offered in Japan's telecommunications market, its role has expanded into testing the wired portion of wireless telecommunications equipment, with yet another organization charging a separate fee for testing the wireless portion of the same equipment. An official of Nokia, the European cellular telephone company most active in the Japan market, appeared on Japanese television in June 1994 to complain that the various seals of approval required to sell his company's telephones in Japan were the most expensive component in the telephone.[34] One suspects that the JATE's jurisdiction is expanding so that its fee revenue will remain at a level needed to support its personnel expenses in the wake of lower fee levels and a move from wired to wireless telecommunications methods.

In contrast, the method adopted by Japanese industry to prevent harm to the office environment owing to electromagnetic signals demonstrates that even in the Japanese context there are less burdensome methods of certification. Most computer, office, consumer electronics, and telecommunications equipment emits electromagnetic radiation that can interfere with other equipment and that potentially affects human health. Spurred in part by European and U.S. regulations, Japan's electronics and telecommunications industries in 1985 decided voluntarily to create a certification system for compliance with industry standards. The organization in charge of certification, VCCI, is a consortium that has created several secretariats for receiving certification petitions and allows foreign companies and testing organizations to join as functioning members.[35] The necessary testing can be performed overseas by foreign companies themselves. VCCI has not sought nonprofit status and does not have a significant number of ex–ministry officials among its personnel. After an initial period when American companies were unaware of VCCI's existence and concerned about VCCI standards, complaints about VCCI seem to have disappeared. Several U.S. testing laboratories have now developed their business of preparing U.S. exporters to meet the VCCI standards. Since VCCI is not an incorporated entity, but merely a liaison consortium, it does not require ministry approval for formation, and because it does not charge fees for a seal of approval, it is unattractive as a bureaucrat's postgovernment career.

Nonprofit industry groups that *are* sufficiently funded by Japanese industry, and that may not impose burdensome certification requirements, nevertheless pose the problem of anticompetitive behavior toward nonmembers. Much has been written about antitrust law in Japan.[36] Japan's antitrust agency, the Fair Trade Commission of Japan (JFTC), states, "The Antimonopoly Act prohibits firms from . . . conducting private monopolization, unreasonable restraints of trade and unfair trade practices. At the same time, it prohibits trade associations that are combinations or federations of combinations of firms from engaging in conduct which similarly restrains or impedes competition."[37]

As far back as 1979, the JFTC issued Guidelines Concerning the Activities of Trade Associations under the Antimonopoly Act (Guidelines).[38] The Guidelines sought to curb illegal cartels, under the guise of trade association activities, by firms in the Japanese market. The activities of the hundreds of *legal* cartels in the Japanese market remain outside the Guidelines' scope.[39]

Japan experienced a significant increase in foreign-capital company activity after the 1979 Guidelines. General foreign investment increased as a result of investment and exchange liberalizations in 1979–81, and electronics investment jumped after the telecommunications and medical equipment market liberalizations of 1984–85 and the Semiconductor Agreement of 1986.[40] Enough of the new foreign entrants to the Japanese market encountered difficulties in joining Japanese industry nonprofit groups that, by May 1986, the JFTC felt compelled to comment, "Trade associations promote the common profit of their members by providing guidance, information and liaison or cooperation with related industries. This can lead to problems with the smooth conduct of business affairs by companies that are not members of the trade associations."[41]

Primarily as a result of changes in the domestic market, rather than JFTC activity, prominent Japanese trade associations in areas the sub-

ject of results-oriented bilateral trade agreements increased their foreign-capital membership.[42] Nevertheless, for the bulk of the Japanese
market not subject to U.S.-Japan bilateral trade agreements, problems
remained requiring the attention of the U.S. and Japanese governments.

The U.S. government, in the Structural Impediments Initiative 1992
Follow-Up Report, obtained Japanese government assurances of increased
access to Japanese trade associations for foreign-capital companies:

> The Government of Japan, in reconfirming its intention to continue poli-
> cies pursuing the principles of a free and open market, with a view toward
> improving market access to the Japanese market, also restates its inten-
> tion to work toward the guarantee of transparent, nondiscriminatory and
> open activity by every trade organization representing a manufacturing
> industry. In pursuit of this goal . . . every part of the Japanese government
> will take the following measures:
>
> (i) Create a list of the most important nonprofit industry groups under
> its jurisdiction, and make that list available;
>
> (ii) Encourage such groups to prepare reports, to the extent possible, of
> their activities, including activities jointly with the Japanese government;
>
> (iii) Compile the above materials and make them available to foreign
> companies.[43]

Nevertheless, less than a year later, the JFTC felt compelled to recognize in 1993 that "foreign companies in particular complain of cases in
which they are not allowed to participate in the internal workings of the
organization, and other forms of internal discrimination. Where business activities are hampered by an inability to receive the benefits of the
activities of the nonprofit industry group, there must be nondiscriminatory treatment regardless of status as an association member."[44] A 1996
JFTC survey of participation by 500 foreign-capital firms in Japanese
trade associations indicates that 26.2 percent of foreign firms surveyed
were not members of the relevant nonprofit organization(s) for their
industry.[45] Among Japanese nonprofit associations surveyed, 28.7 percent admitted discriminating against "outsiders," and 72.1 percent admitted that their quality "seal of approval" was not available to
"outsiders."[46] Of those foreign-capital firms that were not members of
their industry association in Japan, 33.3 percent found it difficult to obtain information regarding their industry and customers in related industries, and 66.6 percent found it difficult to obtain Japanese government
information.[47]

In addition to the JFTC's statistical information, there is anecdotal information to indicate that foreign-capital companies continue to lack effective representation in Japanese trade associations. One of the first market access problems for the American electronics industry in Japan faced by the author involved discrimination by a Japanese nonprofit industry group against an American-capital company that was a leader in optoelectronics technology.[48] The American-capital company had sought entry into the Japanese nonprofit in charge of technical standardization of optoelectronics technology. The author was told that the American-capital company "was not experienced" in the technology by a spokesperson for the Japanese group. At the time that the spokesperson (himself on loan to the group from a for-profit Japanese competitor of the American company) made this statement, he was flanked by a two-inch thick book on a facet of optoelectronics technology authored by a scientist of the same American company that was being denied admission owing to "lack of experience." Partially as a result of trade friction arising from this incident, the Ministry of International Trade and Industry reformed its JIS industrial standards system to allow much greater participation by foreign interests.[49]

Unfortunately, as the repeated exhortations of the JFTC and other parts of the Japanese government indicate, the problem of exclusion of foreign-capital companies from Japanese nonprofit industry group activities has continued over the years. In sad counterpoint to the problem resolved in 1985 in optoelectronics, the author encountered an incident in 1995 that once again smacks of Japanese competitors in a technology using standards activities to exclude leading-edge American-capital competitors. This time the technology in question was uninterruptible power supplies, devices that prevent data from being lost by computers when electric power suddenly fails. Owing to double-digit growth in Japan's personal computer market, the market for uninterruptible power supplies has ballooned. The basic technology for uninterruptible power supplies in Japan, however, has not changed much in the past thirty years. The new American-capital entrant to the Japanese market brought a much more competitive technology to Japan, one that would, among other things, use software to trigger data protection for entire networks. The Japanese uninterruptible power supply manufacturers, weak in software development and inexperienced in network management, reportedly reacted by using their trade association to develop a new Japanese standard for the product that would implicitly exclude the American-capital manufacturer.

A common Japanese response to charges of exclusionary business practices is to claim that once foreign-capital companies join the Japanese groups, they will be "insiders" that benefit rather than "outsiders" that suffer. Relatively few American-capital companies in Japan belong to the major industry groups regulating their field: the JFTC's most recent survey suggests that this is due to foreign-capital companies' lack of the financial, personnel, planning resources, or business status necessary to participate in Japanese nonprofits.[50] On the other hand, 29.4 percent of respondent foreign companies reported that they could not participate in Japanese nonprofits' major deliberations even though they were members, and 17.6 percent reported that their own trade associations limited their access to government information and held secret discussions without them.[51]

It is possible, although exceedingly rare, for a foreign-capital company to organize its own nonprofit: to the author's knowledge, it has been done twice in the past twenty years.[52] Nevertheless, the most common situation is one of an American-capital company being offered only second-class status in the Japanese nonprofit controlling its industry. The companies on the board of directors of Japanese nonprofits are usually determined at the time of establishment, which was often years before an American-capital company petitioned for membership. The chairmanship of a Japanese nonprofit is often determined years in advance.[53] Foreign-capital companies may be barred from certain Japanese nonprofit committees, such as the trade policy committee of manufactured export trade associations. While there are many useful activities, ranging from standards to foreign missions to receptions, that may be open without discrimination to foreign-capital members of Japanese nonprofits, it is rare that foreign-capital members are treated as equal participants. Accordingly, "get along and go along" is not a viable alternative to more pointed market access tactics.

One of Japan's parties in opposition in 1996, New Party Sakigake, targeted reform of the *amakudari* system in its own Administrative Reform Project but failed to enact its proposals into law because of lack of support from the dominant Liberal Democratic Party (LDP).[54] The LDP's own effort at reform was packaged as two September 20, 1996, Cabinet resolutions concerning "Standards for Establishment, Correction and Oversight of Nonprofit Organizations" and "Standards for the Entrusting of Inspections, etc. to Nonprofit Organizations."[55] The Cabinet resolutions state that (i) directors (officers) of nonprofits who come from the controlling ministry should generally be one-third or less of the total membership of the board of directors (except when the nonprofit inspects and certifies, in which case up to half of the directors can be former supervising ministry officials)[56]; (ii) salaries for senior nonprofit officials should not be "unfairly high in relation to that nonprofit's assets, revenues and salaries in the private sector"[57]; (iii) inspection fees should not result in "excessive revenues" for the nonprofit.[58] And who is charged with effecting these reforms, by the year 2000 at the latest? The same ministry that chartered the nonprofit and that sends it retired officials.[59]

Many of the leading U.S.-manufactured exports to Japan, such as computer equipment and semiconductors, represent technology with short life cycles that need immediate market access if it is not to be obsolete before entry into Japan. For this reason, the stately pace of Japan's attempts to deal with market gatekeeper and exclusionary behavior by nonprofits over a period of years is unacceptable to much of American industry. Against this background, it is inevitable that the United States must once again assist Japan in promoting domestic competition. In seeking to eliminate regulations imposed primarily for the purpose of supporting ex-bureaucrats in nonprofits, the United States will find common ground with Japanese industry. Although Japanese industry is unlikely to identify itself publicly with an attack on ministerial power, for fear of retaliation, properly courted it would likely support the revision of article 34 of the Civil Code to allow nonprofit industry groups to be created without the need for government permission.[60]

In addition to revising the Civil Code to allow nonprofits to be formed in the same fashion as corporations, with tax-free status being determined by the tax authorities and not the ministry in charge of the proposed industrial activity, Japan should remove some of the motive for the proliferation of nonprofits. The loophole in article 103 of the Civil Servants Law that allows bureaucrats to retire to *non*profit organizations under their jurisdiction should be closed with an absolute ban on retiring to controlled organizations, both for profit and nonprofit, for an extended period after leaving the ministry. To counterbalance the reduction of retirement options that a revision of the Civil Servants Law would cause, the retirement age for career civil servants in the central government should be raised to an age, such as sixty-five, in keeping with the life span of modern Japanese. The Japanese government should be urged, perhaps in connection with recent promised liberalizations of the pension fund market, to improve the retirement benefits of national civil servants, rather than allowing them to skim the national economy to provide for their old age.

A bureaucrat is no more capable of promoting deregulation than a surgeon is capable of removing his own appendix. The added reluctance of Japan's legislative and judicial branches to oversee genuine reform justifies vigorous foreign actions that offer Japan no alternative but to eliminate the market-restricting activities of Japanese nonprofit industry groups.

Notes

1. As used here, the term encompasses *shadan hojin*, "trade associations," and *zaidan hojin*, "industrial foundations," but not *tokushu hojin*, "public corporations" or other quasi-governmental entities. The *shadan hojin* and *zaidan hojin* most often conduct activities that would be considered purely private sector commercial activities in the United States, while the plethora of *kodan, jigyodan, kokin, tokushu kaisha, eidan* active in Japan perform a variety of activities impossible to classify simply.

2. *1993 Annual Report of the Fair Trade Commission of Japan* (Tokyo, 1994), p. 158. (Hereafter *JFTC 1993 Annual Report*); and *Tsushosangyosho kankei koeki hojin benran 1996* (Guidebook to nonprofit organizations under MITI jurisdiction) (Tokyo: Tsusho sangyo chosakai, 1996).

3. See, for example, *U.S. Internal Revenue Code* §501. Individual states may have slightly different lists of approved nonprofit activities.

4. The registration authorities in the United States are typically state offices. In Japan, local branches of the Ministry of Justice register nonprofit entities according to national law. Most of the nonprofit organizations that affect foreign-capital companies in Japan are registered at the registrars *(homu kyoku)* for Chiyoda Ward and Minato Ward in Tokyo. The public can obtain a copy of the articles of incorporation of nonprofit organizations for a nominal fee in U.S. states; in Japan, one must have authorization from the nonprofit entity to view most registration documents.

5. Law no. 89 of 1897.

6. More than 2.4 million people are expected to be employed as a result of a nationwide fiber optic network according to *Denki tsushin shingikai, 21 seiki no chiteki shakai e no kaikaku ni mukete* (Towards the development of the intelligent society of the 21st century) (Tokyo: Telecommunications Study Council, May 1994), p. 7.

7. For example, both the Telecommunications Technology Council (*Denshin denwa gijutsu iinkai*), under MPT jurisdiction, and INTAP *(Joho shori sogo unyo gijutsu kyokai)*, under MITI jurisdiction, work on standardization of data transfer over networks. In practice, the staff of these two standards organizations have done a good job of reducing duplication of work.

8. An organization denied the ability to incorporate as a nonprofit association has two options in addition to disbanding: it may operate as a for-profit corporation, minimizing its taxes by operating at a break-even level of revenue and expense, or it may operate as an unincorporated association. An unincorporated association can be disbanded at any time and does not have the power to execute contracts in its own name, so it is an unfavorable form of organization for nonprofit activities.

9. For example, a nonprofit organization dedicated to wireless communications and one dedicated to wired communications were clearly separate for much of their history: one dealt with radios, the other dealt with telephones. The proliferation of cellular telephones in Japan in the past decade, however, has blurred the boundary line between the two organizations' interests.

10. MITI appears to prefer that the Japan Electronics Industry Development Association (JEIDA) handle discussions of intellectual property involving foreigners. JEIDA represents mainframe computer makers that historically have viewed the key to their success as copying foreign computer operating systems. This hampers discussions of intellectual property protection involving personal computer software applications, system integration, semiconductors, and data transfer protocols, each the province of a nonprofit other than JEIDA.

11. In practice, the various bureaus within ministries oversee new nonprofit incorporations.

12. "Oyakusho no atsui kabe" (Thick walls at the ministry), *Nihon kogyo shimbun*, October 15, 1993.

13. The Japan Electronic Products Importers Association (JEPIA), an organization that claims to be responsible for several hundred million dollars of U.S-brand electronic product sales in Japan.

14. Author's observation, based on knowledge of American trade associations in Japan representing the electronics, semiconductor, semiconductor equipment, automobile parts, and pharmaceutical industries, and the European organizations representing electronic components and automobiles.

15. *Jinji In.*

16. *Kokka komuin ho*, Law no. 120 of 1947, article 103.

17. One well-known example is that of former MITI Vice Minister for International Affairs and former Director General of the Patent Agency Kazuo Wakasugi, highly regarded as the principal Japanese negotiator of the first U.S.-

Japan Semiconductor Agreement. Wakasugi's immediate post after leaving MITI in June 1986 was with the Long-Term Credit Bank of Japan (LTCB), because the National Personnel Agency found that Wakasugi had no direct authority over LTCB in his MITI post, *Jinji In, Eiri kigyo e no shushoku no shonin ni kansuru nenji hokokusho* (National Personnel Agency annual report on approvals to work for for-profit enterprises) (Tokyo, 1986), p. 108. After waiting the required two-year period, Wakasugi joined Mitsubishi Electric Corporation as an officer and director, "Wakasugi zen tsusan shingikan Mitsubishi denki e" (Wakasugi, former MITI vice minister, Joins Mitsubishi Electric), *Nikkan kogyo shimbun,* May 26, 1988.

18. Complaint of Keidanren official in charge of contributions to nonprofit organizations, reported in "Kan no ronri hanereru kigyo" (Firms distance selves from bureaucrats' logic), *Nihon keizai shimbun,* May 20, 1994.

19. U.S. pressure has also prevented the growth of *amakudari saki.* In 1984 the U.S. government opposed creation of a Japanese semiconductor production equipment association, the Semiconductor Equipment Association of Japan (SEAJ), arguing that to do so would be deleterious to market access for U.S. products. MITI created the organization anyway but limited its activities in deference to U.S. wishes. Ten years later, with the U.S. semiconductor production equipment industry in a more confident mood, SEAJ was quietly allowed to assume full nonprofit legal status.

20. For example, the author was told by a MITI director *(kacho)* in August 1985 that the new organization would not welcome representatives of foreign-brand semiconductor makers on its board of directors; by October 1985 MITI was complaining to the foreign press that representatives of foreign semiconductor makers were boycotting the board of directors.

21. *Senmu riji.*

22. The desire of senior bureaucrats to retire to second careers in which they can quickly multiply their pensions, which for some second careers are lump-sum payments exceeding ¥30 million (over $300,000 at certain exchange rates) after a few years of service. One of the complaints of labor unions is that these payments deplete financial resources available for other employees of the nonprofit organization, *Seiroren amakudari hakusho* (Amakudari White Paper of the government employees' unions) (Tokyo: Seifu kankei hojin rodo kumiai rengo, 1992), pp. 172–223.

23. "Kan no ronri hanareru kigyo," *Nihon keizai shimbun,* May 20, 1994. These frequent requests are addressed by the long-standing "Department of Contributions" *(Shakai koken bu)* of the Keidanren.

24. Ibid.

25. Ibid.

26. "Kore de ii no ka, Nippon? (Series Part 3: "Japan, are you satisfied with this?), *Nihon keizai shimbun,* January 23, 1992.

27. Ibid.

28. *Nihon dendoshiki yugiki kogyokai.*

29. "Kore de ii no ka, Nippon?" *Nihon keizai shimbun,* January 23, 1992.

30. The JATE's formal name is *Zaidan hojin denki tsushin tanmatsu kiki shinsa kyokai,* the Japan Approvals Institute for Telecommunications Equipment.

31. Articles 68-72 of the Telecommunications Business Law *(Denki tsushin jigyo ho),* Law no. 86 of 1984. In theory, the Ministry of Posts and Telecommunications could name multiple testing organizations under this law.

32. JATE literature claims that the average time for gaining approval in the previous year was twenty-five days and that 90 percent of approvals were processed in forty-one days. "Message from JATE," March 1993.

33. American Chamber of Commerce in Japan, *United States–Japan Trade White Paper* (Tokyo, 1995).

34. The Ministry of Posts and Telecommunications asserts that the Nokia official's statement was inaccurate. Nevertheless, most American, European, and even Japanese merchants of cellular telephones for the Japanese market at the time viewed the regulatory approvals thicket as the primary reason why cellular telephone handsets in Japan were priced much higher than the same telephones in the United States.

35. Voluntary Control Council for Interference by Information Technology Equipment, *Joho shori sochi nado dempa shogai jishu kisei kyogikai.*

36. For general discussions of the antitrust environment for trade associations in Japan and the United States, see Andrew A. Procassini, *Competitors in Alliance* (Quorum Books, 1995) and Leonard H. Lynn and Timothy J. McKeown, *Organizing Business* (Washington, 1988).

37. *Shiteki dokusen no kinshi oyobi kosei torihiki no kakuho ni kansuru horitsu,* Law no. 54 of 1947. See *FTC/Japan Views,* no. 18 (October 1994), p. 64. *FTC/Japan Views* is a JFTC translation of Japanese-language materials.

38. *Jigyosha dantai no katsudo ni kansuru dokusen kinshi ho jo no shishin* (Guidelines concerning the activities of trade associations under the Antimonopoly Act), August 27, 1979. The most recent edition of the Guidelines for this article is dated October 30, 1995.

39. *JFTC 1993 Annual Report,* p. 59, lists 161 legal cartels, a stunning number in the American context but down from the 506 legal cartels at the debut of the 1979 Guidelines.

40. In 1981 nineteen U.S.-capital U.S. electronics companies established

permanent offices in Japan; in 1986 that figure climbed to forty-one in a single year, according to statistics kept by the American Electronics Association Japan Office.

41. JFTC, "Shijo access kaizen no tame no kyoso seisakujo no taio" (Competition policy response for improved market access), Tokyo, May 29, 1986, p. 7.

42. For example, the Electronic Industries Association of Japan (EIAJ), in charge of semiconductors, and the Communications Industry Association of Japan (CIAJ), in charge of wired telecommunications equipment, both increased their foreign-capital membership during this period. The CIAJ has gone on to place two foreign-capital companies, Nippon Motorola, Ltd., and Northern Telecom Japan, on its board of directors. Several Japanese telecommunications standards organizations, such as the Telecommunications Technology Committee, the Research Center for Radio Systems, and the Japan Mobile Telecommunications Systems Association, have foreign-capital companies on their board of councillors. In general, standards-related nonprofit organizations under the Ministry of Posts and Telecommunications have a good record of foreign participation at senior levels of the organization.

43. Translation from Japanese text of Second Follow-Up Report to the Strategic Impediments Initiative, July 30, 1992, quoted on p. 87 of "Jigyosha dantai no katsudo to dokusen kinshiho jo no sho mondai" (Business groups activities' and antimonopoly law problems) (Tokyo, JFTC Study Group on Trade Associations, March 1993). (Hereafter "1993 JFTC Business Groups Study.") The author is not aware of this pledge being carried out: the details of activities of Japanese nonprofits in connection with pending Japanese legislation or technology funding, for example, are not revealed to outsiders.

44. "1993 JFTC Business Groups Study," p. 87.

45. "Gaishikei kigyo kara mita wagakuni jigyodantai no katsudo ni kansuru chosa hokokusho" (Survey of Japanese industry associations as seen from the viewpoint of foreign-capital companies) (Tokyo, JFTC General Affairs Office, September 1996), p. 7. (Hereafter "1996 JFTC Business Groups Study.")

46. "1993 JFTC Business Groups Study," pp. 16, 17. More than 12 percent of companies polled replied that their business would be "difficult" *(konnan)* or "impossible" *(fukano)* without the quality mark.

47. "1996 JFTC Business Groups Study," p. 15.

48. Lasers and optical fiber cables are examples of optoelectronics technology that affect a growing number of readers.

49. *Electronic Engineering Times,* August 5, 1985. The optoelectronics sector of the JIS system has had representatives of the U.S. and European electronics industry in Japan since 1985.

50. "1996 JFTC Business Groups Study," p. 13. Many Japanese nonprofits require incorporated status (not representative office) and manufacturing facilities (not merely sales) in Japan as a prerequisite for membership.

51. "1996 JFTC Business Groups Study," p. 11.

52. One such nonprofit was organized by an American-brand fast food hamburger merchant to serve as a counterpoint to Japanese agricultural associations protesting the import of the foreign beef used in the fast food hamburgers sold by the merchant. The other example is in the mobile radio field, in which an American company organized a nonprofit to counterbalance an organization controlled by the American company's competitors. In both cases, an official from the controlling ministry received a position in the new nonprofit.

53. An executive who was simultaneously chairman of the major electronics, the major computer, and the major telecommunications equipment trade associations in Japan in 1984 told the author that his company was next scheduled to hold these three chairmanships simultaneously 120 years in the future.

54. In May and June 1996, Sakigake and other non-LDP parties in the Japanese Diet proposed legislation making it harder for bureaucrats to retire into controlled industries but failed to win LDP endorsement. Author's conversation with staff of New Party Sakigake Administrative Reform Project Team Chairman Hon. Yukio Edano.

55. *Koeki hojin no setsuritsu kyoka oyobi shido kantoku kijun* and *Koeki hojin ni taisuru kensa-to no itaku-to ni kansuru kijun,* Tokyo, Soridaijin kanbo kanri shitsu, September 20, 1996. (Hereafter "September 96 Cabinet Resolution on Nonprofits" and "September 96 Cabinet Resolution on Standards.")

56. "September 96 Cabinet Resolution on Nonprofits," 4(5); and "September 96 Cabinet Resolution on Standards," 1(5).

57. "September 96 Cabinet Resolution on Nonprofits," 4(6).

58. "September 96 Cabinet Resolution on Standards," 2.

59." September 96 Cabinet Resolution on Nonprofits," 8(1); and "September 96 Cabinet Resolution on Standards," 4.

60. The Keidanren has supported this idea in principle for several years, "Oyakusho no atsui kabe," *Nihon kogyo shimbun,* October 15, 1993.

CHAPTER TEN

Bureaucrats in Business

Ulrike Schaede

THE JAPANESE POLICYMAKING environment is characterized by many institutions that serve to lubricate government-business relationships and facilitate policy formulation and implementation. Examples of such institutions include the *shingikai* (deliberation councils) that bring together businessmen and bureaucrats at the policy design stage, or the *shukko* mechanism of seconding corporate employees to work at a government agency.[1] The single institution that is most often cited as an indicator of close government-business relationships is the Old Boy network associated with the *amakudari* ("descend from heaven") system.[2] An *amakudari* Old Boy (OB) is a former government official who, after retirement from long years of civil service, is reemployed in the private or quasi-private sector and begins a "second life" in which he draws heavily on the expertise and the personal relations that he accumulated in his "first life" as a bureaucrat.

Although Japanese and foreign journalists and politicians have criticized the phenomenon with some regularity over the past three decades, the scope of the *amakudari* OB phenomenon is not at all clear. If OBs are a tool of the developmental state, for instance, then their number and relevance should diminish with economic growth.[3] Also, while some anecdotal evidence says that OBs occupy important positions in private

This chapter is an abbreviated version of Ulrike Schaede, "The 'Old Boy' Network and Government-Business Relationships in Japan," *Journal of Japanese Studies*, vol. 21 (Summer 1995), pp. 293–317.

firms, we do not really know what they actually do. And most important, why are firms interested in hiring an OB? Do all firms hire OBs, or
are there patterns across industries showing where OBs are employed?
And if there are indeed such patterns, what do these suggest?

The *Amakudari* Retirement Process

There are OBs in every country. However, important differences in
the regulatory environment in which they operate translate into very
different roles and functions. For instance, in the United States, ex-con-
gressmen, fixed-term commissioners, and political appointees, rather
than long-term administrators, are the preferred insiders. The revolv-
ing-door mechanism allows these short-term civil servants to switch back
and forth between the government and the private sector. A successful
OB in the United States will be able to switch his loyalties on a short-
term basis accordingly.[4] In contrast, the French *pantouflage* system does
not provide for revolving doors, but it allows bureaucrats to go on leave
from civil service in order to be in the senior management of a large
firm. Under this system, the bureaucrat can at the same time be a civil
servant and the CEO of a large public corporation. Because civil service
provides for the better pension system, his loyalties are likely to remain
with the government.[5]

In Japan, the system is strictly unidirectional and exclusive. Once a
bureaucrat has left civil service, he cannot rejoin. Moreover, even after
leaving civil service, the incentive structure is such that the bureaucrat
is likely to stay loyal to the interests of the government. To understand
these incentives, it is important to appreciate how the *amakudari* process unfolds.

Japanese professional long-term civil servants follow a standard career path. They are hired after graduation at around age 22. The large
ministries hire about twenty-five new civil servants every year. For the
first two years, the group goes through a joint training program, which
also includes bonding exercises. Even when the careers of the group
members begin to take different paths in the ministerial hierarchy, the
group stays in close contact. As group members get older, there are fewer
and fewer positions, and winnowing begins. Only a few members of
each class can make it to the upper echelons. Realizing that, some leave
early to enter politics. Other are consecutively retired beginning at around

age 50. Because the salary of a bureaucrat is low compared with salaries of employees in private industry, and the pension system for civil servants is poorly endowed, bureaucrats are dependent on further employment and income at that point.[6]

The National Public Service Law (*Kokka komuin ho*) prescribes a two-year waiting period before the former bureaucrat can join the private sector. The same law also grants the National Personnel Authority (*Jinji-in*) the legal power to govern the further career path of the bureaucrat. That is, the Personnel Authority becomes the de facto employment agency for the rest of the OB career.[7] Therefore, upon joining the firm, the bureaucrats do not shift their interests exclusively to the firm but remain loyal to the interests of their former employee, the government.

The OB Network

By being hired and trained in groups, the bureaucrats early on begin to develop close relationships. Three major mechanisms serve to reinforce their network. First, each class of bureaucrats in a certain ministry holds regular lunch meetings, in which members exchange news and opinions. Because of the progressive retirement process, some members of the group are still in the ministry, while others are politicians or in private business. Second, the smooth flow of information to and from the ministry is ensured even after all members of one year have eventually retired in so-called OB meetings (*OB kai*). During the *bento*-lunch box meeting, an incumbent bureaucrat delivers a speech concerning policy issues currently discussed in the ministry. Both mechanisms therefore serve to guarantee the OBs' value as insiders, even long after their retirement. Third, there are personal connections that extend the core group of one class of bureaucrats. These build on school ties, marital alliances, deliberation councils, and acquaintances through secondment to other ministries or agencies.[8] Therefore, by the time former bureaucrats join the management boards of private firms, they can build on a vast network of personal acquaintances.

OBs in Numbers

Bureaucrats can "descend" to different destinations, such as public corporations (for example, electric utilities or public policy firms such as the Kansai Airport Corporation), private associations for which the government deems regulation essential (for example, the Tokyo Stock Exchange), trade associations, or government agencies (for example, the Bank of Japan, the Japan Development Bank). The largest number of retired bureaucrats, however, retires into private firms, either directly after the two-year waiting period or by way of a first employment at a public corporation. In 1992 a total of 1,111 ex-bureaucrats were employed in Japan's 2,131 largest companies.[9]

The question is, however, why firms are willing to hire former bureaucrats that remain loyal to the government into leading management positions. This firm behavior can be evaluated on the basis of a more detailed data analysis. The database constructed for this purpose consists of the largest 100 stockholding corporations as of 1991.[10] For these, data on board members and prior affiliations were collected from *Kaisha Nenkan* biannually for the years 1979 through 1991.[11] Since the typical employment of an OB lasts for two years, biannual data capture all important movements.

Table 10-1 summarizes the overall findings.[12] As of 1991, 4.9 percent (or 177) of all directors of the largest private firms were OBs. As a yardstick to evaluate this number, the table also lists the number of retired bankers, retired directors of other firms, and interlocking (concurrent) directors. Although these are often considered an important factor of corporate networking in Japan, the retired bureaucrats clearly outnumber these "corporate OBs."

Table 10-1 also shows that the total number of "bureaucrat OBs," that is, board members who retired from a ministry or indirectly via a public corporation, tripled between 1977 and 1991. One explanation of the absolute numbers is that the total number of directors as well as the number of OBs has increased since the 1970s because of the so-called inflation of directors in the 1980s.[13] However, the increase in OBs is steeper than the increase in total directors. Moreover, not only is there an increase in the total number of OBs hired, but there is also a 90 percent increase in the number of firms that hire OBs. In 1979 one-third of the largest 100 Japanese firms employed a former government official. In 1991 more than two-thirds did. This finding is counterintuitive to the argument that large Japanese firms have gained some independence from the tight controls of the "developmental state." It suggests an increase in external constraints, so that more large firms felt they needed direct access to the government by hiring an OB.

The nature of such constraints can be explored by dividing the data

Table 10-1. General Data Summary—Government OBs between 1979 and 1991

| Year | Total number of board members | Total number of firms with OBs | Bureaucrat OBs | | | Former bankers | Former corporate directors | Concurrent interlocking directors[a] |
			Government OBs	Public Corp. OBs	Total[a]			
1979	2,715	35	35	23	58 (2.13)	41	35	80 (2.94)
1981	2,727	40	41	37	78 (2.86)	36	32	85 (3.12)
1983	2,965	39	50	37	87 (2.90)	34	31	94 (3.20)
1985	3,122	50	71	59	130 (4.20)	43	30	109 (3.50)
1987	3,216	62	68	102	170 (5.30)	40	21	112 (3.50)
1989	3,423	65	69	103	172 (5.02)	38	12	127 (3.71)
1991	3,605	67	85	92	177 (4.91)	44	31	95 (2.64)

Source: Nikkei, Kaisha Nenkan, various issues.
a. Number in parentheses is the percent of the total number of board directors.

set into industry groups: if there are specific constraints that lead to an increased hiring of OBs, an analysis by industry may expose the characteristics of these constraints. Statistical analysis reveals that the data set falls into two groups. The first group consists of industries related to trade (imports and exports) and consists of automobiles, electric machinery and electronics, and steel. The second group consists of industries that are primarily domestic in focus: commercial banking, investment banking, and insurance. There is a significant difference between these two groups: almost all firms in the "trade" group hired OBs in the second half of the 1980s, while the firms in the second group hired almost no OBs at all.[14] This result is surprising, because one might initially have assumed that those firms known for their "stubbornness" and resistance to industrial policy (for example, Honda, Toyota, Sony, and so on) would hire the fewest OBs. The opposite is the case. There is a straight increasing line of OBs in the 1980s in these industries. Further, there is a significant correlation between the origin of the OB (ministry) and the industry; that is, automobiles, electric machinery, and steel tend to hire MITI retirees, construction tends to hire OBs from the Ministry of Construction and the Ministry of Agriculture and Welfare, and so on.

The OB Logic

These data findings can be explained powerfully by a "management of regulation" logic. From a firm's perspective, regulation can be regarded as an external constraint on its behavior. The larger the constraint (that is, the more prohibitive the regulation), the more efforts the firm will undertake to manage the regulator (that is, lobby or try to otherwise influence the regulatory decisionmaking process).[15]

The Japanese regulatory framework has two features that differentiate it from Western economies: its wide range, especially in the form of specific industry laws (for example, the Petroleum Industry Law); and a large number of ad hoc rules based on noncodified administrative guidance (*gyosei-shido*). Administrative guidance is not based on any one law.[16] Rather, one ministry acts within its scope of jurisdiction in order to induce specific behavior. Administrative guidance is not transparent and often involves delicate conversations between ministry officials and firm management. Rules can be implemented or revoked at the discretion of the ministry in charge and without any prior notice. Enforcement is based on a carrot-and-stick principle. Corporations know that by following "advice" they may reap rewards later. If, however, the ministries find a noncompliance with administrative guidance, they have numerous options to obstruct future business.[17] Effectively, there is no legal recourse to regulation in the form of administrative guidance. The discretionary and situational nature of the rules makes it hard to forecast changes, and regulation therefore creates a high degree of uncertainty.

Informal industry estimates claim that this regulatory practice may constitute 60 to 90 percent of all regulation in a given industry. The extensive use of situational administrative guidance has two implications. First, there is a high need for direct access to government information and for influencing regulatory decisionmaking. Since OBs provide for direct information channels, this is one reason for the overall large number of OBs hired by large Japanese firms. Second, there will be differences across industries in the need of hiring OBs, depending on the degree and predominant character of regulation; that is, whether it is primarily codified or situational.

Accordingly, the explanation for the finding that the "domestic" industries (banking and insurance) hire fewer OBs than the "trade" industries is that the "domestic" industries (here: banking and insurance) are subject to specific industry laws that tend to align primary lobbying needs. Therefore, firms in these industries can lobby their industrywide interests through their trade associations. In contrast, the "trade industries" are subject to constraints that do not apply industrywide but rather to individual firms. In particular, trade constraints in the form of voluntary export restraints (VERs) restrict market share of the firms within an industry, so that they compete with one another for allotment quotas.

The automobile and electronic machinery industries are major exporters in an environment characterized by trade policy battles with the United States and the European Community. One reaction to the increasing Japanese trade surplus was the introduction of VERs in TV sets (1977, USA), VCRs (1983, EC), semiconductors (1986–91, USA), automobiles (1980s, USA and EC), and steel (1980s). The VERs force firms to turn to MITI to ensure a large (or at least unchanging) share of the limited pie. Effectively, VERs elevate MITI to a control position over export shares of individual manufacturers within one industry. Because this is intraindustry competition, firms cannot lobby through their trade association. They need to hire their own OB.

The division of firms into two large groups—those that hire more OBs and those that hire none or only a few—suggests that firms need to be differentiated in terms of their OB structure into those that are involved in industrywide lobbying and those that are involved in intraindustry competition under external constraints controlled by the regulator. A primary strategy behind hiring a retired government official is to ensure direct access to information and to incumbent bureaucrats under intraindustry competition. The need is even more pronounced if the regulator controls the degree of intraindustry competition. In other words, the primary reason for a firm to hire a former government official is to affect relations with the regulator under policy-induced, intraindustry competition.

Conclusions

Contrary to widespread assumptions, the phenomenon of government OBs in large Japanese firms has increased over the last decade. This contradicts the notion that the regulatory system of the "developmental state" is slowly disappearing.

The "management of regulation" model supports the concept of "consultative capitalism" in that it shows why government and business interact in the process of public and corporate strategy formulation. It is based on three different sets of incentives by the three parties involved. One, the government aims to ensure the implementation of regulation. Two, the government official aims to increase his lifetime employment income by assuming higher-paying positions after early retirement. Three, corporations pursue three simultaneous goals: to ensure access to information in an environment of nontransparent regulation; to ensure intermediation in times of clashes of interests with the government; and to lobby under the framework of encompassing regulation and thereby manage the dependency on the regulator in an environment of administrative guidance.

The model offers two predictions concerning when and why large firms might hire OBs. First, the specific form of Japanese regulation leads to the OB phenomenon. Accordingly, the phenomenon will not disappear as long as administrative guidance prevails. Second, managed trade elevates the ministry in charge into the position of a referee of intraindustry competition, since it is in control of export (or market share) allotments. Therefore, managed trade increases the power of bureaucrats and the need of firms to hire OBs. While managed trade is not the only reason for the extensive OB network, a decrease in market share prescriptions would most likely lead to a decrease in OBs in the strongest Japanese export industries.

In the mid-1990s "*amakudari*-bashing" has again become a major pastime of journalists and politicians of the opposition parties, similar to the waves in the mid-1970s and the early 1980s. The arguments presented in favor of a complete abolition of the system include a fear that bureaucrats, while in office, are more apt to fall to capture and bribery attempts because of future employment considerations. Some also argue that Japan's regulatory system, to the detriment of the national interest, is increasingly based on nepotism.

However, two structural factors clearly stand in the way of abolishing the system. First, the pension system for civil servants is critically underfunded. From the government's perspective, the *amakudari* system is a substitute for state welfare services. Second, without the *amakudari* system, Japanese ministries and government agencies will be unable to attract the best young students from the nation's leading universities into civil service. Abolishing the *amakudari* system would require a complete reorganization of the political economy and the regulatory system of Japan. No one in Japan has yet signaled a willingness to even discuss such an overhaul. If past experience is any indicator, no change will occur any time soon.

Notes

1. *Shingikai* are discussed in Frank Schwartz , "Of Fairy Cloaks and Familiar Talks: The Politics of Consultation," in Gary Allinson and Yasunori Sone, eds., *Political Dynamics in Contemporary Japan* (Cornell University Press, 1993), pp. 217–41.

2. For instance, see Chalmers Johnson, "The Reemployment of Retired Government Bureaucrats in Japanese Big Business," *Asian Survey*, vol. 14 (November 1974), pp. 953–65; Chalmers Johnson, *MITI and the Japanese Miracle—The Growth of Industrial Policy 1925–1975* (Stanford University Press, 1982); Masahiko Aoki, *Information, Incentives, and Bargaining in the Japanese Economy* (Cambridge University Press, 1988); Daniel Okimoto, *Between MITI and the Market—Japanese Industrial Policy for High Technology* (Stanford

University Press, 1989); Clyde V. Prestowitz, *Trading Places* (Basic Books, 1988); and Karel van Wolferen, *The Enigma of Japanese Power—People and Power in a Stateless Nation* (London: Macmillan, 1989).

3. Johnson, *MITI and the Japanese Miracle.*

4. For a detailed discussion of lobbyists and commissioners, and how one lobbyist may end up serving contradicting interests simultaneously, see Jeffrey Birnbaum, *The Lobbyists—How Influence Peddlers Get Their Way in Washington* (Times Books, 1992). U.S.-style OBs are also analyzed in Ross D. Eckert, "The Life Cycle of Regulatory Commissioners," *Journal of Law and Economics,* vol. 24 (April 1981), pp. 113–20.

5. The *pantouflage* system is discussed in Ezra Suleiman, *Elites in French Society—The Politics of Survival* (Princeton University Press, 1978).

6. For a detailed description of these processes, see Tetsuro Murobushi, *Kokyo kanryo* (Career bureaucracy) (Tokyo: Kodansha Bunko, 1987); Makoto Sakata, *Nihon kanryo hakusho* (White Paper on the Japanese bureaucracy) (Tokyo: Kodansha Bunko, 1989); and Ichiro Murakawa, *Nihon no kanryo* (Japanese bureaucrats) (Tokyo, Maruzen Library, 1994), p. 131.

7. In the actual process of finding firms for the retiring bureaucrats, the secretary of the ministry (*kanbocho*) is often the primary intermediary. Personal relations (*jinmyaku*), trade associations (*gyokai*), and "related interests" also play into this process. However, in strictly legal terms, the Personnel Authority has to grant permission for the retired bureaucrat to join a specific firm, and it can also revoke this permission.

8. More than 50 percent of all bureaucrats are graduates of the University of Tokyo. See Ikko Jin, *Keibatsu* (Family ties) (Tokyo: Mainichi shinbun-sha, 1989) for a map of personal ties within the political, bureaucratic, and business worlds.

9. Toyo Keizai Shinbun-sha, ed., *Kigyo keiretsu soran* (Tokyo: Toyo Keizai Shinbun-sha, 1994).

10. This is the equivalent of the Fortune 500.

11. *Nihon Keizai Shinbun-sha,* various issues.

12. See Schaede, "The 'Old Boy' Network," for a more detailed analysis of this database.

13. The "inflation of directors" is ascribed to demographic changes in the Japanese promotional system: a large number of postwar "baby boomers" advanced to the position of director in the corporate hierarchy, not all of whom could be dispatched to affiliated firms. Because the implicit lifetime employment system rules out dismissal, more managers had to be promoted to the board of directors.

14. These data are detailed in Schaede, "The 'Old Boy' Network." Commer-

cial banking is a special case, because some of the large banks in the sample have historical affiliations with the government, such as Bank of Tokyo or Hokkaido Takushoku Bank; these banks usually hire several OBs. In contrast, most of the large private city banks do not hire any OBs at all.

15. Resource dependence theory as spelled out by Jeffrey Pfeffer and Gerald R. Salancik, *The External Control of Organizations—A Resource Dependence Perspective* (Harper and Row, 1978), provides an analytical framework for this intuition. Since organizations (for example, firms) are not internally self-sufficient, they are interdependent with the outside elements that control important inputs or resources. In response, the organization will develop strategies to make the external constraints less burdensome. The smaller the organizations that are controlled, or the more unified their interests, the higher the likelihood that they will form associations to increase bargaining power. Regulation is an external control attempt. In their compliance to regulation, firms will try to influence the formulation of demands in order to mitigate the effects of regulation on their strategic choices.

16. The Japanese regulatory set consists of four layers: (1) the pertinent statute (*horitsu*); (2) supplementary ordinances (*seirei* and *shorei*) issued by the cabinet; (3) written notifications (*tsutatsu*) by the ministry concerned; and (4) informal, often oral, "invitations" to certain actions addressed to an individual or a group of market participants. Notifications and "invitations" constitute administrative guidance.

17. For a more detailed discussion, see George C. Eads and Kozo Yamamura, "The Future of Industrial Policy," in Kozo Yamamura and Yasukichi Yasuba, eds., *The Political Economy of Japan—Vol. 1: The Domestic Transformation* (Stanford University Press, 1987), pp. 423–68; and Frank K. Upham, *Law and Social Change in Postwar Japan* (Harvard University Press, 1988) .

CHAPTER ELEVEN

The Land Factor:
An Economic Disaster

Richard Koo

ECONOMIC DISTORTIONS generally describe a situation in which certain resources are not used economically and effectively. In other words, there is waste. Most such distortions that have attracted attention in the past, however, concerned nations that had balance of payment *deficits*. There have been few instances when those of nations with a heavy surplus like Japan have been studied. Yet there are indeed major distortions—unseen in other nations—hidden within the Japanese economy. Possibly the worst one comes from the surprising inefficiency of land use.

Land is an indispensable resource that supports the lives and production activities of human beings. Despite its obvious importance, land, compared with other resources, rarely is the subject of economic debate. That is because such debate is premised on two assumptions: first that the supply of this resource is fixed, neither decreasing nor increasing, and second, that throughout history, available land has been put to effective use. In Japan, where land is limited, the second assumption simply does not hold.

This becomes evident when one recognizes that buildings in the Tokyo metropolitan area average only 2.5 stories in height, even though land already costs 100 million yen per 3.3 square meters (1 *tsubo*). If this had been the case in any other country, measures would have long since been taken to put a halt to rising land prices. Mega skyscrapers, for example, might have been built before land became even one-tenth as costly as it is today. At the least the balance between demand and supply for housing and office space might have been improved. Buildings with 2.5 stories may be acceptable in the countryside of the United States or Australia where land is plentiful. In Japan land is scarce. The problem is all the more serious when one considers the scarcity of land in central Tokyo. Of all the industrialized economies, Japan's distortion of land values is the most serious.

Basically, three factors hinder effective land use. Of the three, the simplest reason is resignation. Many people have given up hope of spacious housing comparable to that available in the West because the supply of land in Japan—level land, in particular—is limited. Most Japanese learn from their elementary school days not to expect bigger housing. In fact, however, population density in central Tokyo's twenty-three wards is much lower than in Manhattan or Paris. Thus neither absolute population size nor the amount of land available explains why people live in cramped apartments ridiculed by foreigners as "rabbit hutches." It is too early to give up for this reason.

The next often-cited reason is the occurrence of earthquakes. It is true that earthquakes in Japan, including the recent Great Hanshin earthquake, have wrought great damage. From the viewpoint of modern architectural technology, however, the problem of earthquakes is virtually a thing of the past. Actually, if one is seriously worried about earthquakes, it is more troublesome that houses are built close together, along streets that are too narrow for fire engines to navigate with ease. When earthquakes occur, damage has been all the greater because small houses are cluttered from floor to ceiling. People would be much better protected from earthquakes if land were used effectively, allowing the construction of wider roads and larger modern buildings incorporating the latest in earthquake technology.

The principal reason why land cannot be used efficiently lies in the tax system and the nature of government regulations. The property tax rate in Japan, when compared to that of the United States, is extremely low. The tax rate varies from state to state in the United States. But as an example, I sold my house in New Jersey in a suburb of New York, where I had lived until 1984, for $92,000. The property tax at the time was $3,000 a year. This amounted to 3.2 percent of the market price.

Contrast this with the situation in Japan. I once lived in a house that was sitting on a lot measuring 100 *tsubo* in Shirogane, Minato-ku, Tokyo. While I was there, a developer offered an equal-value trade for real estate with a market price of 800 million yen. The property tax on this house currently stands at 250,000 yen a year. Even if a calculation is made for 400 million yen, or half the "market price" of the above-mentioned equal-value trade, the tax rate would be 0.065 percent. This is one-fiftieth of that on my New Jersey home. What effect does this difference have? In the United States, if the price of land goes up and the person owning the land cannot put it to good use, he will be unable to pay the tax. Thus he will have no choice but to rent or sell the land to someone who can use it more effectively. [1]

The tax on land in Japan, however, in comparison with the tax in the United States, is almost nil. Even if land prices surge suddenly, there is almost no pressure to use the land more effectively and to gain a profit. This becomes apparent when one see that there are many shops and houses no taller than two stories in areas such as Tokyo's Chiyoda-ku or Chuo-ku, where land prices have already reached astronomical levels.

The other problem concerning taxes is the capital gains tax that is levied on profits made from land sales. In the United States, the maximum rate of such taxes is under 30 percent, but in Japan, the tax is progressive with the maximum rate at over 80 percent. This situation works as a further disincentive, making it less desirable for people to sell their land.

It is often said that in Japan, land is sold only at the time of inheritance. Many such sales involve fragmentation of ownership, making it more difficult to put land to more effective use. Owners must parcel out their land and sell it in order to pay the inheritance tax. As a result, land ownership becomes even more segmented. As a result of these tax systems, Japanese construction companies must spend enormous sums of money and an unbelievable amount of time in order to assemble a plot that is large enough to sustain high-rise buildings. Those who cannot wait or do not have the requisite resources often end up constructing what are called "pencil buildings," generally five- to ten-story structures on extremely small lots. This makes for a most inefficient use of land. The United States and many European countries prohibit the selling of land in such small pieces.

Construction regulations such as restrictions on height limits or floor area ratios, however, prevent effective use of land that is already available in the form of large lots. Although cities everywhere have some sort of height limit on buildings, the limit is set at extremely low levels in Japan. This, together with so-called sunshine laws, makes effective use of land difficult even for owners of large plots. Unless there is major deregulation if not abolition of restrictions on floor area ratios, effective land use will be hampered. It will prove correspondingly difficult to promote economic growth based on stimulation of domestic demand.

One of the reasons for the restrictions on floor area ratios is to prevent the environmental damage that may result from the trend toward high-rise buildings. Yet this very restriction encourages environmental destruction in another very important sense. It is true that in terms of outward appearance, Japanese cities with low-rise buildings do not seem claustrophobic. There is plenty of sunlight. The cramped interiors of buildings, however, rank worst among industrialized countries. So do commuting conditions to them. Witness the well-criticized "rabbit hutches" and the terribly crowded trains. It is questionable whether it is worthwhile to sacrifice so much in interior living conditions in Japan for slightly more sunshine on the sidewalks.

It is just not possible to build housing profitably at current land prices and floor area ratios. Thus the number of people living within the Tokyo metropolitan area continues to decrease. Communities continue to deteriorate. In some areas, only employees of real estate agencies are left to carry the *mikoshi* (portable shrines) at local festivals. Major deregulation of floor area ratios applicable to residential land is necessary to prevent the creation of slums in urban areas—the inevitable result of decreasing urban population. When the number of floors is limited to ten, only an office can be built profitably. On the other hand, if a forty-story high-rise is possible, apartments can be built that the ordinary salaried worker can afford.

Some Japanese point out that even if such high-rise apartments are built, not many people will choose to live in them because Japanese like single-family homes with land. It is true that high-rise apartments in Japan are expensive. Perhaps because of their short history, there are many buildings that are simply not attractive. Most of the apartments they contain have low ceilings and are small; their layout is unnatural and not well planned. Such apartments are indeed a product of costly land and merciless floor area ratio restrictions. Given such a choice, almost anyone would prefer a single-family house. If deregulation on land use succeeds, however, and competition for quality buildings increases, one could expect an increase in quality of Japanese high-rise buildings to reach levels that are comparable to those in the United States and Europe.

As we see, land policy in Japan and the United States is revealed as totally opposite. Ironically, the difference has resulted in effective land use in the United States, which is blessed with an abundance of land, while forcing inefficient land use in Japan, where land is so limited.

Consumers desire cheap and roomy housing. If all regulations, however, including floor area ratios and the right to sunlight, are satisfied and land remains as expensive as it is today, housing with only very limited floor space will be affordable for consumers. If only a three-story building can be built on a piece of expensive land, then regardless of the ingenuity put into its layout, the builder's only choice is to offer very expensive or very small-space housing. While wealthy consumers may pay high prices, in general domestic demand stagnates. Sluggish demand at home forces the Japanese economy to become highly dependent on exports. Although the Japanese have been successful in increasing exports, their living standards have failed to improve, even as international criticism of Japan's large trade surpluses intensifies.

The only way out of this dilemma is deregulation of domestic land use. For example, suppose that in a certain area, regulations on the right to sunlight are relaxed, and floor area ratios for buildings are also bettered. Such a change will increase return on investment severalfold. With regulations loosened, it then becomes possible to construct a building up to thirty stories high on a lot that was originally limited to three-story structures. Even if rent is halved for each unit of floor space, there will be plenty of investment projects that will pay for themselves. Only then will it become possible to supply the cheap and roomy housing that Japan's consumers have long desired.

People need floor space, not land, to live. As long as they can acquire floor space cheaply, then it matters little whether one *tsubo* of land costs one trillion yen or one yen. If someone with the average pay of a salaried worker could afford to live in a condominium with 150 square meters of floor space, then land prices would not become a social issue.

Land prices rarely become an issue in the industrialized regions of the United States or Europe. The reason is simple; there is an effective substitute for land. This substitute is floor space. As long as this is readily available, then land is not necessarily needed. The reason why only Japan faces such an acute housing problem is because the supply of floor space cannot keep up with demand. There are too many regulations.

Conventional economic principles apply in the United States and Europe. For example, if interest rates fall, then naturally real estate prices rise; what happens next is that various people enter the real estate business because it is profitable. Entering the real estate business does not mean speculating on land. People enter the business by building more floor space to profit from higher rents.

If many people enter the business, however, and build housing hurriedly, in two or three years there will be a surplus of supply. Rents will plummet. As a result, even if real estate prices surge in the short run owing to falling interest rates, in the long run prices will be stable because of the increase in floor space. The subsequent fall in rent as a result of the glut may hurt some developers. But newly supplied buildings and housing are net additions to the wealth of society. With the increase in floor space that people can use, people's lives become richer by that amount.

In Japan, the policy debate on land is fundamentally flawed. If land becomes more expensive, then what needs to be discussed is how to increase the supply of floor space, which is an effective substitute for land accretion. However, in Japan, people first discuss how to bring the land prices down.

In the industrialized areas of the United States and Europe, floor space is increased in response to increased real estate prices. This results in stable real estate prices over the long run, and people's lives are made that much richer. In Japan, however, there is no discussion about expanding floor space, but people fear only a short-term surge in land prices. Regulations are tightened out of such fear, and increasing the supply of floor space becomes more difficult. Yet people's lives will not become at all richer unless floor space is increased.

The outside world can no longer accept the restrained domestic demand and high dependence on external demand that this land problem has foisted on Japan's economy. The Japanese government, in order to counter rising international criticism, has committed itself to expand domestic demand and promote imports. Inevitably, proposals to increase floor space came up as part of this discussion. As usual, however, this initiative was treated on a small scale, limited to designated projects. What is needed, however, is a comprehensive and serious study aimed at improving general urban living standards in this important respect. Without drastic measures, the foreign surpluses that Japan enjoys today cannot be resolved even after several decades. By that time, the international free trade regime, unable to hold up against this heavy imbalance, may collapse. If that happens, Japan will be hardest hit.

To rectify these major distortions, it is necessary to reconsider urban planning on a national level. Any such review should include a major relaxation of floor area ratio restrictions, along with plans to lower the capital gains tax and raise the property tax. The need for such reform comes not only from the imbalances in the Japanese economy and intensified trade friction but also from Japan's rapidly aging population. By the beginning of the twenty-first century, it is estimated that the number of elderly will double, and the national savings rate will be halved. The urban redevelopment as proposed here, however, will require large amounts of money. Because the working population is currently relatively young, there remains an abundance of savings. Despite the heavy volume of foreign investment, it is still possible to redirect much of this savings to domestic use. In later years, Japan will probably have to borrow from abroad when the need to rebuild its housing infrastructure is realized. If Japan fails to remove the largest distortion now plaguing the Japanese economy, the country may never get another chance. Conversely, if Japan accepts the status quo, then the savings that people have generated for their old age will be converted into financial assets in the form of foreign bonds, rather than in real assets in the form of domestic housing.

The greatest gift that Japan can give to the world today is to remove the reasons for restrained domestic demand, through the effective use of land, and thus provide an opportunity for Japan and other nations to follow a more balanced path of development. Economic growth founded on domestic demand will also bring autonomy and independence to the Japanese economy, which until now has been largely dependent on the U.S. economy as it looked to exports as the major means of growth.

Note

1. There are many arguments about the economic effects of property tax on land. To be most accurate, it is necessary to consider the tax rate on other capital goods, the price of land before taxation, and the relationship between the collected tax and the quality of public goods in the area. Here I have focused on the effect on the landowner's cash flow.

CHAPTER TWELVE

The Making of Japan's Failed Land Policy

Koichi Mera

THE LAND POLICY ADOPTED by the government of Japan during the past decade has been a remarkable failure. Even though it achieved its intended objective of lowering the price of land, it did so by economic overkill. The price of land went down much more than anticipated, causing serious damage to the economy, extending economic stagnation for more than five years—a severe recession unprecedented in postwar Japan and rarely seen anywhere else in the developed world. Since 1992, the Japanese economy has been operating substantially below its productive capacity, with an estimated cumulative loss in gross domestic product (GDP) of more than 1 trillion U.S. dollars.[1] As of 1993, the economy was not able to utilize about 4.6 percent of its productive capacity, and this gap was widening.[2] When the gap is eventually eliminated, taking possibly several more years, the total forgone GDP could reach $2 trillion, nearly half of Japan's current annual GDP. The economic fallout from Japan's land policy may not be responsible for all of the forgone GDP, but it nonetheless accounts for a significant part.[3]

The author wishes to thank a number of individuals who have contributed in various ways to the completion of this paper. They include Takahiro Miyao, Niraj Verma, Eric Heikkila, Rosalind Greenstein, Junichiro Yonehara, Hiromitsu Ishi, Daniel Baron, and Masuo Masuda. However, they are not responsible for any shortcomings of this paper.

Although land policy is typically a political issue, Japan's was devised largely by bureaucrats. Indeed, the once highly regarded bureaucrats of Japan appear to have become a serious liability to their country. This chapter examines the process by which land policy was made and identifies the roots of its weaknesses. Measures to improve the decisionmaking system of the country are also discussed.

The Process of Making Land Policy up to 1990

When the price level of land rose sharply in the middle of the 1980s, it became an issue widely publicized in the mass media. The mass media reported mainly two aspects of land price inflation: the extralegal process of land purchase for land consolidation and the diminishing ability of salary earners to purchase adequate housing in large cities. The extralegal process refers to cases of land acquisitions with the help of organized crime members, called *boryokudan*, who used coercive measures to persuade landowners to sell their property. In Japan, it was and has been very difficult to purchase land, because no matter what the price is, landowners for the most part have not been willing to consider selling. This is partly because of the tradition of living at the same place for generations and partly because in the past the price of land consistently rose at rates greater than the interest and inflation rates combined. To acquire a lot large enough for a sizable office building, small lots need to be assembled. In most parts of central cities, such land assembly was necessary.[4] During the 1980s, the process of land assembly advanced in Tokyo because some developers started paying unexpectedly large sums of money to land owners. Those who sold land in the center of the city moved to a suburb and purchased a decent lot and had a house built, thus raising the price of land in the preferred suburban areas. Although *boryokudan* were responsible for some pressured sales, the media probably sensationalized the extent of their role.

It was indeed true that the cost of housing went up, and the purchase of a housing unit by most first-time home purchasers became increasingly difficult. But the rising land price signaled an increasing scarcity of land in large cities. It was an economic signal indicating that within regular commuting distances from the center, single, detached houses should be a rare exception, and most residents in the central areas should be living in apartments or condominiums. The price of condominiums was also high but was much more manageable. Such economic messages were not received by ministries. Instead, the government considered that the rise in the land price was based on speculation, that the price level had become excessive, and that the market must be controlled. In particular, it condemned land speculation and tried to stamp out such activity through almost every conceivable means.

The Choice of Policy

The reasons why Japan's bureaucrats embraced this notion of a defective land market are not hard to find. To start with, Japanese bureaucrats do not have faith in the market. They tend to think that they should build a market rather than that they should follow it.[5] Also, it is possible to conceive a direct link between the bureaucrats' concern and land price increases. Although about 60 percent of the households in the country own the house they live in,[6] and get the benefit of land price increases, most career bureaucrats live near the center in houses provided by the national government at nominal rents and must obtain their own housing after retirement. Unlike those in the private sector who start homeownership much earlier and are paying off the mortgage for twenty-five or thirty years, most bureaucrats are in quite a different situation. Those who are housed in government housing must start homeownership at their retirement, which usually takes place when they are in their fifties. They do not have very many years to pay off the mortgage. It is quite possible that they were seriously worried about their own housing situation in the future and favored measures to reduce the land price.

The land price issue has been widely debated in Japan since the middle of the 1980s, with a wide variety of explanations and proposals advanced. However, the government's position on this issue quickly focused on a single objective: lowering the land price by any means.[7] All other objectives, such as to maintain a viable economy, to develop a reliable banking system, to defend and further develop the market-oriented economic system, or to utilize urban land efficiently, were disregarded. In short, the government's land policy became a land *price* policy.

The Process of Determining Land Policy

When the government decided to take action to lower the price of land, not only did it take excessive actions, but it failed to coordinate among various ministries—a failure aggravated by Japan's weak political leadership.

Let us examine government decisions chronologically. When signs of land price escalation became evident, the Land Agency, which is in charge of issues related to land, started to introduce the Land Price Surveillance System in Tokyo before the National Land Use Law was amended to accommodate this system. The agency did this by requesting the Tokyo Metropolitan Government to enact a prefectural law that empowered the prefectural government to require prospective partners of land transactions to report the intended land price. The transaction of a parcel of land below a certain size was exempted from this reporting requirement. At the urging of the Land Agency, the Tokyo Metropolitan Government adopted such a code in 1986. This system was incorporated into the National Land Law in 1987. Importantly, this system of direct interference with the market was introduced to the prefectural government before the Diet (which is the Congress of Japan) took any action on it. As the Land Agency is closely linked to the Ministry of Finance and the Ministry of Construction, these two ministries must have supported the Land Agency on this antimarket measure.

This price control mechanism represented an extraordinary public interference with the private market. The private sector was left in the dark about how the government would evaluate the reported price. Under this system, the local government received a report and either approved the proposed price or gave advice to lower the price to a certain level. In either case, the local government was not obliged to give reasons for its decision. There was, however, no strong resistance to this measure, which clashed head on with the concept of a market-oriented economic system. That this kind of authoritarian rule could emerge in an economically developed country such as Japan is amazing. It reflects a culture that is distinctly different from that of the West.

When this system was added into the National Land Use Law, an increasing number of prefectures, cities, and towns started to employ the system within its jurisdiction as shown in table 12-1. At the same time, an increasingly large number of land transactions were reported until 1991. Similarly, the percentage of the applications that received "advice" increased until 1990, reflecting the increasingly rigorous attitude of the government as well as the confidence of the people in the economy. Those who received advice abandoned the transaction or followed the advice. Although this surveillance system has been applied

Table 12-1. Governments Employing the Land Transaction Surveillance System

Year	Local governments[a]	Reported transactions[a]	Percent reports receiving advice
1987	39	60,562	12.7
1988	163	157,605	21.8
1989	420	219,367	26.2
1990	652	236,607	39.1
1991	1,070	310,737	31.9
1992	1,188	228,068	29.0
1993	1,211	253,342	27.0
1994	1,210	135,822	23.9
1995	444	14,243	18.3

Source: Land Agency of Japan, *The White Paper on Land* (Tokyo), annual issues since 1988.
a. Denotes number with an active surveillance system and number of reported transactions.

mainly to highly urbanized areas, this control contributed to reducing the number of land transactions within the country. In doing so, this system has prevented those potential economic gains from being realized through landownership changes.

The second crucial step in the formation of land policy was the enactment in 1989 of the Fundamental Law of Land. This law was prepared by a group of the members of the Diet rather than a party or a ministry on behalf of a party. The main thrust of the legislation was to affirm the overriding importance of public welfare over individual interest in the use of land. What was legislated was the declaration of a few principles without specifying applicability of the concept in specific cases. Many writers thought the price inflation of land at that time was due partly to the abuse of land by private parties such as speculation or illegal land assembly. Many legislators were persuaded by this argument.[8] The initial draft legislation for the law was submitted to the Diet by the coalition of four opposition parties in 1988. The Liberal Democratic Party modified this draft and passed it in both houses in December 1989. This legislation declares four principles regarding land: the priority of the public purpose over the private interest in the use of land; the importance of planning in land use, the prevention of speculative transactions; and burden sharing based on benefits obtained from the land. Although this law simply states basic principles, it has played a significant role.

Because it allows open interpretation of these declared principles, bureaucrats have used it to defend discretionary decisions not endorsed by specific legislation. As described subsequently, the Aggregate Control of Real Estate-Related Loans was said to be based on this law.

The third step was the quick increase in interest rates by the Bank of Japan, the Japanese central bank. It raised the discount rate from 2.5 percent to 6 percent within a span of fifteen months. The first was the raise from 2.5 percent to 3.25 percent on May 31, 1989. It went up to 6 percent on August 30, 1990. As the bank is authorized to change the official discount rate for the purpose of achieving economic objectives, the actions themselves were legitimate, but the objectives may not have been. The Bank of Japan explained its actions as necessary to combat inflation.[9] But at that time there was no sign of inflation except in the asset market. This shift in the interest rate changed the business climate drastically. Business people were taken by surprise, as they were seeing nothing but encouraging signs: low interest rates, increasing demand, increasing asset prices, and stable prices. Many firms had borrowed heavily for investment, anticipating bright economic prospects. They borrowed with their land as collateral. As the price of land was going up, the banks assessed its price liberally. Suddenly, those firms that undertook heavy borrowing found their prospects turned upside down. The determination of the Bank of Japan to raise the interest rate was felt more deeply soon after it raised the official discount rate to 4.25 percent in December 1989. The stock market started crumbling from the opening day in 1990.

The most notorious step of all was the decision of the Ministry of Finance to regulate the quantity of lending from the banks to real estate–related sectors. The ministry issued a directive to the banks to restrict the provision of new loans for the purpose of real estate development in such a way that the growth of the cumulative loan balance in these sectors did not exceed the growth of the cumulative loan balance to the rest of the sectors combined. This directive was issued to be effective on April 1, 1990, by the director of the Banking Bureau in the ministry without any authorization by the cabinet or minister, much less by the enactment of a law for this effect.[10] What was more, it was a virtual ban on new loans in the real estate–related sectors. In spite of the specific phrasing of the directive, the banks perceived it as a prohibition.

This decision took the real estate firms and those in other sectors engaged in real estate development by surprise. The price of property started to dip, as they started feeling the pain when money that had been promised was not forthcoming. They had to abandon certain projects that were under way or in the planning stage. This decision, so important for those engaged in banking and property development, was made by the judgment of a director of a department in the ministry, and without any political process. There was no interaction between the ministry official and the true sovereign voters about the desirability of this action. This ban was imposed for twenty-one months, until the end of December 1991, and was highly responsible for freezing the real estate sector and also cooling the economy as a whole.

The final set of policy tools was the major revisions in land taxes. The Ministry of Finance was the organization behind the scene, but it did not appear in the forefront. The Deliberation Council on Taxation was given the task of revising the land-related taxes. The council established a Subcommittee on Land Taxation in the beginning of 1990. This committee produced a set of recommendations toward the end of 1990. However, as shown below, it was widely understood that the discussion in the subcommittee was led by the Ministry of Finance. After about four months of sincere and mostly free discussion, the discussion was subsequently guided by the ministry, and the subcommittee produced recommendations that included the initiation of the new land-holding tax, the Land Value Tax, and the strengthening of almost all land-related taxes, notably the inheritance tax through the upward revision of the assessment and increases in rates of capital gains taxes.

These recommendations were, after minor revisions, approved by the Diet in 1991 and became an important factor for depressing the price of land thereafter. These changes in taxes were instituted through formal legal channels. Therefore, the ministry appears to be innocent. The ministry was far from a silent bureaucratic secretariat for processing the deliberation but was rather a player in instituting the changes.

What was more, the Ministry of Finance was not alone in changing land taxes. In November 1990, the Ministry of Local Autonomy, which oversees the local property tax, also decided to increase the assessment of land significantly, that is, from about 20 to 40 percent of the Land Agency's announced price to 70 percent. The ministry did not do this by a revision in local property tax law or a cabinet decision, but merely by a directive from the director of the Local Finance Bureau in the ministry. This director was able to multiply by a factor of 2 to 4, though with an adjustment period, the tax burden of 70 million tax payers who were paying about U.S.$60 billion at that time.[11]

The decisionmaking process of the government of Japan depends very heavily on decisions made by bureaucrats. Some of the decisions on land policy were channeled through the formal process, but many were implemented without the legislative process or without an endorsement by the cabinet although key political leaders might have been consulted. The minister might have been informed, but his consent was not necessary. Matters were decided among professional bureaucrats, in some cases, only within a department within the ministry, as in the case of the lending controls described above.

The Process of Deciding Land Taxation Reforms

For those interested in the course of Japan's land policy and the economic debacle that it produced, the deliberation process pursued by the Subcommittee on Land Taxation deserves close study. The recommendations of this subcommittee in 1990 led the government to strengthen significantly all land-related taxes. The recommended reforms were legislated, with some modifications, into law in 1991. This was the final and most powerful measure in driving down the price of land. It has contributed significantly to depressing the economy. Drawing in part on public opinion polls conducted in the course of my previous research, I would like to focus on various aspects of the subcommittee's deliberations.[12]

The Selection of Subcommittee Members

When the Deliberation Council on Taxation decided to establish a Subcommittee on Land Taxation at the end of 1989, the council was faced with the task of appointing members for this purpose. According to the government ordinance that authorizes the establishment of the council, subcommittee members were appointed by the council's chairperson.[13] Therefore, there was no procedural fault. But, as the conclusions of the deliberation would depend largely on the orientation of the constituent members, the selection of the members was very important. On the basis of the public opinion polls that I conducted, the selection process of the committee members was not well known to most laymen (76 percent reserved judgment) (table 12-2).[14] But more than half of corporate representatives thought the selection was reasonable (53 per-

Table 12-2. Opinion about the Land Taxation Subcommittee, 1990

Question	Group[a]	Agree	Somewhere between	Do not agree	Cannot judge
1. The members were selected fairly.	Ind	7	31	16	46
	Fm	53	18	21	8
	RE	10	31	15	44
2. The process of deliberation was conveyed to the public well.	Ind	4	12	72	12
	Fm	10	16	70	4
	RE	0	27	61	12
3. The deliberation reflected public opinion well.	Ind	4	17	62	17
	Fm	0	18	74	8
	RE	1	27	56	16
4. The deliberation outcomes reflect the views of the Ministry of Finance significantly.	Ind	45	20	7	28
	Fm	72	14	2	12
	RE	66	17	4	13
5. This subcommittee contributed significantly to solving the problems related to land.	Ind	6	34	36	24
	Fm	0	47	39	14
	RE	6	49	32	13

Source: Author's survey. See Koichi Mera, "The Failed Land Policy: A Story from Japan," Working Paper (University of Southern California, Los Angeles, School of Urban Planning and Development).

a. Ind, individuals; Fm, firms; and RE, real estated–related firms and individuals

cent approved). This implies that the selection of the members was made without letting the general public know the process, but some groups of corporations were consulted in the process or were given to understand that they were represented. The selection process was not open to everybody, but a representative was deliberately chosen from principal sectors. Most major corporations belong to an association of sectoral or more general business associations. Thus most corporations must have considered themselves represented by someone in the subcommittee.

However, no deliberate effort was made to represent the general public in the subcommittee. (See the Appendix for a list of subcommittee members.) A more fundamental problem is how the members were chosen. As Hiromitsu Ishi, the chairman of the subcommittee, has written, as all of the members of the parent Government Taxation Deliberation Council volunteered to be a member in the subcommittee, the composition of the subcommittee must have been seriously biased because the Ministry of Finance must have influenced some members' decisions.[15] The subcommittee also contained a large number of former Ministry of Finance officials, estimated at nine out of the forty-two members in total—one way that the ministry used to ensure acceptance of its proposed policy.

The Process of Deliberation

According to the public opinion polls, a large majority in each category of respondents replied that the process of deliberation was not conveyed well to the public. Only 4 percent of the general public, 10 percent of corporations, and none of the real estate sector respondents thought the process was reasonably well conveyed to the public (table 12-2). This was expected, because the subcommittee or its parent council did not disclose its entire proceedings, and its records were kept confidential.[16] After each session, the chair of the subcommittee responded to questions from reporters. In this way, the government was able to control its exposure to the media.

Furthermore, the subcommittee did not have any specific procedural rule for making decisions.[17] The chair of the subcommittee led the discussion, and when there was no strong opposition, the proposition advanced by the chair was declared to be supported.[18]

There was one exception, however. Toward the end of a long period of deliberation on September 18, 1996, the subcommittee was to decide on a proposal for a new national land-holding tax. Ishi asked every member of the subcommittee about his or her view on the new tax. When every member had completed a statement, he summarized the statements by saying, "There were 20 members supporting this proposal, 9 opposing it in favor of improving the existing property tax, and there were some [who] proposed a combination of the two."[19]

However, this was not voting. And even if the counting was accurate, this spread did not necessarily represent the spread of views in the general public. First, there was no proportional representation by the members of the general public. Aside from academic members, most members represented the interest of a certain sector. Not all the sectors were represented, and some sectors were overrepresented. Second, as stated above, there were a significant number of former officials of the Ministry of Finance in the members. They were strongly bound by the policy held by the ministry. Third, many of the members were contacted by Ministry of Finance officials before important meetings and were requested to support the ministry's position. Even academic members were forced to think about the consequences of not following the ministry's request.[20] As the ministry has enormous power, many tended to go along with its policy.

Reflection of Public Opinion in the Deliberations

Almost none of the survey's respondents thought the deliberation reflected public opinion very well. Although about 30 percent reserved judgment, only 4 percent of the general public and none of the corporations thought it did (table 12-2). The recommendations made by the subcommittee were far from the general view of the voters.[21] If the subcommittee had followed the authentic Confucian tradition, no explicit interaction of views would have been necessary, but the resulting deliberation would have reflected the view of the general public through reading of the minds of the general public by leaders. That did not happen. The decisions reached were undesirable even according to the traditional Eastern criterion.

Influence by the Ministry of Finance

For the majority of the respondents in the survey, it was apparent that the Ministry of Finance had influenced the subcommittee decisions significantly. Aside from those who reserved judgment, an overwhelming majority perceived that the Ministry of Finance had significantly influenced their decisions. This view is supported by interviews with some of the members of the subcommittee. In fact, many respondents preferred the alternative of reducing land prices by increasing the supply of usable land space.

Results of the Subcommittee

Very few thought that the subcommittee contributed to solving the problems associated with land. Aside from those who either reserved judgment or took no sides, a large majority thought that the subcommittee did not do much to alleviate land problems.

These findings are very revealing about the way the government made decisions concerning land taxes. It was largely an elite-driven process in defiance of popular opinion. Of course, elected officials are given the prerogative of taking actions even against the will of the voters, at least for the short term, but it is hard to find an excuse for public servants to do so.

Causes for Inappropriate Decisions

As presented above, the land policy adopted by the government of Japan around 1990 was not supported by many people surveyed by the author in 1994. If the government is supposed to serve the general interest of the people in the nation, the policy package chosen was inappropriate. Decisionmakers could even be accused of criminal negligence of public welfare. The value of properties in the nation dropped by $5 trillion from 1990 to 1995.[22] The government did not follow the basic procedure for rational decisionmaking outlined by Herbert Simon.[23] Even if it is granted that human beings are not able to have perfect knowledge or foresight, the government should have set up rational procedures for ascertaining whether the decisions it was going to make would improve rather than harm the welfare of the people in the nation.[24] A rational choice should have three features: identification of the set of alternatives open to choice; identification of possible future state of affairs associated with each alternative; and comparative evaluation of the possible future state of affairs.[25] Even if each governmental unit actually went through these exercises, there is no public information that they followed this procedure.

Instead, each unit of the government, such as the Land Agency, the Bank of Japan, the Ministry of Finance, and the Ministry of Local Autonomy, made their decision within the organization in secrecy, and those units brought together their decisions. These decisions were simply overlaid and accumulated. No single organization in the government was coordinating the decisions. Although the cabinet was technically in charge of coordinating these decisions, it was merely approving the decisions made by each unit. In this situation, it was not possible to follow the procedure required for rational decisionmaking. Even if the consequences of the decisions, which were going to be made by one unit of the government, could be predicted by the decisionmaking unit, it could not have predicted the consequences when its decisions were overlaid with those decisions made by other units. Without having an effective coordinating unit for the decisions that were going to be made by all relevant units, rational decisionmaking was not possible. Even if the Economic White Paper and the White Paper on Land issued by their respective units of the government declared that the policy decisions were made to correct some aspects of the problems caused by the rise in the land price, they were not in a position to declare that the decisions would improve the situation for the country. Each unit is concerned only with the policies within its own jurisdiction.

One might argue that the governmental units were not able to predict the consequences of any policy with any confidence. But, if so, why could they propose policies for adoption if they were unable to predict their consequences? Each governmental unit must have known what it was doing even though it did not make public what it was aiming at. There might have been a real objective besides the publicly announced objective. In such a case, the real decisionmaking process had to be concealed, rather than publicized. As the decisionmaking procedure was not made public, there is good reason to suspect that the objective was to advance not the public interest but the interest of the decisionmakers themselves. As revealed in the public opinion survey, most of the respondents were in favor of increasing the supply of land into the market as a way of solving the land problem.[26] But the Ministry of Finance was apparently aiming at initiating a new national tax on land value.[27]

Characteristics of Japan's Decisionmaking

To understand better the behavior of the various governmental units in the making of land policy during the 1990s, it would be useful to note some well-known characteristics that affect Japanese government decisionmaking. These include the following:

- Trust in the power of control and distrust of the market;
- A bandwagon mentality among the mass media;
- Lack of political leadership;
- Lack of a sense of mission in the ministries;
- Self-interest of each ministry;
- Competition among ministries; and
- Popular attitudes that led bureaucrats to take the lead.

Trust in Power and Distrust of the Market

This is an Eastern tradition. Although the economy is said to be market oriented, most bureaucrats do not trust the market. Instead, they regard themselves as the leaders of the market. In the past, they have controlled the market in various ways, and on the whole they were successful in achieving major objectives as demonstrated by Chalmers Johnson.[28] In the case of the Ministry of Finance, they have control over the banking and securities sectors as well as budget and taxation. Even in the case of currency exchange, they have intervened quite frequently. As it can control the budgets of all government activities, including the judicial branch, the Finance Ministry can control everything under the sun within the territory of Japan. Since the collapse of the stock market in 1990, it has been well known that the ministry was trying to keep the stock price at a certain level (the so-called PKO, or "price-keeping operation"). Thus it is no surprise that the ministry tried to control the price of land through the means available to it, such as controls on lending and taxation. It can be argued that the introduction of a new Land Value Tax represented an effort by the Ministry of Finance to strengthen its power base.

The Media Bandwagon

During this period, the mass media carried article after article condemning the rising price of land. In fact, all the major newspapers struck an identical theme. It is well known that mass media in Japan have strong connections to government agencies, which must therefore have supported such reports, in particular the influential documentary series on Japanese land prices televised by the Japan Broadcasting Corporation in

1987.[29] The basic fault of these reports was that they did not question why land prices went up, focusing instead on the problems associated with the increase. Some articles attributed the rise of land price to real estate agencies that were buying and selling the same property several times during a short span of time. They did not reason why such high prices were paid by the purchasers. Real estate agents were not in a position to create artificially high prices. They were simply responding to demand from firms that were planning property development.[30]

The Lack of Political Leadership

The political leadership in Japan has been weak in recent years for a number of reasons. To start with, the prime minister is not given much authority by law. He or she can appoint ministers but cannot force them to adopt a specific policy. All government decisions must be made by the cabinet. So in order for a prime minister to have leadership, the prime minister must have the power of persuasion to ministers and other political leaders.

During recent years, Yasuhiro Nakasone had such leadership when he was in the position from 1982 to 1987. He obtained leadership by his ability to organize political strongmen and by the popular support that resulted from his clear message to the public. However, his successors from the Liberal Democratic Party were not able to lead the nation as influentially as he did. Noboru Takeshita, a shrewd politician, did not have any clear message to the public and was tainted by the Recruit scandal.[31] Most subsequent prime ministers were selected not on the basis of leadership but on the basis of public perceptions of their integrity. Partly as a result, Takeshita's successors, such as Sohichi Uno and Toshiki Kaifu, were poor leaders. Most of the land policy measures were devised and implemented when Kaifu was the prime minister. He was selected by the LDP as a compromise candidate for prime minister by major factions. Thus he was not able to exercise leadership, and in addition, he was not a leader by character. As a result, bureaucrats ran the show.

The Lack of a Sense of Mission

Each ministry is expected to work for the good of the country. During the reconstruction years immediately after World War II, the Ministry of Finance as well as other ministries appear to have worked hard to achieve the best for the country. But this discipline seems to have been lost in recent years. The ministries seem to be working for the benefit of those working in them rather than for the general public. Recently, this type of criticism has become widespread in the newspapers and magazines.[32] On the whole, all these writings assert that the ministries have lost their sense of mission. From the viewpoint of an institutional economist, this argument hardly seems novel. If a bureaucrat sees that his or her interest would be better served by taking a measure that would increase his or her long-term income and power than by taking a measure that would improve the national welfare, an institutional economist will declare that the rational choice for the bureaucrat is the former. However, the issue is not that simple. Any public exposure of the selfishness of bureaucrats will damage the reputation of the bureaucrats and the respective ministry, and if it goes far, the bureaucrats and the ministry will be punished by the voters. Japan is still capable of that degree of democracy and justice, as demonstrated by the arrest of Prime Minister Tanaka in the 1970s. A rational strategy for the bureaucrats will be, thus, to improve their own situation while pretending that they are serving the general public. They need to adopt those policies that appear to be supported by many.

In the case of the land price issue, it can be postulated that government officials who resided in well-located rental housing provided by the government feared at least one immediate consequence of rising land prices. If the price of land were to keep rising, as it was at that time, they would never be able to purchase a house upon retirement. This fear may have been a factor behind the government's policy of reducing the price of land and behind its unwillingness to consider land policy from a broader perspective.

From this perspective, all the ministries were in the same situation. This factor might have united all the ministries behind a simple-minded policy of lowering the land price. This being the case, the ministries needed to defend their policies. Indeed, they did this by giving four reasons why high land prices were a problem,[33] while also claiming that a fall in land price would not adversely affect the economy.[34]

The Self-Interest of the Ministry

The Ministry of Finance is in charge of revenue collection and expenditure allocation. The power of the ministry is partly derived from its revenue collection authority. Naturally, the ministry was eager to expand its revenue collection authority. A national crisis is a good opportunity to expand power. Thus it can be argued that the ministry promoted a new national tax on landholding and strengthened land-related taxes to bolster its authority. Moreover, the ministry was also facing revenue shortfalls that were projected to increase over the years owing to rapid increases in welfare-related expenditures. Therefore, it was searching for new sources of revenues. The inflation of land prices was therefore an excellent opportunity to increase taxing power. This was evident even when the subcommittee started deliberations, as newspapers reported the ministry's proposal to introduce a new national tax on landholding.[35]

The mistake the ministry made was not its decision to seek new revenue sources but its failure to examine the possible implications of strengthening taxes. The subcommittee did not examine the consequences of strengthening land-related taxes or of initiating a new landholding tax to the economy or the general welfare of the population. Members just argued that the land price needed to be reduced, and taxing the beefed-up land price was a just and righteous public policy as landowners gained excessively through capital gains. There was no quantitative analysis of the consequences of stepped-up land taxation.[36] These actions support the hypothesis that the ministry was primarily concerned with expanding its taxing power at that time.

Competition among Ministries

An objective observer would have seen at that time that the ministries competed with one another for the sake of self-interest and not for the sake of promoting public welfare. The Ministry of Local Autonomy, which has jurisdiction over the property tax levied by local governments, was not in favor of strengthening the property tax at the time when the subcommittee started deliberations in the first half of 1990. This judgment was based on its assessment of public sentiment, which was against tax increases. But once the Ministry of Finance had started, through the work of the subcommittee, to campaign for the strengthening of land taxes, and had been making progress in this effort within the subcommittee, the Ministry of Local Autonomy decided to increase local property taxes. It decided to do so by raising the assessments of land, rather than by increasing the tax rate, because the latter would have required legislative action. This proposition was adopted by the subcommittee. However, the Ministry of Finance remained skeptical.[37]

The combined effect of various tax increases on the economy or land prices was not examined by the subcommittee or any other governmental organization. The general public had to suffer from highly arbitrary decisions of various ministries. The ministerial competition had led, in short, to a lessening of the public welfare.

One fundamental problem was the lack of a coordinating mechanism among the ministries. As a council reporting to the prime minister and assisted by the Ministry of Finance and the Ministry of Local Autonomy, the Deliberation Council on Taxation should have played this role. But it was not able to do so. The council was heavily managed by the Ministry of Finance, and the prime minister's office did not play any significant role. Other than the council, the cabinet could perform this function. It required the leadership of the prime minister. But he did not have a competent staff under him. Even if he had had the right staff, he would not have had the level of leadership needed to coordinate ministerial proposals. This was no accident. It was, and is, a structural problem. Because the prime minister is generally selected among competing factions within the LDP or a coalition of parties as a compromise head of the party, and because he is not given any great authority by law, most recent prime ministers are coordinators, not leaders.

Popular Attitudes

Democracy is not yet well established in Japan despite the great effort made by the Allied Powers after the World War II. Many voters still believe that government bureaucrats can and should take care of the people, and when there is a crisis, they are inclined to depend on the government. As a result, many people, even though they do not like the policies advanced by the government, do not openly express their opinions. There is still a popular feeling that the government is above the people. This behavior was reinforced during the two and a half centuries of feudal rule under the Tokugawa shogunate and two-thirds of a century of imperial rule until the end of World War II. The American occupation policy made deep inroads into Japanese thinking, but long traditions are hard to uproot.

There are no significant grass-roots political organizations, and most people wait for guidance from the government and depend on political initiatives by the government. Two factors have enhanced this behavior. One is the Confucian tradition of social hierarchy and order. The general public has been trained to depend on the governance provided by wise leaders. Second, the current system worked well during the postwar decades until recently. Many people simply voted for the LDP and worked faithfully in the company where each was first employed. This was the most effective way of improving their income and quality of life. The situation has changed significantly since then, but most have not realized the importance of the change yet.

Implications of the Factors Identified

These seven points indicate the following: One, the society still maintains some aspects of traditional values and behavior patterns as revealed in the perception of the bureaucrats toward the market and people's dependence on the government for guidance. But two, the underlying discipline that supported traditional society has already disappeared from those who are supposed to provide guidance. The sense of devotion to the good of the nation, the unwritten code of ethics that governed past bureaucrats, and the autonomous coordination among actors have disappeared significantly from the present bureaucrats. Certainly, the entire society is in transition. It is moving away from the traditional model and possibly toward the Western model in a modified way. But a new mode of thinking is not yet well established.

Conclusion

In the foregoing analysis, the decisionmaking system of the Japanese government has been found grossly inadequate for coping with present day issues. This is the reason why a serious mistake was made on land policy around 1990. For Japan to perform an economic and political role commensurate with its population and economic size, it must orchestrate a significant structural change in government. That change should consist of reducing the power held by bureaucrats, improving their accountability to political representatives, and improving the decisionmaking process. Deliberation Councils that are now used to conceal the hidden plans of ministries by consensus decisionmaking should be replaced by a transparent system. In such a system, alternative policy options should be examined and the consequences of the recommended policy predicted, and all deliberations should be explicitly documented and made available to the public.

Such changes would mark a significant departure from the current administrative system and might seem impossible. However, recent developments in the country tend to encourage optimism. In recent years, for example, the media have been taking a more critical role, scrutinizing bureaucratic policy choices, highlighting narrow bureaucratic views, and investigating bureaucratic scandals. Public opinion is going through a corresponding shift.

Achieving the necessary changes, however, is not an easy task. As a prerequisite, Japanese voters must be clearly aware of the undesirable consequences of the current bureaucratic system. This needs to become an important election issue. Second, political pressure from outside Japan needs to be applied consistently to amplify the concern of the voters in the country. As the present political situation in Japan is very fluid, this is an opportune time to undertake change. Before the political system is solidified, which may be in five to ten years, drastic changes can and should take place.

In this reform, the most important element is strengthening the power of the elected political representatives relative to the power of bureaucrats. The power of the members of the Lower House and the House of Councilors must be increased. The power of the prime minster should also be enhanced so that he or she can effectively coordinate different ministries.

When these changes are achieved, the welfare of the people will be better served, and the country will emerge as an attractive, advanced nation capable of playing its proper role in world affairs.

Appendix: Members of the Land Taxation Subcommittee of the Taxation Deliberation Council

Status	Name	Position
Status	*Name*	*Position*
Chair, Council	Buichi Ogura	Chair, Food & Agricultural Policy Research Center
Vice Chair, Council	Jiro Yoshikuni	Chair, Yokohama Bank

Status	Name	Position
Chair Subcommittee	Hiromitsu Ishi	Professor, Hitotsubashi University
Vice Chair	Eiko Ohya	Essayist
	Takashi Igarashi	Member, Editorial Board Sankei Newspaper
	Ken Ohtani	Ex-member, Editorial Board Asahi Newspaper
	Hiroto Ohyama	News Analyst, Japan Broadcasting Corp.
	Hidesane Orimoto	President, Japan Tax Research Center
	Ichiro Kato	President, Seijo Gakuen
	Hiroshi Kato	Professor, Keio University
	Ryoichi Kawai	Chair, Komatsu Seisaku Corp.
	Masaru Kurihara	Mayor, Hamamatsu City, Shizuoka-ken
	Arata Kohayakawa	Mayor, Hisayama Township, Fukuoka-ken
	Yugoro Komatsu	Chair, Kobe Steel Corp.
	Takayuki Kondo	President, Public Enterprise Financing Corp.
	Kikuji Sasaki	Governor, Akita-ken
	Satoko Tanaka	Secretary General, Tokyo Regional League of Women's Associations
	Eisuke Toda	Deputy Editor, Mainichi Newspaper
	Taizo Hata	President, Fuji Bank
	Takeshi Hijikata	Chair, Sumitomo Chemical Corp.
	Seigo Yamada	Secretary General, Japan Federation of Labor Unions
	Yoshio Yokota	President, Japan Securities Association

Status	Name	Position
Special Members		
	Tetsuro Aki*	President, Tokyu Real Estate Corporation
	Hitoshi Ikeda*	Managing Director, National Agricultural Board
	Shunsuke Ishihara*	Professor, Meikai University
	Keimei Kaizuka	Professor, Tokyo University
	Hiroshi Kaneko	Professor, Tokyo University
	Ryu Kiyomiya	Political Analyst
	Shozo Kohno*	President, Housing Financing Fund
	Mitsuo Kohno	Economic Analyst
	Yoshio Suzuki*	Vice President, Nomura Research Institute
	Ryo Takeda	Certified Public Accountant
	Takeshi Tateyama	Social Analyst
	Hiroshi Niida	Professor, Yokohama University
	Yukio Noguchi*	Professor, Hitotsubashi University
	Tokunosuke Hasegawa*	Director, Building Economics Research Institute
	Hisao Hari	Advisor, National League of Tax Return Associations
	Ichiro Hirose	Editorial Advisor, Chubu Newspaper
	Yoshio Hirose	Essayist
	Yoshiharu Matsuo	Editorial Board, Kyodo Press
	Sakue Matsumoto	President, Agricultural, Forestry and Fishery Fiancing Corp.
	Junichiro Yonehara*	Professor, Ohtemon University

*Refers to a member newly appointed in 1990.

Notes

1. An analysis of these costs is provided in Koichi Mera, "The Failed Land Policy: A Story from Japan," Working Paper (University of Southern California, Los Angeles, School of Urban Planning and Development, 1996).

2. Economic Planning Agency of Japan, *The Economic White Paper* (*Keizai Hakusho*) (Tokyo: Ministry of Finance Printing Bureau, 1994), p. 146.

3. See Mera, "The Failed Land Policy."

4. It took the Mori Group twenty-one years to assemble the land and complete the buildings of the large-scale project called ARC HILLS located in the Akasaka area of Tokyo. For most developers, that is too long a time span.

5. This mindset can be considered a product of the society's adherence to traditional Confucian thought: The ruler and his mandarins are expected to guide the populace, and not vice versa.

6. According to the Land Agency, 57.4 percent of all households own land of some sort, and 53.8 percent of all households own the land they live on. Excluding-single person households, the ratios are 62.3 percent and 66.0 percent, respectively. The Land Agency of Japan, *A Basic Land Survey: Households* (*Tochi Kihon Chosa-Shotai Chosa*) (Tokyo: Land Agency, 1995).

7. Until April 1990, the focus of government strategy was to increase the supply of usable land to reduce the price of land. But in June of that year, the Ministry of Finance and the Subcommittee for Land Taxation Reform led the way in shifting that strategy to one of strengthening land taxation in order to reduce land prices.

8. A TV documentary series by Nippon Hoso Kyokai (Japan Broadcasting Corporation) played a significant role in forming public opinion. This series was published soon afterward as Nippon Hoso Kyokai, *Japan in the World: To Whom Does Land Belong?* (*Sekai no Naka no Nihon: Tochi wa Dare no Mono ka*) (Tokyo: Nippon Hoso Kyokai, 1987).

9. Economic Planning Agency of Japan, *The Economic White Paper* (*Keizai Hakusho*) (Tokyo: Ministry of Finance Printing Bureau, 1990), p. 98. It states that the raising of the official discount rate was for preventing future inflation and for maintaining continued growth of the domestic demand. This statement in part admits that there was no imminent inflation. As it is common knowledge that a sharp rise in the interest rate would not be consistent with continued growth of domestic demand, the second reason cannot be accepted as a real reason. Thus the real reason must have been for the reduction of the land price.

10. It was issued on March 27, 1990.

11. It was 6.0 trillion yen in 1990. See Bank of Japan, Research and Statistics Department, *Annual Economic Statistics* (Tokyo: Bank of Japan, 1995).

12. See Mera, "The Failed Land Policy," for full details on the public opinion polls.

13. Government Ordinance 156 issued on April 24, 1962, by Prime Minister Hayato Ikeda.

14. See Mera, "The Failed Land Policy."

15. In Hiromitsu Ishi, Land Taxation Reform (*Tochi Zeisei Kaikaku*) (Tokyo: Toyo Keizai Shimposha, 1991), Ishi states that "the Subcommittee constituted with 43 members among the Government Taxation Deliberation Council, who volunteered to be a member in the Subcommittee" (p. 59). He acknowledged the accuracy of that statement through direct communication with the author in June 1996.

16. One person familiar with the subcommittee proceedings informed the author that those invited to testify were allowed to be in the meeting only for their own testimony. Keidanren, the Federation of Economic Associations of Japan, the largest business group, was allowed to have one person observe all the meetings.

17. This is based on a conversation with a former member of the subcommittee in October 1994 and is confirmed by a transcript of the meetings.

18. This was the case when the subcommittee chair announced an interim summary report to the press on May 29, 1990. There was no voting on the report, although various views were expressed in the summary document prepared by the chair, according to the available transcript of the meeting.

19. From the confidential transcript of the meeting.

20. This observation is based on conversations with several members of the subcommittee.

21. As table 12-2 shows, a large majority opposed the recommendations of the subcommittee. When the issue was debated in 1990, most business groups were against the introduction of the new national tax.

22. There was a reduction of ¥580 trillion. See Economic Planning Agency of Japan, *The Economic White Paper* (*Keizai Hakusho*) (Tokyo: Ministry of Finance Printing Bureau, 1997), Appendix, Long-Term Statistics, p. 18.

23. See Herbert A. Simon, "A Behavioral Model of Rational Choice," *Quarterly Journal of Economics*, vol. 69 (February 1955), pp. 99–118; and Herbert A. Simon (1956), "Rational Choice and the Structure of the Environment," *Psychological Review*, vol. 63 (May 1956), pp. 129–38.

24. See Herbert A. Simon, "From Substantive to Procedural Rationality," in S. J. Latsis, ed., *Method and Appraisal in Economics* (Cambridge University Press, 1976), pp. 129–48; and Herbert A. Simon, "Rationality as a Process and as Product of Thought," *American Economic Review*, vol. 68 (May 1978), pp. 1–16.

25. See Simon, "A Behavioral Model," pp. 100–01.

26. Mera, "The Failed Land Policy."

27. *Nihon Keizai Shimbun* of May 9, 1990, reported that the Ministry of Finance started to study the conversion of the rate on business properties from a local tax to a national tax with a view toward possible adoption of a national land-holding tax in Japan.

28. Chalmers Johnson, *MITI and the Japanese Miracle: The Growth of Industrial Policy, 1925–1975* (Stanford University Press, 1982).

29. See note 8.

30. See Koichi Mera, "Examining the Bubble Hypothesis: Land Policy and the Japanese Economy," Working Paper (Willamette University, Atkinson School of Management, 1995).

31. In 1989 the Recruit Corporation sparked a political scandal when it provided politicians, including Takeshita, with an opportunity to purchase advance shares of its stock before they were offered to the public.

32. See, for example, Ikuhiko Hata, *A Study of Bureaucrats (Kanryo no Kenkyu)* (Tokyo: Kodansha, 1983); Chalmers Johnson, *Japan:Who Governs? The Rise of the Developmental State* (Norton, 1995); Nobuhito Kishi, *Those Who Steer the Ministry of Finance (Okurasho wo Ugokasu Otokotachi)* (Tokyo: Toyo Keizai Shimpo Sha, 1993); Atsuo Mihara and Takahiro Miyao, *A Scenario for the Revival of Japan: A Drastic Change of Vision Is Required (Nihon Keizai Korega Fukkatsu no Shinario da: Imakoso Hasso no Daitenkan wo)* (Tokyo: Diamond Publishing Co., 1992); Takahiro Miyao and Ken Tobioka, *The Japanese Economy Was Ruined by Bank of Japan President and Finance Ministry Bureaucrats (Nihon Keizai wo Dame nishita Nichigin Sosai to Okura Kanryo)* (Tokyo: Nisshin Hodo, 1993); Nihon Keizai Shimbun, *Bureaucrats: The Derailing Big Power (Kanryo: Kishimu Kyodai Kenryoku)* (Tokyo: Nihon Keizai Shimbun Sha, 1994); Kenichi Ohmae, *A Critique of Japan's Bureaucracy (Kanryo Hihan)* (Tokyo: Shogakkan, 1994); Taichi Sakaiya, *The Satisfactory Society: An Answer to Today's Confusion (Manzokuka Shakai no Hoteishiki)* (Tokyo: Nihon Keizai Shimbun Sha, 1994); Makoto Sataka, *Breakup of the Ministry of Finance: Ace for Economic Revival of Japan (Okurasho Bunkatsu Ron: Nihon Keizai Saisei no Kirifuda)* (Tokyo: Kobunsha,1996); Ushio Shiota, *Failures of the Ministry of Finance (Okurasho no Fukaku)* (Tokyo: Nihon Keizai Shimbun Sha, 1993); Takarajima Journal, *The Profound Problem of the Banks in Japan (Ginko no Dao Mondai)* (Tokyo: Takarajima, 1996); Peter Tasker, *The End of the Japanese Golden Age? (Nihon no Jidai ha Owattaka)* (Tokyo: Kodansha,1992); Katsuto Uchihashi, *Collapse or Revival (Hatan ka Saisei ka)* (Tokyo: Bungei Shunju Sha, 1994); Karel Van Wolferen, *The Enigma of Japanese Power* (Vintage Books, 1989).

33. As stated in the Economic Planning Agency's 1991 *Economic White Paper,* those four reasons were increasing disparity in wealth holding, the difficulty of home purchasing for medium-income families, increasing distance of housing locations from places of work, and increasing expense for land acquisition by the public sector. Economic Planning Agency of Japan, *The Economic White Paper* (*Keizai Hakusho*) (Tokyo: Ministry of Finance Printing Bureau, 1991).

34. Economic Planning Agency, *The Economic White Paper*, 1991, chap. 2, sec. 2, pp. 167–82; and Economic Planning Agency, *The Economic White Paper,* 1992, chap. 1, sec. 6, pp. 86–95.

35. The *Nihon Keizai Shimbun* reported the ministry's interest in this new landholding tax on May 9,1990.

36. There were several research papers done by scholars, but they were not commissioned by the Taxation Council or the Land Taxation Subcommittee.

37. Conversation with Hiromitsu Ishi, chair of the subcommittee.

CHAPTER THIRTEEN

●

The Myth of Regulatory
Independence in Japan

E. B. Keehn

IN JAPAN'S DEREGULATION and reform campaigns of the 1990s, the Ministry of Finance has come under an unusual amount of scrutiny and criticism, inside and outside of Japan. The changes under discussion have been complex and varied. They include everything from Prime Minister Ryutaro Hashimoto's desire for a "big bang"–style deregulation of domestic financial markets in the year 2001 to a dismantling of the entire ministry.

The thrust of the discussions about changes to MOF are not about increasing bureaucratic efficiency; they are about reducing that ministry's authority and increasing its responsiveness to political leadership.[1] This would include creating a more transparent regulatory climate, altering an overly dictatorial relationship with the Bank of Japan, and addressing problems with conflict of interest and corruption in regulating Japan's securities houses, banks, and mortgage operations.[2]

How likely is it that there will be a wholesale diminution of MOF's power? Not very. One problem is that the ministry has a long history of drawing up its own reform proposals, the logic being that those changes most acceptable to MOF stand the best chance of being put into place. This approach naturally limits the pace and depth of reform. Moreover, the idea that Japan's politicians should come up with these reforms, or that MOF should be more responsive to political leadership, has little acceptance within the ministry. As one senior MOF official put it, "It is doubtful whether politicians are doing what they should do. We have a sense of mission. We should do more than just formulate policies."[3] In fact, the inflexibility of MOF to accept real change in its affairs now provides rich fodder for Japan's television and print satirists.[4]

As a result of the difficulties inherent in asking a powerful organization like MOF to reform itself, a number of Japan's politicians, academics, and business elites argue that the best way to make inroads into its powers is to create new, independent organizations that take over some of the ministry's activities.

At first glance this seems a good approach, until we consider the success of previous attempts. As it turns out, virtually all new bureaucratic oversight organizations created in Japan since the end of the U.S. occupation in 1952 have been manipulated from the inside by the very ministries they were designed to regulate.[5]

To get some idea of the likely tenor and depth of future MOF reforms, it is useful to look back a few years at the last "reorganization" of the ministry's power. This was the highly publicized creation of the Securities and Exchange Surveillance Committee (SESC), which was supposed to be an independent watchdog organization. An examination of the history of the SESC not only demonstrates how the Japanese bureaucracy effectively manages reform movements, but also raises important questions about the very possibility of independent regulatory agencies in Japan.

MOF's Actions Lead to Demands for Reform

In the summer of 1991 MOF, reacting to stories in the press, confirmed that a number of Japan's securities houses and trust banks had been regularly reimbursing favored corporate clients for losses on their market investments. Interestingly, this did not lead to public calls for the punishment of brokers who were involved. Instead, the loss compensation scandal resulted in an international condemnation of MOF's regulatory style. This dissatisfaction led to attempts to move control of regulation of the securities industry out of MOF's Securities Bureau, culminating a year later in the creation of the SESC.

During the debates leading up to the creation of the SESC Anthony Rowley of the *Far Eastern Economic Review* commented, "The scandals are woven too deeply into the fabric of Japanese society to be dismissed as a legacy of financial excess. They demonstrate, in fact, how far business practices, governance and accountability are lagging in Japan."[6] There is no question that the loss compensation scandal would have been regarded as a regulatory failure in New York or London. But in Japan this sort of "failure" is by design and is an integral part of the way in which the bureaucracy influences the nation's economy. Universalistic ideas about how markets should be regulated are secondary to the flexible use of bureaucratic power to bring about specific market results. The case of the SESC, and the philosophy behind its creation, highlights how this flexibility helps to shape Japan's system of capitalism. Nathan Rosenberg has suggested that "economists who purport to have something to say that is pertinent to the contemporary operation of capitalism have the obligation to deal with certain distinctive patterns of capitalist behavior and to explain their consequences."[7] The case of the SESC, and the philosophy behind its creation, highlights part of what is distinctive in Japan's system of capitalism.

The SESC began operations in July 1992. It was touted by Japan's financial press as the functional equivalent of the Securities and Exchange Commission (SEC) in the United States, an independent regulatory agency that relies on the skills of in-house lawyers and financial specialists to oversee the securities business in the United States.[8] If Japan's SESC were to approximate the operations of the SEC, it would need to demonstrate levels of transparency in regulatory behavior new to Japan.[9]

This makes the creation of the SESC an important test case for claims that Japan's government began a process of fundamental change in its relationship with the economy in the 1990s. If, as a regulatory office with a new philosophy, the SESC succeeded in working around the entrenched power of MOF, it would be an important piece of evidence supporting the idea often heard in the press that Japan is reshaping its marketplace to more closely resemble that of the United States. But an SESC that failed to gain independence from MOF and its old regulatory approach would mean business as usual and provide evidence that we are still waiting for fundamental change in the collusive relationship between the bureaucracy and the market that has long characterized Japan's approach to its economy. An SESC without operational independence would mean not only a failure to challenge MOF's authority, it would also mean that Japan's political leadership had failed to meet public demands for regulatory changes. Similarly, it would suggest that Japan's securities industry is still unable to wean itself away from MOF's particular brand of regulatory behavior.

In fact, the creation of the SESC turned out to be a textbook example of how reformist sentiments can be systematically short-circuited by the entrenched power of the bureaucracy. As Hiroshi Mizuguchi explains, the SESC turns out to be only "superficially similar" to the SEC in the United States, with the Japanese agency "muzzled" because it was designed to remain under MOF's control.[10]

Scandal and "Reform"

The circumstances behind the cycle of scandal and "reform," which created the SESC, demonstrates the bureaucratic logic that structures the reshaping of the Japanese marketplace. In the early days of the loss compensation scandal it was reported that Japanese brokerage houses and trust banks had paid out as compensation a total of ¥78 billion to corporate clients who had taken market losses. But it soon became clear that Japan's Big Four securities companies—Nomura, Nikko, Daiwa, and Yamaichi—as well as thirteen second-tier firms, had paid at least ¥171.9 billion in compensation to 608 corporate clients.[11] In all likelihood this is a low estimate. The true extent of loss compensation practices has never been made public by MOF, nor were the companies and individuals involved required to publicly disclose the full dimensions of their involvement. This in itself highlights one of the problems associated with MOF's self-interested approach to regulation, which often falls short of thorough disclosure on information important to markets and to the making of public policy. In part, this is what an independent SEC-style approach to regulation would have helped to correct.

Loss compensation was one of the ways brokerages and trust banks in Japan competed for deposits by corporate clients throughout the years of the bubble economy. But it was a practice that was increasingly difficult to sustain in the shrinking market that began in 1989. Japan's Big Four securities companies were all criticized by the Ministry of Finance for this practice, as were a number of trust banks. Yet when MOF went public with its information on loss compensation practices and forced their halt, Yoshihisa Tabuchi, the president of Nomura, argued that this practice was not only well known to MOF but was informally approved as a way to keep the Tokyo market buoyant during the bubble economy and its early aftermath. MOF denied this, and Tabuchi was forced to resign, though it was widely acknowledged by market watchers that loss compensation was indeed informally supported by MOF's Securities Bureau. But if Nomura and others were engaging in a practice with MOF's unwritten approval, why did MOF decide to condemn this practice when it did?

The most commonly accepted theory is that by doing so, the "guilty" brokerage houses would no longer be held liable for their clients' losses. By June 1991 the Tokyo stock market had fallen 42 percent from its high in 1989, but most clients who were promised compensation had only had their losses reimbursed up to March 1990. MOF's "disciplining" of firms for compensating clients for their losses—an action apparently sanctioned by MOF bureaucrats—potentially saved Japan's brokerage houses billions of yen in further compensation payments.

If correct this meant that regulators had allowed the nation's equities markets to function as a source of risk-free profit for a small number of privileged Japanese firms. And when the practice became unsustainable—as the Nikkei index continued to search for the bottom of the market—MOF stepped in to end it. This suggested that the Tokyo market was anything but a level playing field, whether or not one accepts the theory that the market was rigged at the highest levels by its regulators. As Peter Tasker suggested at the time, "The way in which Japan responds to the securities scandals will be an important indicator of how capitalism Japanese-style develops in the 1990s. . . . Do the authorities attempt to preserve their arbitrary power over the nation's economic life or will the principles of an open economy triumph?"[12]

The damage to public confidence as a result of the loss compensation scandals was enough to lead to demands, at least in some segments of the popular press, for a basic change in the regulatory framework governing the securities industry in Japan. MOF was judged by its critics to be too close to the industry to act as an impartial regulator. But in a market where insider trading was not even made illegal until 1987, the selective use of regulations, and informal approval of questionable practices, had long been the norm and used as a flexible tool by Japan's financial authorities. Even in the case of loss compensation MOF's Securities Bureau never made it clear whether the practice was or was not illegal, only that they wanted it stopped.

The loss compensation episode suggested that MOF's role as both advocate and regulator of the securities industry raised natural questions about conflict of interest and was inconsistent with principles of transparent and equal protection of small and large investors alike found in markets such as New York and London. It would appear that the disregard for small investors was not unlike that expressed by the president of the American Sugar Refining Company, voiced in 1900 in opposition to the idea of full disclosure and the public's purchase of shares: "Let the buyer beware; that covers the whole business. You can not wet nurse people from the time they are born until the time they die. They have got to wade in and get stuck, and that is the way men are educated and cultivated."[13]

The fact that less-favored clients of brokers were left to take their losses, combined with Tabuchi's charge that loss compensations were done with MOF's knowledge and at least tacit approval, did little to inspire public confidence in the ministry's regulatory impartiality. This led to debates over the need to place some regulatory distance between MOF and the securities industry.

The debate covered two options. One option was to create an independent commission with full regulatory and investigatory powers, including the ability to subpoena evidence, similar to the SEC in the United States. The Provisional Council on Administrative Reform, a quasi-official government, made it clear it preferred this option. This option was seen as "impractical" by MOF because of the fundamental changes it would introduce into Japan's marketplace. MOF advised keeping regulation within the ministry but removing it from under the direct administration wing of its Securities Bureau, though regulation would still follow the bureau's cues. Needless to say, MOF favored this second option. And once the ministry made its position clear, it never lost control of the political debates and the planning process which resulted in an SESC that remains tied to MOF regulatory concerns.

The MOF team that led the battle to prevent the creation of an independent SEC in Japan was led by Akira Ogawa. Ogawa was a powerful figure within his ministry, particularly on tax affairs where he played an important role in getting Japan's VAT (value-added tax) system introduced during Noboru Takeshita's prime ministership. He was closely connected to LDP grandees, particularly to Takeshita whom he served twice, first as personal secretary when Takeshita was finance minister, and again as personal secretary while Takeshita was prime minister. For his efforts in limiting the powers of the SESC, Ogawa was awarded the directorship of MOF's Securities Bureau,[14] the same bureau whose regulatory interests he protected by preventing the creation of an independent U.S.-style SEC in Japan.

The SESC began operations in July 1992. Its executive includes a chairperson and two commissioners with a tenure of three years, appointed by the Ministry of Finance.[15] A staff total of 202 is divided between the Coordination and Inspection Division and the Investigation Division. However, this is a misleading figure since market surveillance was designed to be in the hands of only 12 staffers, with another 26 involved in inspections. This small number is responsible for tracking the operations of 265 firms with about 3,000 branches and around 153,000 employees nationwide. This compares with approximately 2,600 staffers in the SEC in the United States, about 800 of whom are engaged exclusively in surveillance and inspection work.[16] There is no question that staff and resource shortages seriously hamper the SESC's ability to carry out its appointed tasks. When it prepared its first case, against a small group of speculators charged with driving up the price of Nihon Unisys between October 1990 and May 1991, its inspection staff members were overwhelmed with the preparations. There simply were no resources left over for the investigation and preparation of other cases.

SESC staffing levels are likely to increase over time. Even if staffing were not an issue, the problem remains that the SESC is an organization with limited independent powers of its own. It is responsible for examining the books of securities dealers and financial institutions, but it can only turn its findings over to the Ministry of Finance and the Japan Securities Dealers Association.[17] MOF is then free to use or ignore this information as it sees fit. There are no clear regulations or procedures requiring the ministry to act on SESC findings in any preordained or predetermined way. Moreover, MOF made sure that the SESC's establishing law would allow the ministry to carry out the same work as the commission if it so desired.[18] In practice this means that the SESC follows MOF's lead on investigations to insure against pointless effort. As if this were not enough, the watchdog abilities of the SESC are hamstrung in still other ways. The commission has no subpoena power and it cannot assess penalties without prior MOF approval. Even if penalties are assessed, they are not particularly severe, with a maximum fine of ¥3 million and jail sentences of up to three years.[19]

Virtual Reality

In the Japanese context, an SESC without independence makes sense. The selective enforcement of vague regulations, coupled with bureaucratic discretion, is viewed by MOF and other ministries as a crucial part of its economic management tool kit.[20] Eamonn Fingleton points out that "even top Japanese lawyers have difficulty understanding regulatory nuances."[21] This is reinforced by a political culture in which "Most Japanese citizens are not even aware of the [constitutional] principle that interpretation of the law is a matter for the courts, and instinctively turn to the bureaucrats if they need a law interpreted."[22] Under these conditions, an independent SESC without accompanying reforms that would put an end to MOF's discretionary use of vague regulations would have done little to create a more transparent regulatory regime.

This situation raises the question of whether deregulation campaigns can hope to deliver fundamental change without clearer and more objective regulatory arrangements. As a reading of the Deregulation Research Group's (*Kisei Kanwa Kenkyukai*) 1994 study makes clear, despite the numerous deregulation measures that are likely to pass into law in Japan throughout the rest of this decade, there will be no fundamental changes made in the bureaucratic behaviors that so often leave Japan's marketplace dependent on informal rules and selective enforcement of regulations.[23]

The lack of true independence in Japan's regulatory agencies contributes to this state of affairs. This does not result from simple bureaucratic intransigence, as is often portrayed by deregulation campaigners.[24] It is brought about by design. In East Asian systems of state-guided capitalism, pioneered by Japan, compromised regulatory agencies are a basic component in the successful implementation of strategic economic policy. Truer regulatory independence could too easily contradict the plans of the leading economic bureaucracies and frustrate their use of flexible and informal regulatory tools.[25]

From the state's perspective, independent regulatory agencies would introduce unwanted levels of uncertainty into the already difficult tasks of goal-oriented economic management. Regulation based on universalistic economic principles would complicate the state's ability to influence markets with flexibility, speed, and favoritism. Neutrality in regulation—a simplistic "rules of the game" approach— would too easily permit industries to seek their own market outcomes, separate from the strategic interests of the state.

For these reasons the SESC's lack of independence from MOF follows a consistent pattern in Japan's governmental system of binding the behavior of regulatory agencies to the interests of the economic ministries. In fact, all postwar regulatory agencies have been made dependent upon the very ministries whose interests they were designed to assault.[26] This can be done, as in the case of the SESC, by keeping the new regulator under the influence of the ministry most affected. Or it can be achieved by sabotaging new agencies from the inside, by using personnel exchanges as an organizational weapon.[27] In this case ministries reserve the new agency's key executive and research positions for their own elites, who are rotated through these posts on a regular basis.

This is the "reserved seat" (*shiteiseki*) system, and it is used in all of Japan's regulatory agencies, from the Fair Trade Commission to the Environment Agency. These rotated individuals control the internal life of these agencies to ensure that decisions are not taken that threaten the interests of their ministries. This is the regulatory equivalent of virtual reality. Regulatory agencies appear on government organization charts, but they do not have independence and generally are subservient to the strategies of the economic bureaucracies. Tensions and policy contradictions between regulatory agencies and the manipulatory economic ministries do occur, but these differences are rarely sustainable in the long term.

It is significant that other ministries in Japan have taken MOF's creation of the SESC as a model for their own "virtual" regulation. A year after the SESC was established, the Ministry of Construction announced its intention to set up its own "independent body to oversee the bidding process for public works."[28] As the ministry singularly responsible for encouraging and entrenching the practice of bid-rigging (*dango*) on public works in the first place, any "independent" body it creates is likely to have more public relations value than genuine regulatory effect.

The SESC in Action

By 1997 we had come full circle with the scandal that produced the conditions which forced the creation of the SESC in the first place. Charges of loss compensation for favored clients again surfaced and were soon substantiated by the Tokyo Public Prosecutors Office and the SESC. However, this time the story had a new twist and involved the illegal practice of buying off *sokaiya*, a particularly Japanese form of corporate racketeer. In this case, part of a payoff for a *sokaiya* was the guarantee—also illegal—that his investments would not lose money.

This particular scandal centers around one *sokaiya*, Ryuichi Koike. When the story about Koike first broke, it was assumed to be a limited incident that involved Nomura Securities. By mid-July 1997, the SESC believed it had dug as far as it needed and sent out a press release on its findings.[29] This was followed by premature reports in the United States that the scandal was "winding up."[30] However, once the digging had begun and the Tokyo Public Prosecutors Office became involved, the problem turned out to be more far-reaching than expected, including loss compensation and the involvement of all of Japan's Big Four securities houses—Nomura, Nikko, Daiwa, and Yamaichi. The Daiichi Kangyo Bank was also implicated in cooperation with Koike.

Though *sokaiya* is normally translated as "corporate racketeer," that does not fully capture the meaning. These are individuals who specialize in blackmailing the management of major Japanese corporations by demanding payment from companies in exchange for promises *not* to publicly reveal potentially damaging information about these companies during their annual meetings. The *Japan Daily Digest* brilliantly summarizes how this was done by Koike:

> Just before the 1992 annual meetings, Koike sent thick lists of questions he proposed to ask about a 1991 scandal that had turned up strong ties between Nomura, Nikko and the late mob boss Susumu Ishii. Like his counterparts at the other two brokerages, Nikko president Kichiro Takao saw Koike to "thank him in advance" for not asking. That gave Koike enough clout at Nikko to win some very special favors. The firm set an account for his front company, promised it would make profits no matter what—and when losses cropped up, it pumped a ¥300 million loan to a friend of Koike through an affiliate, Nikko Credit. Later it also—illegally— pushed ¥10 million of its own trading profits into Koike's account. Nikko's behavior. . . . so closely resembled what the rest of the Big Four did for Koike, because the general affairs *sokaiya* specialists of the four brokerages got together regularly to swap information.[31]

As of this writing, none of these companies nor Mr. Koike has been brought to trial, and they have not had an opportunity to publicly mount their defense. However, the case has taken its toll. More than four dozen senior directors have been removed at Japan's Big Four securities houses, and one suspicious death occurred—the stabbing of Yamaichi executive Koichiro Tarutani in which the murderer did not bother to take the ¥143,000 (approximate $1,200) in cash Tarutani had on him at the time.

It is possible that this latest round of financial scandal, about which we still have much to learn, may yet force the creation of truly independent regulatory agencies in Japan. But for now it is business as usual, with the creation of yet another MOF-captive organization, the Financial Supervisory Agency.[32] Considering that Japan's bubble economy—and the hard landing, bad debt mountain, and lengthy slowdown that resulted—are nearly all MOF creations, it is difficult to agree with the optimism of the Japanese Diet that MOF's powers should actually be expanded through legislation. But it is a logic consistent with Japan's approach to political economy.

Why Change?

If transparency and neutral enforcement of regulations are at fundamental odds with the economic bureaucracy's interactive and strategic role in Japan's marketplace, what are the prospects for fundamental change? The arguments for true liberalization, both by American trade negotiators and Japan's own domestic critics, are well rehearsed in the press and need not be restated here. Instead I would suggest that, despite the ongoing discussion on deregulation in Japan, the prospects for liberalization may actually be weakening, and this includes changes to dependent systems of regulation as represented by the SESC. Japan faces increasing economic competition from the high-growth economies of East Asia on the one hand—most of whom have adopted some form of state-led economic development—and a United States that is increasingly interested in managing its international trade with Japan (which amounts to an implicit industrial policy, if not particularly well thought out). Under these circumstances an economy in which the government exercises less strategic control may not be regarded by Japan's collective leadership as the wisest way forward in an increasingly complex and challenging global marketplace.

Added to this is the weight of Japan's existing economic institutions, which, when all is said and done, have consistently produced good economic results. As Taichi Sakaiya explains, "Japan's system of firm bureaucratic guidance was greatly strengthened in the days leading into World War II, and it has been left largely intact throughout the postwar period. Until recently the Japanese were virtuously unanimous in the view that the features of this system were virtues. . . . Any attempt to discard a bureaucratic system that has been in place for half a century will naturally meet with strong resistance. After all, virtually every existing organization has developed under this system, and almost all the leading figures in society have benefited from it and have had their ethics and aesthetic values shaped by it."[33] It is worth noting that Japan's economy, despite high levels of regulation, has consistently proven itself highly adaptable to new economic challenges, including the oil shocks of the 1970s, the bubble economy of the 1980s, and the high yen and sluggish economic performance of the mid-1990s.

This does not rule out the possibility of unanticipated economic shocks too severe for Japan's marketplace to absorb in its current guise. But short of that, history will continue to set the terms of Japan's internal debates about the reshaping of its marketplace—as it does in every other country—with decisionmakers at least as influenced by their own experiences as by demands or expectations on the part of Japan's trading partners.

This is not to say that Japan's economic structure and regulatory philosophy will remain static. It will continue to evolve within the context of preexisting institutions, with the changes consistent with the lessons Japan's decisionmakers learned over several decades of state-influenced economic development. As the case of the SESC suggests, this is at least as likely to result in the reorganization of old practices as it is in fundamental change.

In fact, the possibility of fundamental change is receding into a mythical future. Throughout the 1990s, a good deal of discussion on further economic reforms and regulatory changes has stemmed from concerns over Japan's sluggish economic performance. As this logic goes, the longer Japan's economy remains mired in slow growth, the more far reaching the program of deregulation and economic reform. Broader philosophical concerns, such as the proper balance of power between the policymaking prerogatives of politicians and bureaucrats, have also been widely discussed. But at the practical level, successful reforms have been market directed and highly specific.

If poor economic growth is crucial to further reform and deregulation in Japan, we may be in for some disappointment. By early 1997 Japan's economy began to show signs of growth, creating more jobs in 1996 than did the U.S. economy.[34] If policymakers and trading partners are relying on disastrous economic indicators to make the case for further change in Japan, they may have to wait until a worse economic situation prevails than the recession of the 1990s.

Notes

1. There are numerous sources for stories on the inequalities inherent in the relationship between bureaucrats and politicians in Japan. A good source of case studies and anecdotal evidence can be found in Jinyo Kaneko, *Sei wa kan o do shinogu ka* (How can politicians stand the bureaucrats?) (Tokyo: Kodansha, 1995).

2. For an introduction to thinking on bureaucratic reforms in Japan, including the Ministry of Finance, see Shukan Toyo Keizai Henshubu, *Kasumigaseki o kaitai-seyo* (Dismantle the bureaucracy) (Tokyo: Toyo Keizai Shinhosha, 1997).

3. Yuichiro Tanaka, "Ministry Still Meddling in the Market," *Asahi Evening News,* April 17, 1997.

4. Teruo Itoh, *O-warai: okurasho himitsu joho* (A good laugh: secret files of the Ministry of Finance) (Tokyo: Asuka Shincho, 1996). For the classic on this sort of thing in the English language, see Jonathan Lynne and Anthony Jay, eds., *The Complete Yes Minister* (London: BBC Books, 1984).

5. E. B. Keehn, *The Mandarins of Kasumigaseki* (London: Macmillan, forthcoming).

6. Anthony Rowley, "Ministry of Myopia: Japanese Scandals Lay Bare the Nexus between Bureaucrats and Brokers," *Far Eastern Economic Review*, September 12, 1991, p. 48.

7. Though he makes this comment with regard to Schumpeter's interest in economic change instead of economic stability, it is a comment that is equally relevant to the study of state-guided capitalism. See Nathan Rosenberg, *The Emergence of Economic Ideas: Essays in the History of Economics* (Aldershot: Edward Elgar, 1994), p. 158.

8. Nihon Keizai Shimbunsha, *Okurasho no yu-utsu* (MOF's melancholy) (Tokyo, 1992), pp. 61–62.

9. Studies of the SEC suggest that it is not an organization that is historically above reproach and that the effectiveness of its operations has varied with the leadership of its commissioner. Yet the principles of SEC regulation have remained relatively clear over the years. See Joel Seligman, *The Transformation of Wall Street* (Houghton Mifflin Company, 1982).

10. Hiroshi Mizuguchi, "Political Reform: Much Ado about Nothing," *Japan Quarterly,* vol. 40 (July–September 1993), p. 253.

11. Ibid.

12. Yas Idei, "Securities Scandals Expose Holes in Ministry Guidance," *Nikkei Weekly*, September 14, 1991, p.1.

13. Industrial Committee, *Preliminary Report on Trusts and Industrial Combinations*, H. R. Doc. 476, 56 Cong. 1 sess. (Government Printing Office, 1900), p. 123, cited in Louis Loss, *Fundamentals of Securities Regulation* (Little, Brown and Company, 1983), pp. 25–26.

14. Nobuhito Kishi, *Okurasho o ugokasu otokotachi* (The men who move the Ministry of Finance) (Tokyo: Toyo Keizai Shimposha, 1993), pp.100–01.

15. MOF's selection of the chair and two commissioners is in the hands of the finance minister and requires Diet approval. However, to date, recommendations of MOF's bureaucrats on these matters have been followed.

16. Michael L. Magdich, "The Failure of Financial Market Regulators and Regulations in Japan to Meet the Needs of a More Efficient Securities Market" (University of Essex, Contemporary Japan Centre, 1993). I would like to thank David Campbell, Essex University for directing me to this excellent thesis. This article would not have been possible without it.

17. Masato Hotta, "Securities Watchdog Chained by Limited Staff," *Nikkei Weekly*, August 2, 1993, p. 2.

18. Magdich, "The Failure of Financial Market Regulators," p. 29.

19. Ibid., p. 35.

20. Leon Hollerman, *Japan Disincorporated* (Hoover Institution Press, 1988).

21. Eamonn Fingleton, *Blindside: Why Japan Is Still on Track to Overtake the U.S. by the Year 2000* (Houghton Mifflin, 1995), p.157.

22. Michio Uchida, "The Iron Triangle: Bureaucrats, Businessmen and Politicians at the Core of Corruption," *Tokyo Business Today*, November 1993, p.7.

23. Kisei Kanwa Kenkyukai, *Kisei kanwa de Nihon ga kawaru* (Through deregulation Japan will change) (Tokyo: Japan Times, 1994).

24. See, for example, Yayama Taro, *Kanryo bokokuron* (Bureaucrats ruin the country) (Tokyo: Shinchosha, 1993).

25. Mark Tilton, "Informal Industry Governance in Japan's Basic Materials Industries," *International Organization*, vol. 48 (Autumn 1994), pp. 663–85. See also Tilton, "Why the 1991–1992 Anti-monopoly Law Reforms Have Not Curbed Japan's Cartels," paper presented at the annual meeting of the Association for Asian Studies, 1995.

26. Edward Barry Keehn, "Managing Interests Inside Japanese Bureaucracy: Informality and Discretion," *Asian Survey*, November 1990, pp. 1021–37.

27. Philip Selznick, *The Organizational Weapon: A Study of Bolshevik Strategy and Tactics* (Glencoe, Ill.: Free Press, 1960).

28. This was a development that rapidly disappeared from sight. See "Ministry to Set Up Watchdog," *Nikkei Weekly*, November 8, 1993, p. 2.

29. The full text of the press release is as follows:
SECURITIES AND EXCHANGE SURVEILLANCE COMMISSION
Press Release   July 15, 1997

The Securities and Exchange Surveillance Commission (SESC) conducted the investigation of Nomura Securities Co. (Nomura) on the charge of loss compensation that is prohibited by Securities and Exchange Law (SEL), and found legal violations and improper activities described below.

The SESC sent recommendation to the Minister of Finance to take disciplinary action against Nomura and other appropriate measures, pursuant to Article 19 (1) of Ministry of Finance Establishment Law on July 15, 1997.

1. Providing property gains to compensate for losses

Nomura, by involvement of the president, two board members, and a director of the division, for the purpose of compensating for a part of a customer's losses incurred in securities trading, offered to the customer:

1) approximately yen 47,500,000 in total by disguising its own five equity-buying transactions between January 1995 and July 1995 as the customer's transactions;

2) approximately yen 2,200,000 in March 1995, by disguising as if the customer had bought the profitable warrants which Nomura held on its own account at the old price and repurchasing them immediately at the current price on Nomura's own account; and

3) yen 320,000,000 in March 1995 by providing that amount of cash.

(violation of SEL 50-3<1>(3))

2. Entering into an agreement to make discretionary trading account

From February 1989 to July 1996, Nomura entered into agreements with the customer that gave Nomura discretionary powers for aspects of share trading transactions to decide, without consulting the customer, whether to purchase or sell, shares issued, number of shares and prices, and executed the customer's order based on this agreement. Making such contracts after January 1992 violates SEL Article50 <1>(3).

3. Problems with internal controls

The SESC recognized the following problems with Nomura's internal controls underlying legal violations mentioned above:

1) In providing loss compensation and executing discretionary trading, officers and employees in several divisions were involved in such improper activities as making false order slips;

2) The officers responsible for internal controls and business activities in relevant divisions failed to properly recognize long-lasting and frequent discretionary trading account transactions, and to give proper direction and supervision concerning customer management. The Compliance and Guidance Department at Nomura did not adopt appropriate measures as well; and

3) In the SESC's investigation, the officers in the trading compliance and administration department, whose responsibility was to investigate questionable transactions, along with the officials and employees involved in the loss compensation, did inappropriate operations so that the truth would not be easily revealed.

The SESC thus recognized that the officers and employees involved in such improper activities were not mindful of compliance with laws and rules at all, and that there was serious defect with [the] internal control system of Nomura.

30. Jon Choy, *JEI* (*Japan Economic Institute*) *Report*, no. 29B, August 1, 1997, p. 3.

31. "Nikko President, Too, Is Likely to Step Down over Koike Affair," *Japan Daily Digest*, September 22, 1997.

32. *JEI Report*, no. 24B, June 27, 1997.

33. Sakaiya Taichi, "Kanryo no shinwa" (Bureaucratic myths), *Bungei Shunju*, vol. 72 (February 1994), p.157.

34. Kenneth S. Courtis, "Japan Comes Roaring Back," *Japan Times*, April 11, 1997.

CHAPTER FOURTEEN

Japan's Financial System

Christopher Wood

JAPAN'S FINANCIAL CRISIS has continued to rumble on long after the speculative bubble burst at the beginning of the 1990s. True, the perils of Japanese finance no longer seem as dramatic as they once did. The world has become used to the spectacle of Japanese banks weighed down by bad debts, which for the most part they still do not want to own up to. It is also used to a Nikkei index whose performance has remained decidedly lackluster. There is growing understanding, however, that the authorities' continuing interventionist efforts to prevent a greater financial crisis, by the application of various Band Aids and numerous acts of expediency, have had unfortunate ramifications throughout this period. For their actions have inhibited the financing of the entire economy.

It is likely that Japan's financial crisis reached its nadir in August 1992, when the Nikkei index plunged to near the 14,000 level, some 60 percent below its all-time high. At this shrunken level the integrity of the financial system itself was in question, since many major banks and also many major life insurance companies had by then no capital gains left on their long-term share holdings. This mattered for the banks because the capital gains they held on these long-term share holdings were about their only effective buffer against bad debts given their then still minimal level of loan-loss reserves. Japan's banks, which just a few years before had seemed poised to take over the world, were suddenly left wondering where all their money had gone.

The disappearance of capital gains was equally as life-threatening for the life insurers, Japan's other financial behemoths, for their solvency

220

was also suddenly put into question. Since 1945 Japan's life insurance companies have always paid policyholders out of cash flow. Money flowing into the general account has always exceeded the money paid out. Much slower growth in assets and net new business, combined with too-generous guaranteed payoffs made during a period of higher interest rates, have now undermined this once cozy arrangement. Hence the growing fears prompted by the stock market's slump that life insurers would be forced into massive selling of securities to meet policyholders' claims. Yet as their capital gains vanished, so did their buttress against just such an emergency.

The Japanese government averted this late summer crisis, which attracted worldwide headlines, with an official support plan to inject public sector funds into the stock market. In late September of 1992 a total of ¥1.7 trillion of beneficiaries' money held in public sector savings institutions was handed over to institutional investors, principally trust banks, to invest in shares. The funds came from the postal insurance fund, the postal savings fund, and the national pension system which is also run through the post office. A further ¥1.1 trillion was released in November. The trust banks, emboldened by considerable political prodding, were given every incentive to invest in shares. Rather than meet an annual performance target as is usual, they were given five years in which to earn an average annual return of 5.5 percent. This means their investment performance will not be measured until September 1997 by when, it is hoped, the bear market will be a distant (though no doubt still painful) memory.

Thus began the Japanese government's naked intervention in its own stock market. It was to have longer-lasting consequences than the Ministry of Finance bureaucrats who devised it as a temporary expedient could ever have imagined. Stockbrokers were quick to give the official stock market support operation a catchy name. They called it the PKO (price-keeping operation), a term borrowed from Japan's peacekeeping operation in Cambodia conducted under the United Nations umbrella. The exercise's initial apparent success at putting a floor under the stock market soon encouraged the ever-meddling officials to allocate more funds to the effort. Thus, for the fiscal year that began in March 1993, a further ¥6.6 trillion was allocated to the support operation. However, precisely how much public sector money was being spent propping up share prices was, initially at least, beside the point. For investors were increasingly prepared to assume the government had underwritten the market until such time as a genuine earnings rebound occurred as a result of a recovering economy, which would justify the stock market's then still extremely lofty level of valuation in terms of a price-earnings ratio around ninety times prospective earnings. So, confident in their belief that the government would not countenance a stock market decline, investors began buying shares again. The bureaucrats had seemingly created a virtuous circle.

The stock market support operation was also accompanied by a veritable blizzard of administrative guidance, since the bureaucrats in the interventionist Ministry of Finance were determined to leave nothing to chance in their efforts to prevent further financial distress. There was a frenzy of improvisation to plug all possible holes before the conclusion of the financial year that ended in March 1993. This is the key date in the Japanese corporate calendar because it is when balance sheets are drawn up and capital ratios are fixed. A case in point is when the life insurance companies were told by the Finance Ministry in January 1993 that they could use unrealized capital gains to pay dividends to policyholders that year. This amounted to a temporary revision of Japan's insurance law, which states that life insurers can only pay policyholders out of income, not capital gains. Clearly, paying dividends out of only paper capital gains that could disappear should share prices subsequently fall seems extraordinarily imprudent.

The direct rigging of the stock market, the increasingly prevalent attempt to use administrative guidance techniques such as arbitrary changes in accounting rules to prevent shares being sold at a loss or underwater investments being made market to market, combined with increasingly absurd attempts to regulate the futures markets, all formed part of the same trend. This was an increasingly overt attempt by the Ministry of Finance to reregulate. The direction of policy was in direct contrast to the process of gradual deregulation, which had been under way in the 1980s, particularly in the area of liberalizing interest rates.

By the middle of 1993 the mandarins at the Finance Ministry had begun, prematurely, to gloat. After presiding since 1990 over a series of humiliating banking and securities scandals, which had occurred on their own watch, not to mention deeply shaming (in the Japanese context) policy errors, they had begun to feel vindicated again. They were being lauded for rescuing the Japanese stock market by ordering public sector savings institutions to buy Japanese shares. This was all grist to the mill to those foreign observers of Japan who like to argue that Japan has been so successful because it works by different rules than does the West. Administrative guidance was back with a vengeance, they asserted approvingly. And officialdom showed disturbing signs of believing the flatterers. It was to prove a Pyrrhic victory, for the celebrations were far too premature.

The Ministry of Finance had in fact made a major error in its crude support operation. For it assumed, wrongly, that the most effective way out of Japan's troubles was to indulge in what is anyway its strongest instinct. That is to reregulate everything, a process that also has the benefit of consolidating the ministry's own power. It was to become increasingly obvious that this was precisely the direction in which the ministry was heading again. The Finance Ministry had been intent on retaining a degree of centralized bureaucratic control wholly inconsistent with what is normally implied by the term deregulation. As a result, Japan still risks being saddled with the same primitive financial services industry that created the late 1980s boom-bust cycle in the first place. That is an industry with a nannylike dependence on bureaucratic guidelines and where clear winners and losers are not allowed to emerge as they have, say, in Japan's auto and electronics industries. That in turn will lead to a continuing lack of product innovation and a further loss of competitiveness. Japanese banks and securities firms remain far behind their American and even European counterparts. As a consequence, capital will continue to be allocated inefficiently in Japan; and risk will be measured badly if at all. Regulatory overkill explains why Japan still has no efficient corporate bond market though it desperately needs one since the banks want now to lend only to those with the safest credit, while the stock market has for the most part remained virtually closed to new equity issues during the period since early 1990 because of officialdom's concern that added supply would further depress share prices. Stifling regulation and traditional hidebound attitudes also explain why Japan has not yet properly exploited securitization, an available technology, which, as America's example in the early 1990s has shown, has the potential to alleviate at least some of the distress in Japan's property market.

The detrimental consequences of this policy bias are clear from a closer look at the way the PKO operation has worked in practice. The PKO's main feature has been the use of public funds to buy the stock market. Its other notable feature is that it does not officially exist. Still Andrew Smithers, a London-based investment strategist with long experience of analyzing the Japanese market, reckons that the direct support given to the stock market has been running at around ¥5.7 trillion annually.[1] He derives this figure by taking 70 percent of the funds allocated for portfolio investment through the extremely important but little understood Fiscal Investment and Loan Program (FILP). The FILP is essentially a device for rechanneling the excess savings of the Japanese public for the purpose of running a government-funded financing plan. Its main element consists of the long-term lending of funds that have accumulated in the Finance Ministry's trust fund bureau. This shadowy entity manages up to ¥300 trillion of public sector funds including the ¥200-odd trillion deposited in the giant piggy bank that is Japan's postal savings system, as well as the surpluses accumulated in the state's insurance and pension plans. In this sense the Japanese government has ready access to a huge amount of cash as a result of the public sector running its own financial services businesses, which compete directly, of course, with banks and insurance companies in the private sector. It is also from this cash hoard that the PKO was sprung. Never mind if the members of the public who had entrusted their savings to public sector savings schemes in the first place did not want this nest egg invested in the stock market.

The PKO definitely had the effect of keeping the stock market at a higher level than it would otherwise have been. As a result, prices have not been allowed to clear. This has prevented companies from issuing new equity since prices have not been allowed to decline to levels at which investors are happy to buy the shares, knowing that they are not doing so at an artificially supported price. Smithers argues cogently that holding up the market at unrealistic levels and thus limiting the supply of new issues is turning out to be a cure that may be worse than the disease.[2] For the constraint that is put on new equity issues severely restricts the banks from raising new equity capital. Yet the issuance of more equity would make the banks' capital ratios less vulnerable to stock market fluctuations. The same point applies to other sorts of companies, many of which are undercapitalized. Thus, as late as the summer of 1996, Japanese banks were still having problems raising badly needed equity. The life insurers shocked Japan when they let it be known, via a public statement, that they were not prepared to buy proposed Japanese bank-preferred issues because they knew the equity would only be used to fill the hole left by bad debts. The implication of their statement was that the banks should shrink their assets rather than raise more equity.

So, the life insurers, the largest owners of Japanese bank shares, have clearly had enough. In all, the Japanese banks will try to raise about ¥3 trillion of badly needed equity during the next year. They may find it easier to sell their shares to foreign investors, rather than domestic players, since foreigners have remained net buyers of equities throughout the bear market, doubling their ownership of Japanese shares in the process. The reasons for this sustained *gaijin* optimism are hard to fathom, though their buying has kept the Nikkei higher than it would otherwise have been.

The key point then about the PKO is that it kept share prices at artificial levels. This is reflected in the demonstrable failure of the stock market to provide risk capital at current prices. This in turn is aggravating an existing problem, which is that Japanese companies tend to have too much debt and too little equity. As long as the stock market is not really functioning properly as a capital-raising vehicle, which is after all its primary *raison d'être*, that problem can only get worse.

Still the PKO has one positive virtue. It shows clearly that Japanese government policy has been quite simply to get the stock market up and, above all, to do whatever it took to prevent it from falling again. This is positive in a perverse sort of sense because it shows a greater awareness of and respect for market forces by the bureaucracy. For the stock market is now no longer disdained as a vulgar casino not worthy of attention, the traditional mandarin attitude at both the Ministry of Finance and the Bank of Japan. Evidence of the official change in attitude came with the publication in February 1993 of a Bank of Japan special paper titled "Functions of Stock Markets: Implications for Corporate Financial Activities." The message from this report is that officialdom has been humbled at the savagery of market forces as reflected in the Nikkei's extended slump. The conclusion is that market moves can have broader rnacroeconomic consequences. The Japanese government's bet with the PKO seems to have been that by rigging the stock market it could improve sentiment sufficiently to lure in enough suckers, in particular foreign investors, to pull off the same sort of giant debt-for-equity swap that occurred in America in the early 1990s when a rising American stock market allowed many undercapitalized banks and other companies to rebuild their capital base by raising equity. Sadly for Japan this approach has not worked.

The continuing bear market is one reason why Japanese banks continue to remain under financial pressure more than six years after the bubble first burst. Another culprit is the way the banks' bad debt problems are being addressed or rather not addressed. Problem debts stemming from the burst bubble probably totaled some ¥100 trillion, though not all of these rest with the banks. The agricultural credit cooperatives, to give just one example, have lots of questionable debts, the extent of which the world may never know about because of the extreme political sensitivities involved. The agricultural lobby still wields great political power. Japan's bad-debt problem has always been more serious than in the West because Japanese banks have had, by international standards, minute loan-loss reserves to set aside against bad debts beyond a mandatory reserve or 0.3 percent of total loans. There are two historic reasons for this. First, there has been almost no tax incentive for Japanese banks to reserve against their problem loans since the tax authorities traditionally have only allowed a bank to make such a reserve and deduct against its taxable income where the borrower is declared officially insolvent. The banks, it should be noted, have long been Japan's biggest taxpayers. Second, loan-loss reserves were considered unnecessary because banks regarded the capital gains on their long-term share holdings, their so-called hidden reserves, as their effective loan-loss reserves. Needless to say, as these gains shrank in size with the stock market's decline, so did the banks' ability to withstand the impact of bad debts reduced.

So the debt problem represents a formidable challenge to a system that no longer really works. Sumitomo Bank became the first Japanese bank to declare a loss in fifty years when it made a ¥800 million provision for bad loans in 1995. This action marked at the time a precedent. Sumitomo could afford it, though it is worth noting that Sumitomo had only ¥1.2 trillion in unrealized gains on its long-term share holdings as of the end of September 1994. Other banks duly followed Sumitomo's example after it had broken the mold. In the financial year to March 31, 1996, more than a dozen of Japan's biggest lenders announced losses that enabled them to write off a total of ¥10 trillion of bad loans.

The hitherto longstanding reluctance of Japanese banks to declare a loss reflected political as well as financial pressures. Unlike in America, Japan has no organized hierarchy of independent bank examiners. Nor has it been acceptable public policy to spend taxpayers' money bailing out banks as American taxpayers, however reluctantly, accepted the need to pay for the savings and loan disaster to prevent an outright depression. And clearly if American depositors in these thrift institutions and similarly insolvent banks had seen their savings wiped out, there would have been just such a deflationary debacle.

The result in Japan has been a continuing official reluctance to own up to the size of the bad-debt problem. Instead the preferred course has been to try to hide it in the hope that the problem will eventually correct itself. It should be noted that this is the exact opposite of the American strategy. In dealing with banks' bad debts, most of them property-related, during the early 1990s American banks were encouraged and even compelled by zealous regulators, burned badly by the savings and loan disaster, to reserve aggressively against their questionable property loans as soon as possible in a proactive attempt to force banks to recognize reality and start working their way out of their problems. This approach worked remarkably well considering the scale of the problem. In Japan, a country that culturally prefers the opaque over the transparent, there has been no such initiative. Instead there is a continuing collective attempt on nearly all sides to pretend the losses never happened.

Consequently, a big, formal, taxpayer-financed bailout of the banking system remains unlikely. Instead the way the problem has been dealt with so far has involved a form of surreptitious taxpayer-financed bailout that the ordinary Japanese citizen may never know about. This bailout has primarily taken the form of debt restructurings in which bank lenders have reduced the interest rate charged to troubled lenders to the level of the official discount rate (1.75 percent by September 1993) or even lower, and therefore below the cost of what the banks themselves pay for funding. This has not been quite as painful for banks' operating profits as might be thought because the Finance Ministry agreed in late 1992 to let banks subtract from their taxable income the difference between the interest received on such concessionary loans and the cost to the banks of funding them. The growing popularity of deals involving interest-rate concessions soon became clear. Loans at the official discount rate or less were growing in early 1993 at a rate of 50 percent per annum though admittedly from a low base. By contrast, total bank loans were barely growing at all.

Clearly there can be no guarantee that the principal amount owed will ever be recovered in full in the case of borrowers for whom interest rate concessions have been granted. Still the Finance Ministry has been fully behind the strategy despite the obvious risks. Its intentions seem clear. First and foremost it has wanted to buy time in the hope that over, say, a ten-year period the debt problem will right itself, thanks to a combination of inflation and economic growth. Second, to encourage banks to write loans off would quickly unmask glaring qualitative differences among Japanese banks. The result would be to shed a degree of daylight on the differing credit quality of Japanese banks, which the Ministry of Finance would probably be most unhappy about. For officialdom continues to dislike in principle the idea of conspicuous winners and losers in the supposedly deregulated banking industry over which it presides. Far better the traditional convoy approach to banking, which at least suggests the bureaucrats are still in charge. The unmasking of losers would also cause the public to focus more on the Finance Ministry's own responsibility for the bad debt mess.

For similar reasons of cover-up it has always been naive to expect to learn the real truth in terms of the scale of the bad debt problem. Take as an example what happened when the banks disclosed for the first time ever their level of bad debts at the same time as they announced their final results for the financial year that ended in March 1993. Their discretion as to what to report was deliberately made immense. Bad debts were defined for this purpose as loans to bankrupt companies or loans on which interest had not been paid for six months. But banks did not have to include loans on which interest-rate concessions had been granted nor loans sold to the Soviet-sounding Cooperative Credit Purchasing Corporation. This entity was the then recently established bank-owned loan-liquidation vehicle. It worked as follows: banks bought their own distressed loans with their own money and paid themselves interest. The only merit in this classic fudging exercise for the banks, aside from not having to report as bad the loans thus "sold," was to be able to deduct for tax purposes any loss incurred selling loans to the loan liquidation company at a discount to their face value. The aim of this essentially warehousing exercise was again clear: to prevent loan write-offs and dumping of real-estate collateral in the hope that the passage of time and inflation would eventually cause the problem to go away. Meanwhile the Cooperative Credit Purchasing Cooperation's role was to buy loans and not property itself, unlike the land-buying company originally proposed by the Finance Ministry in the autumn of 1992 in the heat of the stock market crisis, because there were too many unresolved disputes about which lender had first claim on collateral sometimes pledged many times over. The company was also to be financed by the banks themselves and not by the government, as originally proposed, because the politicians dared not admit to the public the need for a taxpayer bailout. Thus, when the Bank of Japan announced in December 1994 that it would go halves with private banks by contributing public money to a proposed ¥40 billion bailout of two bankrupt credit cooperatives, there was such a public outcry that the whole deal had to be called off. The row was fueled by the disclosure that the two busted financial institutions had made a large number of loans to politicians. This episode has, as a consequence, severely inhibited the authorities' ability to use taxpayer money to reliquefy the banking system. The same was true in early 1996 with the public row that broke out over the proposed taxpayer bailout of the agricultural cooperates, known as *jusen*. The remarkable point to this observer was that the authorities had succeeded in keeping the lid on the *jusen* issue for so long in terms of concealing the extent of the financial problem.

The pretense that the problems do not exist has been the essence of Japanese strategy for dealing with its deluge of bad debts. This policy has one major macroeconomic problem with it. Japanese banks have been given every incentive, via the tax deductions offered on concessionary lending, to keep financing deadbeat creditors In contrast, a policy of encouraging more aggressive reserving against dud loans would enable banks to relend funds thus freed up to healthier firms that can better contribute to renewed economic growth. Outstanding loans by Japan's big commercial banks (known as city banks) to the property sector increased by 8.8 percent in the year to March 1993. This hardly seemed healthy at a time when city banks' total ending during the same period grew by just 0.3 percent. Loan growth has continued to be anemic ever since, despite an apparent cyclical economic recovery. The banking system, like the stock market, is not really working as it is meant to. The system is literally gummed up. Instead the major stimulus to economic recovery in recent years has been heavy fiscal pump priming. So intense has this been that Japan's fiscal deficit rose to almost 5 percent of GDP in 1996, considerably higher than America's.

The still unhealthy state of Japanese finance has naturally caused domestic criticism of the once august Ministry of Finance to grow. There has been increasing debate that the ministry is too powerful and that it should be broken up into the component parts that are its different bureaus. This sort of dramatic radical action still seems unlikely in the Japanese context. Still it should not be discounted. The message of recent years in Japan is that seemingly impossible things can and do happen. Few would have predicted the collapse in land prices or for that matter the Liberal Democratic Party's loss of power, even though it was only temporary. Similarly, a humbling of the bureaucracy is no longer out of the question. The only issue is perhaps what form this will take. It is already clear that the Finance Ministry has already lost a huge amount of prestige as a result of the trauma of recent years. In terms of the stock market, the banking system, or indeed the economy in general, it has consistently, since 1990, underestimated the gravity of the problems. As a result, those in the private sector who believed what the bureaucrats were telling them and acted accordingly have been badly misled. In this sense administrative guidance has been dealt a painful if not yet fatal blow. True, the banks will eventually crawl their way out of their problems and the Nikkei will one day touch 40,000 again, though that happy day will probably not be until well into the next century. But in the more immediate future Japan, and in particular its bureaucratic establishment, has received a humbling lesson in the laws of economic gravity. And the class has not ended yet.

Notes

1. *The Japanese Market: Government Support versus Corporate Liquidity,* research report (London: Smithers and Company, 1994).
2. Ibid.

CHAPTER FIFTEEN

Two Years after the Kobe Earthquake

Edith Terry

SATURDAY NIGHT, January 21, 1995. Five days before, Japan's worst natural disaster in decades ripped through the bustling port city of Kobe, killing 6,425 people. In a smoke-filled, unheated room in Kobe's city hall, a glassy-eyed official is doing his best to convince reporters that the local government is firmly in control. "Because we are all Japanese, we help each other," says Manabu Shinya. "There are no homeless in this earthquake."

Shinya was wrong. Downstairs in City Hall, hundreds of refugees from the giant earthquake were bedded down on cold stone floors in the brightly lit lobby of the building. These were the lucky ones. Outside, in darkened city parks and school courtyards, 300,000 newly homeless people huddled in tents or crowded into school gyms and auditoriums. Although they did not know it then, many would still be homeless two years later.

"This industrial port city of 1.5 million people now possesses the half-realism of a Hollywood back lot," wrote Michael Zielenziger, a correspondent for the *San Jose Mercury News* after a visit in January 1997. "Freshly paved main streets beckon with gleaming high-rises and neon-bright department stores. Pedestrians walk briskly through the commercial heart, their packages and briefcases held tightly in the January cold. Yet just a block or two behind the downtown facades, bleak, vacant and mutilated neighborhoods struggle to find a future."[1]

In the spring of 1997, according to official government estimates,

231

some 70,000 people were still living in temporary housing, including 47,000 in remodeled shipping containers. At the time of the quake's second anniversary, more than 200 people were still camping out in the original crude tents that had been set up immediately after the earthquake.[2] Kobe not only had homeless people; it was a city of the homeless. Over two years, 121 died as a result of exposure in these shelters.[3] And while Kobe's citizens faced the disaster and its immediate aftermath with resolute courage, the bureaucratic bungling of the last two years has torn at their souls.

Prior to the Kobe earthquake, the Japanese maintained a consistent, if uneasy, reverence for their leaders. The 1991 Persian Gulf War witnessed similar scenes of political and bureaucratic disarray, but the crisis that provoked them was far away. The aftermath to Kobe shredded the previously seamless fiction of a powerful, benevolent, and all-wise bureaucracy. Poor planning and abysmal lack of preparation moved Kobe from the category of tragic natural disaster to that of preventable human catastrophe.

It is not a lesson that any who lived through the earthquake can easily forget. And its message has been reinforced by the series of scandals and disasters that have dogged Japan's elite bureaucrats and disorganized politicians ever since—from the incompetent handling of the Aum Shinrikyo cult's depredations to the Ministry of Health cover-up in the import of tainted blood products.

Japanese trust for its postwar leadership structure is at a low ebb, contributing to a deepening sense of social crisis. And this downward slide began in the confused first days after Kobe. "I feel strongly that since the (Kobe) earthquake, things are going in the wrong direction," Rokusuke Ei, a songwriter, told a Japanese concert audience early in 1997.[4] Many Japanese agree. Says Isao Nakauchi, chairman of Daiei, Inc., a major retailer based in Kobe, "In emergencies like this quake, someone must exert leadership, but today's Japan is a country where no one dares to take responsibility."[5]

To many observers, the political paralysis, bureaucratic turf wars, self-deception, and sheer chaos that followed the Kobe earthquake were signs of the bankruptcy of the post–World War II Japanese political economy. Hobart Rowen, the late, influential columnist for the *Washington Post*, speculated that public reaction to the earthquake might generate Japan's first consumer revolt against its producer-tilted society. His reasoning: The same problems that blocked relief for Kobe's victims also kept Japanese consumers from receiving the benefits of national prosperity. Surely, Rowen argued, popular revulsion with the botched relief effort in Kobe would spill over into an up-swelling demand for cheap imports, better public services, and drastic deregulation.

Such heady talk was common in the first weeks and months after the disaster. But much as the asbestos clouds that hung over Kobe for months finally settled, so did talk of revolution. Instead of weakening the powers of bureaucrats, or generating the spontaneous emission of obsolete regulation, Kobe created a whole new bureaucratic subindustry—little of which was to the good of the supposedly nonexistent tens of thousands rendered homeless by the earthquake.

The immediate impact of the tragedy was threefold, and in the best tradition of Japanese industrial policy. First, the bureaucracy promised to scrutinize earthquake safety and civil disaster rules, that is, to add to regulations for disaster relief. Second, the government would establish a new set of procedures to involve the central government directly in disaster relief—which would also have the effect of strengthening bureaucratic control. Third, Tokyo announced a 1.4 trillion yen reconstruction program (worth $11.6 billion in 1997 dollars) to put the city back to work.

Such a regulatory crackdown is the natural response of a government accustomed to defining its role in terms of micromanagement. The Kobe earthquake left the bureaucracy in a down but not out position. Nor did it provoke the out-and-out consumer outrage predicted by Hobart Rowen. Japanese consumers, indeed, were depressed, but failed to summon energy to demand change.

There was, however, one positive outcome of the public outcry after the earthquake, and this positive outcome also served to advance the Japanese debate over *kisei kanwa*, or regulatory easing.

This positive outcome was the new idea that the elected head of government should take charge in a national crisis. This idea has gained firm support despite the cynicism of the postwar generation toward politics generally.

Then–prime minister Tomiichi Murayama did not take charge in Kobe. Murayama dithered for hours, refusing to make changes in his daily schedule, even though the visual evidence from scores of television helicopters and camera crews on the ground gave vivid evidence of the scope of the disaster. He waited twenty-two hours to send troops into the city to help search for victims. Murayama followed Japanese tradi-

tion—indeed, Japanese law—in ceding crisis management to the bureaucracy. The bureaucracy was virtually on its own in managing the
crisis, and as a result, hundreds and perhaps thousands of lives were lost
unnecessarily.

The government is unable to declare a "state of emergency" in Japan,
and there is no federal disaster agency. Any involvement of Japan's
euphemism-clad military in civilian affairs is politically sensitive (under article 9 of its constitution, Japan can only engage in military acts in
the event of an invasion or other attack; taboos against the military are
so strong that officers doff their military attire before leaving the pre-
cincts of "self-defense" agencies or bases).

In other countries, particularly the United States, a central command
structure for crisis control is taken for granted. In Japan, it is not. This is
in part because of the history of militarism in Japan, which left many
local authorities opposed to using Japan's Self-Defense Forces for disaster relief. It is also due to the reluctance on the part of local jurisdic-
tions to sacrifice control. The calamity of Kobe, however, left the
bureaucracy with little choice other than to cede some of its powers to
political leaders.

Why this is so has to do with the Japanese bureaucracy's central weakness—the tendency of officials to identify with the interest of their agencies, not with the national interest. Writes Glen Fukushima, a former
American trade official and vice president of the American Chamber of
Commerce in Japan, "What one saw (during the Kobe earthquake) was
tatewari gyosei ('vertical administration,' where agencies jealousy guard
their turf and refuse to cooperate with each other) at its worst."[6]

To take a few examples:

Refusal of foreign help. The reluctance of Japanese authorities to accept
foreign assistance stunned the world. Initially, the Japanese Foreign
Ministry turned down all but two offers of help from abroad. The United
States, for instance, offered to make available the resources of the Sev-
enth Fleet for emergency relief. The Japanese Foreign Ministry grudg-
ingly accepted seventy-eight large tents and a supply of 50,000 blankets
from its closest ally. It took two days for the Japanese government to
give the go-ahead to Switzerland, a less-close ally, to send a thirty-per-
son team with twelve search-and-rescue dogs. When the team with dogs
arrived in Japan, immigration authorities insisted on applying quaran-

tine rules to the dogs despite the urgent need to pull victims out of the wreckage.

The Japanese government eventually accepted thirty-six out of seventy offers of assistance from countries around the world. Nonetheless, the impression remained that national pride came before human welfare.[7] Explained Tadashi Ikeda, deputy vice minister of foreign affairs, "When accepting assistance, it is necessary first to identify the actual needs of the devastated area. We also have to ensure that the local set-up, including transportation arrangements, is in place, in order to carry out rescue operations smoothly. Each time a foreign country makes an offer of help, we contact local authorities to find out their needs as well as their preparedness to accept assistance, and then decide in the order of the most urgent requirements."[8]

What Ikeda failed to mention was that the earthquake had knocked out major communications lines, including lines to computers tracking the quake near its epicenter. Many privately organized foreign volunteers elected to make their way to Kobe on their own. Countries like France and Greece that had offered medical teams waited days for a response or were turned down.

Timid senior officials. From Prime Minister Tomiichi Murayama to General Yuzo Matsushima, commander of the Chubu District Army in central Japan, officials showed extraordinary respect for bureaucratic protocol in a situation that clearly called for risk-taking. The prime minister himself was a model of bureaucratic courtesy. Murayama was not flustered. He delegated the problem to the National Land Agency, which has titular authority over natural disasters. The Land Agency's powers are largely on paper, however. They do not include any system for gathering information in times of crisis or any direct authority over the Self-Defense Forces (SDF).

For the rest of the day on January 17, 1995, Murayama carried on business as usual. He canceled only one appointment, with a local official from Kagoshima Prefecture and his two female staff members.[9] Even the South Koreans reacted more swiftly. While the Japanese prime minister dozed, South Korean Prime Minister Lee Hong Gu was recommending relief measures. The Korean decision came two hours before the Japanese held their first cabinet meeting on the quake. [10]

General Matsushima also took the easy way out, leaning on rules that justified inaction. Rules give SDF units jurisdiction for relief work in designated areas, or *taiku*. At the time of the earthquake, there were about 1,500 SDF troops already in Hyogo Prefecture. General Matsushima waited twenty-one hours before calling for reinforcements. By the time he did so, the known death toll had already reached 2,000. Eventually the SDF deployed about 20,000 troops.[11]

Insular local authorities. A political factor underlying the botching of the relief effort was the reluctance of the left-center Japanese Socialist Party and Communist Party members to have any dealings with the Japanese military. Unfortunately, key politicians in charge in Tokyo and Kobe at the time of the quake were either Socialist or Communist Party members. Both Hyogo Prefecture Governor Toshitami Kaihara and Kobe Mayor Yukitoshi Sasayama had a long history of poor relations with the SDF prior to the disaster. Every year, the SDF participates in earthquake drills in every Japanese prefecture. In Hyogo, however, actual communication between the prefecture police and the SDF amounted to little more than sitting next to each other on review stands. The more than arms-length relationship proved a poor foundation for emergency operations when a real catastrophe struck.

In the first weeks after the disaster, citizens of Kobe were convinced that politics accounted for Governor Kaihara's excruciating delay in seeking emergency relief from the SDF. Kaihara waited two hours before accepting an offer of help from the nearest SDF station at Himeji. The earthquake occurred at 5:46 A.M. on January 17. It was more than six hours, around 1 o'clock in the afternoon, before the first SDF troops arrived on the scene.

Among the more graphic signs of the antimilitary prejudice is a prohibition against the use of sirens on emergency vehicles. This is a matter more of custom and discretion than of regulation and stems from the association of sirens with Japanese military despotism in the 1930s and 1940s. The consequence is that emergency vehicles became locked in the long traffic lines they were meant to dispel.

As they arrived on the scene under the glare of television cameras, the prefectural police and SDF forces appeared to have little idea how to focus their resources. Lacking both training and adequate intelligence on the scope of destruction, the rescuers wandered aimlessly or busied themselves with pointless tasks. In one such episode on January 18, about two dozen riot police ringed a landslide site where bodies were being removed, apparently with no other purpose than to prevent television crews from filming the scene. Meanwhile, soldiers refused aid to victims crying for help if they were outside their assigned sectors.

The governor excused himself by blaming the delays on complicated procedures for requesting SDF assistance. Under article 83 of the Self-Defense Forces Law, a request for emergency assistance must provide an explanation of the disaster, offer reasons for requiring SDF assistance, specify where the troops should go and how long they should stay, and provide details on the number of personnel, vehicles, ships, and aircraft needed.[12]

Local jurisdiction conflicts. Foreign volunteers were not alone in getting a brush-off from local authorities. In the first few days after the earthquake, Japanese medical and other volunteers also learned the hard way that Kobe was less than eager for their help. The rule for emergency medical relief is similar to that for dispatch of SDF forces. The prefectural governor must first issue a request for assistance.[13]

Harried Kobe officials told Japanese medical personnel from outside the prefecture who applied as volunteers to wait until they were contacted. The contacts never came. Inexplicably, the same officials initially turned down an offer of temporary shelter for victims from nearby Osaka. Here, civic pride seemed to be the key point. The Kobe officials claimed they could handle the situation on their own.

Such hubris quickly collapsed. By the day after the earthquake, the shortage of doctors and nurses was so acute that Kobe officials were telling volunteers to come ahead even without the paperwork. By the weekend after the earthquake, volunteers flooding the city had created a new problem. Without any clear distribution system, donations quickly piled up in holding centers. Office clerks, housewives, backpackers, and salary men, moved by Kobe's plight, jammed transportation links into the city. The supplies they brought with them ranged from bottled water to prettily wrapped boxes of tea cakes.[14]

Bureaucratic wrangling made a bad situation worse, but the general panic after the earthquake saw few cool heads. As a nation and the world watched in horror, fires spread relentlessly through the downtown area of Nagata on the afternoon and evening of January 17. Many of the fires were caused by gas leaks from a system that was not shut down until six hours after the quake hit. With most road and rail transportation damaged beyond use, refugees leaving the city and emergency supplies coming in were forced onto the two highways that remained open. The result was 20 kilometers of gridlock. Even after a traffic control system was set up using stickers for authorized vehicles, moving in and out of Kobe by surface transportation was nightmarish.[15]

A Legacy of Bureaucratic Incompetence

As the Kobe earthquake recedes into history, news teams show up only for anniversaries of the disaster. Other scandals, other disasters, in too great profusion, have superseded the problems of Kobe. Yet the problems live on, and many of them have been evident from the start.

Kobe is likely to be a city of the homeless and of temporary shelters for many years to come. The earthquake and fires destroyed some 150,000 homes, but city authorities built only 40,000 temporary shelters, many of them on public lands distant from the city. In mid-February 1995, 60,000 people applied for the first 2,021 temporary housing units and 680 public dwellings made available by the prefecture.[16]

Then word got out of the inconvenience and discomfort of many of the facilities. By May 1995, the government had awarded 10,000 temporary shelters to refugees by lottery, but people were not moving in. Said Sojiro Kawamura, founder of the Hyogo Earthquake Victims Network, "We ask for the government's assistance, but they do nothing. They don't even want to help us out—they just want all of us refugees to go somewhere else so they can build a big downtown with lots of fancy shops."[17]

It took eighteen months for the government to decide how to distribute some U.S.$1.6 billion in donations and relief supplies. The favored methods were lotteries and the long-established practice of *risai shomei*, a document that certifies that the bearer has suffered damage in a large-scale natural disaster.

Victims have to produce *risai shomei* in order to receive tax relief, cheap home loans, medical coverage, or any other of the benefits that have been legislated for them. The system is, of course, intended to prevent fraud. But it also takes time to complete the application procedures, which include a visual inspection of damage by officials. The often lengthy wait has been one more factor eroding goodwill and civic fortitude, as Kobe continues to rebuild its public and private infrastructure.

The elderly have been particularly ill-equipped to deal with the bureaucracy of the relief effort. One man told the *Japan Times*, an English-language newspaper based in Tokyo, "Whenever you apply for anything, quake relief money or public housing, you have to go to the city or ward office, fill out all these forms, then go back a second time to get it. It's very hard for old people to get to the office. They should come here so that we can apply for things at the temporary shelters."[18]

Reconstruction, too, has produced its share of spats, bad feeling, and bureaucratic idiocy. The city and prefecture favored different approaches. The Kobe city government preferred the idea of rezoning the hardest hit areas, while the prefecture wanted to relocate quake survivors to reclaimed land and other unused areas.[19] Neither set of authorities thought to bring the public into the deliberation process. The Kobe city plan was based on force majeure purchase and redevelopment of badly damaged areas. Landowners in these areas were forced to wait until the city acted, even if they had their own funds to rebuild.

Two years later, many former homeowners are still waiting for the 125,000 homes that the city and prefecture are building in rezoned areas. Meanwhile, residents who have rebuilt their homes without official permits face the possibility that they will be torn down. Nor has there ever been any program to provide relief on an individual basis. In January 1995, Makoto Oda, a Vietnam-era activist, organized a citizens' petition demanding reparations of 5 million yen each (about $42,000) to quake victims whose homes were destroyed. According to a report in the *San Jose Mercury News*, this represents the first time in history that Japanese citizens have directly petitioned parliament to introduce legislation, which is normally drafted by the bureaucracy and then rubber-stamped by the Japanese Diet.[20]

The specter of the Great Kanto earthquake of September 1, 1923, haunts the memory of Kobe and its failures. If the Kobe earthquake had occurred just a few hours later, during morning rush hour, the damage might have been much more extreme. In much the same way, Shinpei Goto, the official who was in charge of reconstruction after the Great Kanto earthquake, is a needling reminder to the officials who bungled their way through the Kobe disaster.

Goto, the interior minister at the time of the Kanto earthquake, prepared his bold plan for reconstruction in just one day. He called upon the Imperial Government to buy up vast tracts of rubble to rebuild the capital along European lines. In the end, a much less ambitious plan went ahead, but Goto's vision is preserved in parks and tree-lined roads that were an exotic foreign touch in Tokyo in the 1920s.[21]

In the immediate aftermath of the Kobe earthquake, Japanese bureaucrats seemed to go to some lengths to compound their reputation for incompetence in a crisis. In Febuary 1995, a month after the earthquake, the National Land Agency began holding meetings to revise its basic disaster plan. One of the first ideas that was struck down was to set up a system for emergency rescue and relief operations based outside the damage zones. The concept inflamed local officials. Their argument: "Bringing in outsiders to run activities would run against the Japanese way of doing things."[22]

The Land Agency itself objected to a proposal from seismologists of the Meteorological Agency to provide early warnings to government agencies and the press when it detects precursor earthquakes—flurries that often come ahead of a major fault displacement. Land Agency officials said that the distinction was irrelevant.[23] An early warning system would cause "social confusion and adversely affect business activities," they expounded. This reasoning was based on the existing system, in which a small council of seismologists meets to assess warning signals of a major earthquake and, if they concur, issue an advisory that stops transportation and business activities in some parts of Japan. The Land Agency feared that the inclusion of precursor flurries in such advisories would vastly increase such stoppages, which in fact are exceedingly rare.

Nonetheless, the decision to include the Japanese prime minister in emergency relief operations is one positive outcome of the bureaucratic soul-searching that followed the Kobe earthquake. Among the first recommendations of the newly formed Central Disaster Prevention Council, in March 1995, was for the prime minister to order the SDF to engage in relief work after a disaster. This represented a radical change from the previous system, which was dependent upon decisions by local authorities. Not to insult the locals, the council inserted a one-hour waiting period before the SDF could act, giving local authorities time to join the chorus asking for help. But the intention was clearly to establish a top-down chain of command in place of the existing decentralized structure.

Besides the new command structure, the council's proposals included suggestions for better cooperation between the SDF, local police, and fire prevention authorities; the granting of authority to the Red Cross to organize foreign and domestic volunteer groups; a working relationship with the press to disseminate information on shelters and lists of victims (which the media did unbidden during the Kobe earthquake and aftermath); restrictions on the use of aircraft for newsgathering in the first three days after a major earthquake; the establishment of stringent earth-quake-proofing standards for public infrastructure; and an offer of government funds to purchase lands for reconstruction.[24]

All of these measures will help Japan deal more effectively with the next big earthquake, which seismologists say is likeliest to happen in the Odawara corridor southwest of Tokyo, or in Tokyo itself. The most significant aspect of the recommendations was that they tackled head-on the issue of *tatewari gyosei*, or vertical administration, by establishing a command structure similar to that used by the United States in national emergencies.

Although there is no proposed Japanese version of the U.S. Federal Emergency Management Agency, putting the prime minister in charge of the SDF has given an elected official primacy over the highly professional, but fragmented, civil service. The reforms thus address a problem that most Japanese instinctively recognize as central to *kisei kanwa*, or regulatory easing.

For Japan, the problem is not the number of regulations—whether there are 10,000 or 100,000 rules—but a bureaucracy that has become so insulated and arrogant that it no longer respects the basis of the rules system in public welfare. Critics who cite the excessive number of rules are missing the point. "Regulatory relaxation" means easing Japanese bureaucrats out of the control seat, not just scrapping a few thousand obsolete rules. The Kobe earthquake reminded the Japanese that the bureaucracy, which has performed its postwar role superbly in many ways, has its limits when human welfare is at stake.

Notes

1. Michael Zielenziger, "Kobe Still Reels from Earthquake; Many Are Homeless; Government Aid Lags," *San Jose Mercury News*, January 20, 1997.

2. Reuters, "Japan Quake Refugees Still Seek Homes," January 16, 1997.

3. Zielenziger, "Kobe Still Reels from Earthquake."

4. Ibid.

5. "Daiei Head Hits Failures in Aftermath of Quake," *Japan Times*, February 18, 1995.

6. Glen Fukushima, "The Great Hanshin Earthquake," JPRI Occasional Paper 2 (Santa Monica, Calif.: Japan Policy Research Institute, March 1995).

7. "70 Nations Offer Help; Japan Says OK to 36," *Japan Times,* February 14, 1995.

8. Tadashi Ikeda, "Foreign Aid Was Needed and Appreciated," *Japan Times*, February 15, 1995.

9. "Govt's Slow Quake Response Coupled with Information Lack," *Daily Yomiuri*, May 10, 1995.

10. "South Korea Responded Quickly to Quake," *Daily Yomiuri*, March 31, 1995.

11. "Red Tape Limited GSDF Quake Response," *Daily Yomiuri*, February 28, 1995.

12. "Urgent Decision Delayed by Confusion," *Daily Yomiuri*, March 25, 1995.

13. "Disaster Plan to Focus on Medical Response," *Daily Mainich*, February 23, 1995.

14. Edith Terry, "Kobe Quake Transforms Japanese into Volunteers," *Christian Science Monitor*, January 23, 1995.

15. "Hyogo Police Campaign Fails to Unclog Traffic," *Daily Yomiuri*, February 26, 1995.

16. "Lucky Evacuees Move into New Homes," *Japan Times*, February 16, 1995.

17. Catherine Pawsat, "Tent Cities Brace for Season of Typhoons, Heat, Red Tape," *Japan Times*, May 7, 1995.

18. Cameron Hay, "Evacuees Unite Over Demands," *Japan Times*, February 14, 1995.

19. Asahi Evening News, "Reconstruction Plans Should Be Based on History, Reality," February 18, 1995.

20. Zielenziger, "Kobe Still Reels from Earthquake."

21. "Post-quake Rezoning and Property Rights," *Asahi Evening News,* March 18, 1995.

22. "Disaster Plan Review to Focus on Medical Response," *Daily Mainichi*, February 1995.

23. "Agencies Debate over Issuing Quake Warnings," *Daily Yomiuri*, February 20, 1995.

24. "Plan Would Allow Prime Minister to Call Out SDF in Major Quakes," *Daily Yomiuri,* March 9, 1995.

Whither Deregulation?
An Epilogue to Japan's
Industrial Policy

Leon Hollerman

IT WILL BE RECALLED that in the aftermath of World War II, some time before America began learning from Japan, the Japanese were eager to learn from the United States. The most avid students were the Japanese bureaucrats who, by the courtesy of SCAP (Supreme Command for the Allied Powers), had belatedly won their war with the Japanese military brass. As mentor, SCAP claimed credit for bringing democracy to Japan during the occupation. With some exceptions, however, the predominant result of its activities in economic (as distinguished from political) affairs was just the opposite. SCAP imposed comprehensive economic controls on Japan and suppressed the free market system. Its intervention was especially repressive on the international plane.

Prior to mobilization for the Pacific War, Japan had never had a planned or controlled economy. As the occupation drew to a close, however, SCAP authorized the Diet to pass legislation for economic controls to be employed by successor peacetime governments. A zealous Japanese government bureaucracy with a vested interest in the perpetuation of economic controls took charge of their implementation. The economic control laws, and the bureaucracy to which they were bequeathed, constituted an important part of SCAP's legacy to postwar Japan. This legacy became a primary conditioning factor in Japan's subsequent resistance to economic liberalization—a source of friction in relations between the

243

United States and Japan ever since. Today we can see Japan's regulatory regime in historical perspective. In 1952, when the occupation ended, SCAP naively presided not only over the transfer of its own authority, but also over the institutionalization of the most restrictive set of economic controls ever devised by a major free nation.[1]

At the outset of the postwar period, Japan used its regulatory regime to achieve the purposes of its industrial policy. That policy was designed to promote the national interest as seen from a Japanese point of view. Besides survival, independence, and continuity, which are in the interest of all nations, Japan has an unappeasable passion for stability and economic security. Its national interests also include the goal of reducing its vulnerability to economic threats from without and its overdependence on trade with the United States.

In reflecting these interests, the goals of Japan's industrial policy (as seen by an outsider) included the following: economic concentration (to achieve economies of large-scale production as well as raw business power), guided development of Japan as a "major industrial nation," protection of Japan against the vicissitudes of the world economy and the incursion of foreigners, and control of Japan's foreign markets and sources of supply. Japan's postwar economy was opened for business under the rule that "all is forbidden except that which is expressly permitted." These principles appear to be inconsistent with Japan's free-market philosophy as professed in its "liberalization" program (removing direct controls) that began in the early 1960s, continuing as "administrative reform" (reducing the size and intrusiveness of government), and which now survives as "deregulation." This announced program calls for further removal of direct government controls as well as those imposed by business groups within the "private sector."

The principles of Japan's industrial policy, however, were never changed; they remain intact to the present day. Meanwhile, the approach to economic liberalization was taken with slow and tiny steps, backward as well as forward. In developing Japan as a major industrial nation according to the industrial policy scenario, successive liberalization, administrative reform, and deregulation programs (the terms are roughly synonymous) were synchronized with the process of regulated reform of the structure of industry. Hence, paradoxically, government intervention and control were often applied in the name of liberalization.

In the first structural reform (1955–72), there was a general consensus in favor of the government's policies, including its regulatory regime. In the second phase (1973–85), when Japanese big business (the chief beneficiary of the first reform) had been revived, the consensus was fractured. Government and business became more or less equal partners in the implementation of industrial policy. This was the period of "Japan, Inc." But it was also the period of "Down with GNP!" as economic performance was scarred by environmental and other scandals. In the third period (1986–present) big business had become less monolithic. Thus the national interest was superseded by special interests in industry, agriculture, and finance. These reverberated in inter- and intraministerial rivalries among the business sector's various bureaucratic patrons. An incoherent mixture of regulatory and deregulatory measures became the norm of the liberalization process. Economic planning was history.

The First Structural Reform (1955–72)

In its rehabilitation stage (1945–55), Japan's government tried to go back to where the nation had been before the war. For a decade it concentrated on the production and export of labor-intensive consumer goods such as textiles, toys, and radios. This was Japan's answer to foreign skeptics who doubted that it would ever even return to a condition of self-support. The skeptics were further astounded by the first great restructuring of Japan's postwar economy. During this period, the Japanese government restricted consumption in order to allocate a maximum of resources to producers. This policy has persisted to the present day.

At the outset, government economized on social infrastructure such as hospitals, schools, housing, and public amenities. It even economized on economic infrastructure such as roads, airports, and sewage and water systems. Under the micromanagement of the Ministry of International Trade and Industry (MITI) and the Ministry of Finance (MOF), a system of regulatory carrots and sticks was foisted on the economy. This resulted in shifting the industrial center of gravity from low-tech to middle-tech products and from consumer goods to heavy and chemical products. Key industries—such as steel, petrochemicals, electric machinery, and shipbuilding—were selected for special assistance.

At the same time, Japan became notorious for its exploitation of the surviving labor-intensive small- and medium-scale firms that constituted the backward sector of its dual economy. By the end of the first great restructuring, these firms had been extinguished, upgraded as independent survivors, or co-opted within *keiretsu* networks. A virtuous circle of domestic investment and export promotion gave rise to the economic "miracle" of 1955–70.

Thus the economy grew. As foreign nations (especially the United States) now perceived the potentialities of the Japanese market, they made demands (*gaiatsu*) for the liberalization of its import and foreign direct investment (FDI) regulations. In its public relations Japan's government made much of this external pressure. Spokesmen emphasized the extent to which Japan had bowed to it. Yet, in every case, the accommodation was made only step by step, case by case, and was backed by long-term, cost-benefit calculations. There was probably no case of liberalization that was not consistent with Japan's own national interests, as perceived by the bureaucracy. Moreover, deregulation as a disguise for the protection of big business was accomplished by the very procedures prescribed for "liberalizing" inward FDI. [2]

Finally, the government organized cartels for "designated" industries. These included antirecession cartels (1953–present), rationalization cartels (1953–present), machinery promotion cartels (1972–78), stabilization cartels (1978–83), machinery and information industry cartels (1979–85), and structural improvement cartels (1983–88). Designated cartel industries were exempt from the provisions of the Antimonopoly Law. Moreover, the government took no judicial cognizance of hundreds of informal, unregistered cartels of whose existence it was fully aware. This was "deregulation, Japanese style."

The Second Structural Reform (1973–85)

The second major regulated shift in Japan's postwar industrial structure was performed in counterpoint to liberalization's ripest years. Newly anointed as a major industrial nation, Japan had become a formidable competitor in its chosen fields. Opening the door (somewhat) would reveal no empty spaces to be preempted by foreigners. However, the bureaucracy, in sectors such as international finance, would admit a select few. This would afford Japanese banks a chance, as Mao Tse-Tung might put it, to "learn from your enemy."

In the second restructuring period, middle-tech products gave way to high-tech products on Japan's industrial frontier. The key industries of this period included semiconductors, biotechnology, pharmaceuticals, new materials, and information and international financial services. Control of industrial policy, moreover, shifted substantially from government to the private sector. From having been a junior party in making industrial policy, big business became a powerful force in imposing its own direct controls on the economy. Parallel to liberalization, the *zaikai*, (business leaders of the private sector) could employ their trade associations, cartels, and *keiretsu* affiliations to decide such matters as who could do business with whom, who could find warehouse space to store imported merchandise, who was given access to trade information, and who was eligible for the benefits of what one might call institutionalized collusion. This represented the "privatization" of industrial policy.

In terms of liberalization, the government's role was to shift (partly) from direct to indirect controls. (In Japan, however, it is often difficult to distinguish between them.) Macroeconomic policy began to replace microeconomic intervention. Many foreign exchange controls remained in place, however. Quite obviously, internationalizing its economy, purportedly under the rules of the General Agreement on Tariffs and Trade (GATT), was in Japan's interest. As Japan offered "reciprocity" to other nations, government spokesmen could truthfully assert that, through liberalization, Japan's tariffs had become lower than those of the United States. But by the time this occurred, tariffs were no longer that important. Instead, nontariff barriers became the chief means of protecting local markets. These included regulations concerning standards, certification, and testing, as well as others mentioned above.

The United States proved a disingenuous collaborator in sustaining the direct regulatory controls of the Japanese government. In frequent controversies over "dumping," the United States demanded that Japan adopt "voluntary export restraints" (VERs). These were not subject to the purview of GATT. In effect, VERs were a way of justifying the imposition of government cartels on the industries to which they applied.

MITI was delighted to be in charge of this new job. Dominant firms in the private sector were delighted as well. The VER cartels froze the market shares of firms in relation to a selected base period, thus excluding newcomers. In the case of mature or declining industries, many firms were happy to rest on their laurels and enjoy guaranteed market share. Thus VERs could be popular with almost all concerned, and Japan could appear to be acquiescent to American "pressure" in the bargain.

In proceeding step by step, liberalization served another purpose of industrial policy, namely, the encouragement of economic concentration. It was the government's policy to remove restrictions on major firms before doing so in behalf of minor firms. This gave big business a head start in cultivating new turf. In May 1979, for example, the minimum permissible size of certificates of deposit for which interest rates were deregulated was ¥500 million. Only major banks had many customers in this range. It was not until April 1988 that the minimum was reduced to ¥50 million for the benefit of smaller institutions.

Similarly, in October 1985, ¥1 billion was set as the minimum size of ordinary deposits for which interest rates were deregulated. It was not until November 1991 that the minimum amount was reduced to ¥3 million. Then there was credit rationing. In the early postwar period city banks—under the guidance of MOF—provided major firms in key industries with large loans at low interest rates. Smaller firms were required to pay higher rates. They had to maintain substantial compensating balances (unutilized portions of the proceeds of their loans) as well.[3]

Similarly, large banks were the first to be given permission to engage in securities transactions, provided they were performed by their foreign subsidiaries. In the securities industry, during the 1980s, brokerage firms—with the knowledge of MOF—were allowed to compensate major customers for their stock market losses.

Measurement of Japan's economic concentration is complicated by various statistical problems.[4] According to Japan's Fair Trade Commission, however, as measured by the Herfindahl index, industrial concentration rose by approximately 10 percent between 1983 and 1992.[5] It is clear that exports in Japanese manufacturing are highly concentrated in a few big firms. Aggregate export concentration is much higher than aggregate firm concentration.[6]

As suggested above, one of the anomalies of Japan's liberalization process is its reliance on appearance at the expense of reality. Japan's new bank law (April 1982) is a case in point. In contrast with the previous law (which did not mention the matter) the new law restricted the size of loans a bank may extend to any single borrower to a proportion of the bank's equity. The proportion was to be specified by administrative guidance. The purpose of this provision was not prudential; it was a countermeasure to the increasing independence of private banks from central bank control that occurred during the 1970s. This was the result of an increase in the private banks' nonborrowed reserves. The new Bank Law also imposed a heavier burden of disclosure and auditing requirements than its predecessor. In effect, the new law widened the scope of government administrative guidance. This was regulation rather than liberalization.

The Third Structural Reform (1986–present)

The third structural reform built on its predecessors' industrial policy. In a mature economy, however, the principles of Japan's industrial policy do not apply as well as they did a half century ago. The inconsistencies and erroneous assumptions of that policy are becoming apparent and counterproductive for the goals it seeks. In the event the principle of regulation, rather than deregulation, survived as a basic element of Japan's industrial policy.

Japan's Industrial Policy in the 1990s

In the 1990s, the bureaucracy rarely speaks in public about industrial policy, but below the surface its principles are alive and well. However, there have been changes in the instruments, if not the goals, of industrial policy. In the first two restructurings, policy was imposed by the micromanagement of MITI and MOF, with big business playing a steadily increasing role in the formulation of strategy. The third saw a further shift in emphasis from direct to indirect intervention, but the surviving multitude of microregulations and their counterproductive effects evoked strong criticism even from members of the establishment. This reflected adversely on MITI (the official custodian of industrial policy), but served the purposes of MOF. In bureaucratic politics, the increasing dominance of the financial sector over the nonfinancial sector likewise enhanced MOF's image at the expense of MITI.

The defining episode of the third structural reform was the economic bubble of 1985–90. Its origin can be traced to bureaucratic politics that entwined conflict between the banks and the securities companies with rivalry between the Banking Bureau and the Securities Bureau of MOF, which supervised those industries respectively. The banks were traditional allies of the Banking Bureau and historically under its thumb. By contrast the securities companies were not only enemies of the banks, they were regarded as presumptuous upstarts. MOF needed to defend the banks because it depended on them to transmit its monetary policy throughout the economy. Moreover, in contrast to the securities companies, the banks were reliable landing places for MOF's *amakudari* schemes, as senior bureaucrats retired from the ministry to take jobs in the private sector.

The banks were also sorely disadvantaged by other developments beyond their control. During the early postwar period, business was at the banks' mercy, since they provided its only source of capital. By the time Japan's economic miracle had run its course, however, Japanese business had grown affluent enough to accumulate its own capital reserves. Moreover, the securities companies were eager to float securities for major firms at much lower cost than the price of loans from the banks. The banks were losing the battle.

Therefore, to help the banks hold their ground, MOF adopted a cheap money policy—an indirect regulatory instrument. The remedy included low interest rates and an expanded money supply, together with a tight budget policy. The reduced supply of government bonds for investment forced the banks to rely more heavily on making loans as a source of revenue. Thus the banks had an incentive to lend, business had an incentive to borrow.

This led to a vicious circle. Cheap money borrowed from the banks was used to buy and bid up the price of securities and land; these in turn provided collateral for further bank loans that were used to again bid up the prices of land and securities and so on. Late in 1989 the bubble was pricked. The vicious circle collapsed when Yasushi Mieno, governor of the Bank of Japan, raised interest rates drastically. The ensuing asset deflation led to Japan's longest and deepest postwar recession.

In view of many historical precedents, it is difficult to believe that this debacle was not anticipated by any of the financial authorities who presided over the macroeconomic policies that first created the bubble and then extinguished it. The interesting question is, what was their purpose.

The regulatory strategy of the economic bubble and the recession that followed it induced great structural changes in the Japanese economy. Unlike those that occurred in the first two structural reforms, however, these changes were not *announced* as an object of government policy. Nor was it *announced* that preservation of its regulatory regime was likewise a specific aim of the bureaucracy's policy. However, the government's intentions may well be judged by its actions of omission and commission. First, the liberalization movement has gone backwards and sideways as well as forward throughout the postwar period. Under the new label of deregulation, the program has been ambiguous, selective, and curiously combined with new regulations. Japan remains the most overregulated "free market" nation in the world.

The intentions of the economic ministries can be judged in part from their studied neglect of the postbubble recession. There are four conceivable reasons for MOF's perfunctory response.

First, the ministry was not accustomed to dealing with structural recessions, as in the present case. Japan's typical postwar recession (as during the "miraculous" growth period) was of the cyclical variety, usually induced by tight money policies imposed in response to balance of payments constraints. In the past, when "overheating" of the economy subsided and monetary policy was relaxed, recovery was spontaneous. But MOF's present easy money policy, which is about as far as it is willing to go, has not produced that result.

Second, MOF is traditionally prone to austerity. Throughout the postwar period, as I noted, consumer spending has been repressed in favor of allocating resources to industry.[7] At present, consumption constitutes barely one-half of GNP in Japan while it amounts to two-thirds of GNP in the United States. Nevertheless, after five years of recession, MOF still believed that Japan's lifestyle was extravagant and profligate. Its guardians were in favor of more rather than less constraint.

The exploitation of Japanese consumers is apparent from the statistics of yen appreciation in relation to the change in Japan's wholesale and consumer price indexes. Between 1990 and April 1995, the yen appreciated against the dollar by 38.1 percent. This made imports cheaper, which presumably should have been reflected in the price indexes. During the same period, however, while the Wholesale Price Index (1990 = 100) *fell* 8.4 percent, the Consumer Price Index (1990 = 100) *rose* by 7.1 percent. In other words, the profits of yen appreciation were retained by importers or manufacturers. They were not shared with consumers.

A third reason for MOF's tepid reaction could be its realization that apart from deregulation, there was no other long-term remedy for the structural recession. But MOF had little enthusiasm for deregulation.

A fourth reason was not so obvious but doubtless very important in the bureaucrats' calculations: the recession offered a recipe for invoking the latest structural reform in accordance with industrial policy. That is to say, at Japan's present stage of development, recession would help to squeeze out surviving low and medium-tech industries (by bankruptcy or expatriation). This would further shift Japan's industrial structure toward industries on the technological frontier; it would also promote "globalization."

The high-valued yen (so distorted in terms of purchasing power parity) was another decoy in the bureaucracy's effort to distract attention from its long-term objectives. The high yen had been accused of prolonging the recession by hindering exports. This evoked official expressions of concern. In 1994, however, Japan's exports in dollar terms were the largest in its history. In yen, they almost matched the record high of 1992. This implies that the high-valued yen had contributed to significantly increased productivity in the Japanese economy. It forced producers to reduce their cost of production and reduced the price of imported components. The high yen also makes it easier for Japanese businesses to expand foreign direct investment, in accordance with the goal of globalization.[8] These are among the principal aims of industrial policy.

Globalization

Owing to its high-valued yen, rising productivity, and rising trade surpluses, Japan would seem to be in the strongest position in its history to achieve the purpose of globalization, which is at the heart of current industrial policy. The essence of globalization is the expansion of Japan's FDI position, as well as coordination of its trade and foreign investment. Both the financial and nonfinancial sectors of the Japanese economy and its overseas transplants are to be "globally" coordinated. These are the elements of what I have referred to as Japan's industrial policy on the international plane.[9]

According to this scenario, Japan aspires to become a headquarters nation in the world economy. As manager of a global system, Japan would develop its capability for hedging and offsetting risks in a worldwide context. Moreover, the profits of its global enterprises would enable Japan to become a rentier nation, like England in the nineteenth century. In effect, Japan would reproduce on a global scale the dual domestic economy that was phased out within Japan itself during the 1970s. In Japan's domestic economy, the upper reaches of that dual economy would now include super-high-tech versions of the research-and-development-intensive industries developed during the second structural reform period. Thus, contrary to the alarmist "hollowing out" thesis, this scenario sees one set of domestic industries being replaced by a superior set.

In the meantime, the bureaucrats at Kasumigaseki do their best to restrict access to Japan's domestic markets. This effectively augments the trade surplus, which is a source of capital for the globalization process. Furthermore, according to the Japan Export-Import Bank, Japan's foreign subsidiaries and affiliates now rely on foreign rather than Japanese sources for more than half of their capital requirements abroad.

The Predicament of Japan's Industrial Policy

Presumably some cost-benefit calculations are being made by Japanese authorities in charge of deregulation. They must be asking whether it is in the national interest—as well as their own—to deregulate and thus to overcome the postbubble recession. MOF may believe that a structural recession is good because it works toward realizing policy's goals: changing the structure of Japan's economy in favor of frontier technological industries, expatriating Japan's traditional mass production industries, perfecting a global economic network under central control from Tokyo. After all, the first two postwar structural reforms were successful. Why not the third?

The answer to that is that the self-preoccupied, naive nationalism of Japan's early postwar industrial policy no longer suffices. It cannot serve as a strategy in the postindustrial world because its assumptions are no longer valid either at home or abroad. Domestically, the leads and lags of its social and economic variables are desynchronized and out of phase. Japan's industry is mature; its government is immature. Externally, neither the bureaucrats nor, apparently, the politicians can cope with the new realities of power, responsibility, and scale that now confront them.

Among the inherited erroneous assumptions is the concept that Japan can rely on widespread consensus to protect the national interest in the formulation of policy. Special interests have destroyed the national— even the group—consensus. There is a struggle for power among the elites. (This is not new, but now there is more at stake and the conflict is more vicious than ever before.) Thus Japan can no longer rely on its traditional institutional arrangements to condition and contain power conflict.

During the present recession, moreover, consensus has been fractured by the slippage in social welfare responsibilities that since World War II have been assumed by major firms. In the name of cost-cutting and rationalization, factories have been closed and workers discharged on an unprecedented scale. "Lifetime" employment and seniority wages are being abandoned. Thus in the process of implementing a semiprivatized industrial policy the big business partners of the bureaucracy have helped invalidate some of the institutional assumptions upon which that policy was built. Reciprocal obligation, long-term relationships, and communitarianism seem to be on the way out.

For various reasons, as mentioned above, Japan's deregulatory program began (nominally and cautiously) in the international sector. There was less consensus for deregulation in the domestic sector, where regulation often serves a protective purpose. Vested interests in the domestic sector—especially those that are uncompetitive—are heavily entrenched and have much to lose through deregulation.

Japan's "groupism" in the past has been vitally important for its economic performance—especially in the mass production sector. But it may have become less relevant in a postindustrial society based on information technology. In the present era, it may be that individuals capable of working alone will have an advantage. Some of Japan's major strengths may thus become weaknesses.

In its external affairs, the assumption that central control can be maintained from Tokyo is particularly vulnerable. Already the *sogo shosha* (general trading companies) have been grappling with this problem for over a decade. Traditionally, *sogo shosha* have been Japan's chief instrument for the conduct of foreign trade. Before Japanese manufacturing firms were versed in foreign languages and capable of financing, shipping, warehousing, and distributing their products abroad, the *soga shosha* performed these services for them. As the composition of exports changed, however, and products such as electronic goods and automobiles entered the list, there arose a need for after-sales servicing and repair. This the *soga shosha* could not provide. When major firms began to perform their own export transactions and established their own distribution and repair networks abroad, the *sogo shosha* used their knowledge of foreign markets to engage in foreign direct investment. At present, half of *sogo shosha* business concerns the direct management of foreign firms.

Here a new problem arose. As traders they were masters of the rulebook in exercising central control over their worldwide chain of offices; as direct investors, however, they found no standard rules for decisionmaking. They lacked special knowledge of local conditions, especially in the service industries, that differed everywhere. Thus the *sogo shosha* have had a difficult task in drawing the line between central and local decisionmaking. In the transition process, the share of Japan's total exports transacted by Japan's top nine *sogo shosha* has declined from over half two decades ago to approximately one-third in 1995.

The solution now being proposed for this problem is deregulation in the form of repealing the Antimonopoly Law prohibition against holding companies. This would perhaps bring back central control of a sort. But it would be a return to the old *zaibatsu* form of control. It is generally agreed that the relatively decentralized and less regimented *keiretsu* form of group association is vastly more dynamic than the centrally controlled and regimented *zaibatsu* system. Turning back the clock out of yearning for preemptive headquarters control may be counterproductive.

The *keiretsu* themselves have been a major instrument in the performance of Japan's foreign economic policy. Yet they are likewise in a state of decline. In 1981, for example, intra-*keiretsu* sales among the members of the six leading *keiretsu* averaged only 10.8 percent of their total sales. By 1992 the figure had dropped to 6.9 percent. One implication of *keiretsu* dissolution is that insider information networks will likewise be dispersed. This diminution of joint planning and strategy will conflict with the industrial policy goal of promoting centralized economic control. However, if institutionalized collusion gives way to free market competition, Japan's competitive power may increase. Which of the two will it be?

Paradoxically, bureaucratic bias against free markets is inimical to the globalization process. It is ironic that the bureaucracy here presents the main stumbling block to fulfillment of its own strategy, devised in the interest of industrial policy. At present, however, the national interest and interests of the bureaucracy do not coincide. Moreover, in the globalization era the regulatory regime is no longer in the interest of Japan's major firms.[10] This can be seen in the astonishing fact that big business, which had been the chief beneficiary of regulatory favors, is now in the vanguard of those demanding deregulation. From the snail's pace of deregulation, however, no one would guess that in coping with institutional change, Japan is engaged in a race against time.

These aspects of the predicament of Japan's industrial policy suggest an answer to the baffling question of the past half century: how is it that Japan's mercantilist method of doing business could yield an economic "miracle" while the same policies would lead to chaos and disaster in the United States? The answer is that as a mature industrial nation Japan would find those regulatory policies are as counterproductive as they would be in America.

Where Will Japan Go from Here?

The foundation of Japan's present regulatory regime lies in the control system of the American occupation following World War II. The occupation imposed a comprehensive set of controls on the Japanese economy, which was implemented by indirect rule, namely, through the Japanese government bureaucracy that acted as a surrogate for General MacArthur. When Japan's autonomy was restored after the occupation, these regulations and controls were bequeathed to the bureaucracy, which with samurai zeal assumed command in its own name. The control system was embodied in the form of industrial policy, implemented largely by MITI and MOF.

Industrial policy was based on three principles. First was the principle of bureaucratic preeminence in government and society. One of MOF and MITI's tools was a monopoly of essential economic information that they did not freely share with others at the political or ministerial level. Second was protectionism, to keep foreign predators away from Japanese assets and to restrict the inflow of foreign products that otherwise would preempt the Japanese market. Third was a system of licensing for all the basic activities of entrepreneurship, including foreign and domestic trade, production, and finance. In the process of rehabilitation and growth, licenses were used to allocate scarce resources in accordance with the bureaucracy's concept of optimality.

MITI, whose policy bureaus consist of the International Trade Policy Bureau and the Industrial Policy Bureau, was the nominal custodian of industrial policy. However, in the course of recovery and growth, big business outgrew its government swaddling clothes, and in response to its pressure (not in response to American demands) a liberalization movement began in the 1960s. As that movement progressed, both the International Trade Policy Bureau and the Industrial Policy Bureau were emasculated. Foreign trade licensing and allocation of scarce materials were phased out, and MITI's policy prerogatives were sharply curtailed. Today it is only declining industries that need MITI's help. Indeed, in its rivalry with MOF, whose career continued to flourish rather than decline, and which was reluctant to liberalize, MITI became an advocate of liberalization and deregulation.

In active or inactive form, however, a great many of the regulations of the early postwar period survive, plus a huge set of informal instructions known as "administrative guidance." As a result, by the standards of big business and the wishes of consumers, Japan remains highly overregulated. Moreover, the regulations often precipitate evasion and corruption in the private sector as well as money scandals among the bureaucrats and politicians. Government and business are often on a collision course, and conflicts of interest prevail within government and business respectively.

Ironically, since feudal times Japan's leadership has girded itself against what it perceived as threats from without. Today it appears to be complacent about a palpable threat from within, namely, the threat to governability. That threat was evident, for example, in the results of the parliamentary election of November 20, 1996, in which less than 60 percent of eligible voters bothered to vote (unprecedented in postwar Japan) and in which no party received a mandate to govern. The credibility of Japan's leadership has declined and has been swamped in a morass of power struggles.

Deregulation as a Power Struggle

In Japan's present transition, the issues of regulation, deregulation, and policy reform may be seen as a power struggle in which the national interest has been increasingly subordinated to the special interest of the rivals. These include the bureaucrats, politicians, and business leaders. The struggle is a contest between the dinosaurs of Japan's postwar reconstruction and the avatars of a new millennium. It is also a struggle to straddle the gulf between the short-term and long-term interests of the nation versus those of the parties concerned. Each is engaged in a race against time.

In the economic sphere, the bureaucracy held the reins until the 1970s. Thereafter in a striking reversal it was challenged and constrained by big business, which in effect took charge of the planning of industrial policy. Ceremonially, for example, it could be seen that bureaucrats were often meeting businessmen in the latter's offices rather than the other way around. Historically, major firms first outgrew the *soga shosha*; then they outgrew the banks; now they have challenged the bureaucracy. At present, the pot is calling the kettle black: politicians have barked at the bureaucrats for their scandals and "mismanagement." The postbubble recession, however, was a structural and strategic result of various dilemmas in the Japanese economy. At the center of these dilemmas stood the Ministry of Finance.

A structural aberration of MOF was the enormous scope of its brief (assigned to it in an absent-minded moment by the American occupation): it is a source of conflict as well as strength. The range of its authority includes the budget, taxation, public finance, securities, banking, international finance, customs and tariffs, insurance, and financial inspection. Its regulatory regime performs both micro and macro intervention. For example, besides monetary and fiscal policy, it also controls the Bank of Japan, the Japan Export-Import Bank, and the Japan Development Bank, among other banks. Another example of MOF's micro-macro intervention concerns the foreign exchange value of the yen, which is more tightly managed than any other major international currency. This has a bearing on what MOF can do in applying its strategy for the globalization of the Japanese economy.

What is that strategy? One can only surmise. Unlike MITI, MOF does not publish its "vision" of where the Japanese economy (and the ministry itself) will be in the next century. Relevant factors underlying the scenario that might be inferred, however, are clear. Institutionally, activities within the ministry itself are frequently in conflict; thus sectionalism within MOF is rampant, exceeding that within MITI.[11] For example, conflicts arise between monetary and fiscal policy and between banking and securities policy. Since the Recruit scandal, MOF has been displeased with the securities industry, but the securities bureau has won the fight with the banking bureau in intra-MOF sectional rivalry.[12] In the power struggles over MOF's conflicting interests, the regulatory regime contains seeds of its own undoing.

Apart from its dilemma of conflicting policy interests within the ministry, MOF (like the politicians) is beholden to the beneficiaries of the regulatory process who resist changes in the status quo.[13] Among the chief beneficiaries of the regulatory process are the big business proprietors of key industries that have been favored in accordance with industrial policy. These same firms are important members of Keidanren (Japan Federation of Economic Organizations), which has been in the forefront of those demanding deregulation. This suggests again, as in another context mentioned above, that big business in Japan has outgrown its dependence not only on *keiretsu* but also on the government itself. The strength of those who hold the government hostage to its own paternalistic commitments, however, was evident in the futile exercise MOF was impelled to perform to "stimulate" the economy out of its postbubble recession.[14] Six stimulus packages totaling $U.S. 600 billion were expended between August 1992 and September 1995 to overcome "weakness of demand." Most of the proceeds of that expenditure lined the pockets of construction firms that produced public works (which at best have a low income multiplier) including redundant roads, bridges, and tunnels as arranged by politicians from rural areas. In other words, the very defects of the regulatory system were exploited in a vain effort to remedy the results of that system.

Another impediment to structural reform appears where the status quo reflects a shaky quasi equilibrium of power in which several ministries share overlapping jurisdiction. It may be in their interest to resist reform because of its unpredictable consequences in the power struggle. In an analogous case, as an exception to the familiar conflict between central and local authorities, local protectionists line up with central bureaucrats in the deregulation struggle. Although they are losing the battle with big business, local protectionists include small and medium-scale enterprises such as retail shops that attempt to defend their turf against chain stores and supermarkets.

At the outset of the liberalization movement in the 1960s (which later embraced "deregulation"), it was chiefly perceived as a status symbol rather than as a policy in the interest of the Japanese people. Since the late 1970s, MITI has advocated deregulation on the assumption that it would adversely affect MOF more than itself, thus improving MITI's relative position in the power struggle. In an indirect attack on MOF, MITI supports Fair Trade Commission (FTC) actions against MOF's regulatory interests. Having lost ground in industrial policy, MITI has sought new fields to conquer. Trade conflicts between Japan and the United States are welcome to MITI because they give the ministry a job to do. MITI also plays a role as marriage broker in arranging mergers among its clients.

Returning to the question posed above, what strategy can we infer in the case of MOF? In contriving a strategy that secures its own special interests, MOF faces one of its various dilemmas. In the short run it must accommodate forces for reform while fulfilling its own long-term interest in regulatory power and control. From the point of view of deregulation as a power struggle, how might MOF outflank both its intramural clients and its external adversaries? MOF would have to circumvent both the stubborn beneficiaries of its prevailing policies as well as the reformers. It would need to impose new regulations in the name of deregulation, control in the name of decontrol, and above all, pursue its own interests in the name of the national interest.[15] A conceivable way for MOF to attempt all this would be to concentrate its attention on the international plane.

MOF and Industrial Policy on the International Plane

Japan's asset inflation bubble of the 1980s was ostensibly a domestic aberration. Actually, it was a calculated demonstration by MOF of Japan's industrial policy on the international plane. Its ministerial purpose was to improve MOF's position as the preeminent player in the power struggles within the Japanese government and in the power balance between the Japanese government and big business. Its national purpose was to emancipate Japan from overdependence on the United States and from potential overdependence on China. Big business would be served by being given new political and economic policy support for its initiatives on the international plane.

At the outset, however, what are the categories of the national interest in whose name MOF's strategy had to be presented? They include survival, independence, continuity (legitimacy), stability, and economic security. For the economic ministries, the last of these, "comprehensive economic security"—a phrase attributed to the late prime minister, Masayoshi Ohira—has served as a shibboleth since it was first enunciated. In the 1980s, security came to be seen in terms of financial power, which was clearly ascendant in the world economy. At that time, moreover, in the midst of its asset bubble, Japan loomed as a potential financial "hegemon." In a world dominated by finance, hegemonic financial control would seem to promise the ultimate assurance of security to a nation possessed of an exiguous physical endowment such as that of Japan. The Ministry of Finance would become the chief custodian of

Japan's industrial policy on the international plane, namely, to control foreign markets and sources of supply (a strategy that bears the marks of its genealogy). Japan should become a rentier nation like England in the nineteenth century. By means of the bubble, it would create out of thin air the capital with which to do so.

The rentier nation scenario is conceivable as a proxy for what must be a subject of discussion in the inner circles of MOF. The discussion surely concerns the question of how the ministry might escape the jaws of the domestic power struggle and secure its own interests. Assuming this discussion, and in the context of the bubble economy of the 1980s, the scenario is an explanation of how the national interest, bureaucratic interests, and the regulatory regime have been entwined in Japan during recent decades. MOF's actions in introducing the bubble and allowing it to expand were seemingly perverse because it was entirely preventable, its eventual collapse was clearly foreseeable, and it violated all of MOF's conservative principles of monetary and fiscal policy. In fact, however, MOF's actions were entirely consistent with Japanese tradition and its own principles.

Globalization was the fulcrum of the strategy by which the interests of the nation, the bureaucracy, and big business were entwined. The role of the bubble was to assist in the accumulation of capital with which to finance Japan's acquisition of assets abroad. In this context, interpretation of the Plaza accord of September 1985 is quite different from the usual story. According to that story, Japan generously agreed to assist the United States in depreciating the dollar as a means of overcoming the U.S. trade deficit. Actually, Japan's cooperation in this effort could be construed as a triumph for the rentier nation scenario. It resulted in overvaluation of the yen as a by-product of the bubble, which, while its trade balance continued to soar, made it cheap and easy for Japan to promote foreign direct investment after 1985 to a level unheard of in world history. It did not result in a reduction of the U.S. trade deficit; on the contrary, the deficit increased, both with Japan and other nations. The accord, by the way, was an impressive demonstration of MOF's ability to control the value of the yen—a key instrument in the implementation of the scenario.

In addition to the acquisition of new assets abroad, the bubble impelled the expatriation of labor-intensive and mature industries by raising the cost of labor in Japan. "Hollowing out" in the search for cheap labor elsewhere was not evidence of bungling or mismanagement by

MOF; it was intentional for the purpose of enlarging Japan's global hinterland. It was also intentional for the purpose of increasing unemployment, intimidating the labor force, and constraining union power. Squeezing out low-tech, labor-intensive, and declining industries contributed to the improvement of efficiency, technical advance, and competitive power in the homeland. Firms remaining in Japan (and remaining solvent) are forced to improve their value-added performance, typically by restructuring, downsizing, and outsourcing. In the recession following the collapse of the bubble, these trends were reinforced, thus promoting the rentier nation scenario and contributing to Japan's emergence as a headquarters nation in the world economy.[16] Similarly in the national interest, the collapse of the bubble induced a fall in the price of land, which reduced the cost of production and further improved the competitive power of Japanese industry. Another purpose of the foreseeable recession was MOF's traditional policy of constraining consumption in order to increase saving and capital accumulation. "Deficiency of demand" was intentional. Above all, so were the foreseeable bankruptcies that would enable strong surviving firms to acquire foreclosed assets cheaply and thus promote economic concentration.

Why is economic concentration in MOF's interest? Basically, it is to overcome adversarial relations with big business, to co-opt it as an ally, and to engage its services, just as the occupation employed the bureaucracy (including MOF) in the system of indirect rule. Without that partnership, the Japanese economy has become too big, too complex, and too technically sophisticated to be micromanaged by a small group of civil service generalists. In the past, industry associations, dominated by major firms, were the instrument by which ministerial guidance was transmitted and enforced upon the multitude of lesser firms in the Japanese economy. In recent years, major firms have lost interest in their industry associations because they no longer needed to ingratiate themselves with the bureaucracy by performing its chores. Now, however, they may need to do so again. As a result of economic concentration, giant Japanese oligopolies have entered the political as well as the economic arena on the international plane. As a political as well as an economic ally, they are likely to be better served by and more beholden to MOF than any other ministry in the Japanese government. This may be part of the rationale behind MOF's seemingly untraditional behavior in the bubble episode.

Two types of traditional policy are evident in MOF's behavior. It has revealed both in the banking industry. One type is communitarianism; the other is the nurturing of giant firms and oligopolies with which to confront the West. In pursuing the former, MOF once provided a guarantee against the failure of any minor bank. In pursuing the latter, they have withdrawn that guarantee and assured the twenty largest banks that none of them would be allowed to fail. Again, in the latter case, and in accord with the drive toward economic concentration, MOF has abandoned the "convoy" system wherein the fleet moved at the speed of the slowest ship.[17] From MOF's point of view, economic concentration is in the national interest for the purpose of creating raw business power, if not economies of scale. Through bankruptcies, mergers, and consolidations, the postbubble recession has clearly contributed to that result in Japan.

A progress report of Japan's industrial policy on the international plane could be expressed in terms of the extent to which it has achieved "self-sufficiency in the context of its global hinterland," so to speak. In 1993, as a rentier nation, Japan's net investment income from abroad amounted to $41 billion, almost a fifth of total imports. In July 1994 the net investment surplus from abroad was approximately the same. At the end of 1994, Japan's net external assets were $689 billion, the largest of any nation in the world. Its current account surplus in that year was $129 billion. In 1995 the net investment surplus from abroad amounted to $45 billion. For comparison, however, in the domestic economy the amount of nonperforming bank loans in 1995 was officially estimated at $370 billion; unofficially it was estimated as several times higher.

Fiscally, public policy may be described in terms of three indicators: (1) the level of government spending as a percentage of GDP; (2) the size of the budget deficit as a percentage of GDP; and (3) the level of government debt as a percentage of GDP. Concerning the first, the level of government spending in Japanese fiscal year (JFY) 1994 was 34.5 percent of GDP. In 1975 it had been 26.7 percent. Concerning the second, the JFY 1996 budget had a deficit in the primary balance[18] of 0.9 percent of GDP. If the government's Fiscal Investment and Loans spending is included, the deficit was approximately 8 percent of GDP. (In the United States the figure was approximately 1.6 percent.) Concerning the third, it was estimated that total central and local government long-term debt in Japan would reach 90 percent of GDP at the end of JFY 1996 (31 March 1997). For comparison, under the Maastricht Treaty, members are eligible to participate in the European Monetary Union if their deficit in the government's general account is less than 3 percent of GDP and the total balance of government debt outstanding is less than 60 percent of GDP.

The government's debt service in the JFY 1996 budget amounted to 32 percent of all tax receipts. At the same time, the saving rate is declining because the population is rapidly aging and the elderly save less than the young. The trade balance has been declining since 1992 (partly because Japanese producers have been satisfying foreign demand from their overseas output). Real economic growth for fiscal year 1997 is projected by the Nomura Research Institute to be only 0.7 percent. "In no other major industrial country are government finances in worse shape today than Japan." Moreover, extrapolating from the rates at which Japan's imports and exports expanded in 1993–95, "Japan will have a trade *deficit* in 2003."[19] This translates into a weak prospect for a continuing net increase in Japan's FDI in the near future.

Retrospect and Prospect

Japan's chief resources after the devastation of World War II were the talents, traditions, and tenacity of its people. In charge of the reconstruction was the bureaucracy, led by planners who had supervised Japan's colonial regime in Manchuria. They promptly introduced institutional arrangements based on that experience. Chief among them was industrial policy, which provided for central control of industrial organization and allocation of resources. For purposes of control, they imposed segmentation of authorized activities into narrow categories; in banking, for example, transactions of various kinds were separated and restricted to specialized institutions. The nation submitted to the regulatory regime because it provided the carrot as well as the stick. The carrot took the form of favors, subsidies, and implicit guarantees against bankruptcy for "key industries" and other insiders. The insiders were prevented from encroaching on the turf of small shopkeepers and the like, who were secure in their claim to the crumbs of the system. The crumbs were the social compact component of communitarianism. These arrangements of industrial policy in the immediate postwar period may be described as the institutions of poverty.

A key point in Japan's recent transition concerns the fundamental contribution of the social compact and employment security to the infrastructure upon which the "economic miracle" and "Japan, Inc." were built. Neither would have occurred in the absence of the national consensus they supported. At present, however, the social compact is being associated with overregulation as a constraint on the competitive power of big business in the era of global competition. Institutions of poverty are becoming a casualty of the globalization process.

The details of Japan's regulatory regime have changed considerably since the tentative beginning of liberalization in the 1960s. However, surviving regulations and administrative guidance are a huge burden on the economy. The bureaucracy—having a strong institutional memory— is their defender: it regards deregulation and economic reform as a threat to its interests in central control.

Beginning in the 1960s big business was able to make its case for liberalization in the name of the national interest. It was clear that business had to be unshackled in order to stand its ground in competition with the West. When the "catching up" period was completed, not only had Japan caught up with the West, but big business had caught up with the bureaucracy as well. It had become too big to be controlled. This was the point at which the conflict between the institutions of poverty and economic liberalization began in earnest. The issues of the conflict include the surviving set of restrictive policies and their attached regulations (subject to ad hoc administrative interpretations; nontransparency and lack of accountability in government decisionmaking; and overdue economic and other reforms).

Growing wealth was a catalyst for the emergence of special interests that dissolved the national consensus, especially with regard to the institutions of poverty. A powerful special interest was that concerned with preserving the safety net for those who were "inside" the system. The distinction between communitarianism for the strong and communitarianism for the weak became a new issue.

At the same time, industrial policy received a shattering blow by the crumbling of the *keiretsu* system, which among the institutions of poverty had provided communitarian support for the strong. Industrial policy needed the *keiretsu* as an instrument for economywide imposition of controls through the industry associations that the *keiretsu* dominated. This was the bureaucrats' system of indirect rule (referred to above), which economized on their time and trouble. Why did the *keiretsu* crumble?

As *zaibatsu* successors, the *keiretsu* were associations of the premier firms of the nation. Their rationale was the creation of a safety net by the socialization of risk and by concentration of control in key industries. They were closely knit by information, technological, and financial networks, by interlocking directorates, by internal labor markets (especially for top managers), and by cross-shareholding among group members for the exclusion of predatory outsiders. Their strategies were coordinated by Presidents' Councils. Their domination of the Japanese economy was far greater than any attained by the *zaibatsu*. This rationale was highly persuasive. But it could not cope with the combination of problems of success and problems of failure.

The horizontal *keiretsu* were organized around a "main bank" (such as Mitsubishi Bank), which was surrounded by a miscellaneous group of major firms. In times of difficulty the main bank came to their rescue with financial, management, and advisory resources. Above all, the main bank provided a guarantee against bankruptcy for every member of the group. The vertical *keiretsu* were composed of a headquarters company (such as Toyota Motor Corporation) and its constellation of subcontractors (*shitauke*). Members of the horizontal *keiretsu*, however, found that they could finance themselves more cheaply by floating securities or borrowing abroad rather than by borrowing from their main bank. Already in the late 1980s, Mitsubishi Bank could not lend money to fellow Mitsubishi *keiretsu* firms. Moreover, in the recessionary aftermath of the asset inflation bubble, the main banks were swamped in nonperforming loans and could no longer guarantee group members against bankruptcy.

In the case of the vertical *keiretsu*, pressure of rising costs of production in Japan induced them to abandon some of their subcontractors in favor of outsourcing, either at home or abroad. Furthermore, Japan's domestic market was being opened up and foreign competition was making inroads. *Keiretsu* firms were tired of providing "lifetime" employment and seniority wages to an aging and underemployed work force. In many cases they expatriated some of their plants to less expensive production sites abroad. Substantial *keiretsu* outsourcing began in 1993. Toyota began to procure auto parts from suppliers that formerly had been attached exclusively to Nissan. This movement spread to all major industries. In some cases, however, globalization served subcontractor firms quite well. In China, for example, for efficient production, Nippon Denso needs a minimum-scale capacity larger than the present needs of

Toyota (its parent), and therefore in China it is supplying components to other auto makers as well as to Toyota.

In the postbubble recession, mutual stockholding is being abandoned because shares of *keiretsu* group members not only paid no dividends but also declined in value. Mutual shareholding was a luxury that could no longer be afforded. The decline of the *keiretsu* is also pronounced in the crumbling of their networks; sharing of information, exchanges of personnel, and collaboration in research and development have all decreased. Now Presidents' Council meetings are often mere social events.

In the carrot-and-stick regime, central control was the stick. It was personified in the alliance of bureaucrats, politicians, and big business known as the "iron triangle." The iron triangle was cracked in August 1993 when after twenty-three years of one-party rule, the Liberal Democratic Party was removed from office. Within days following the LDP defeat, Keidanren (Japan Federation of Economic Organizations) announced that it would no longer collect donations from its members for distribution to political parties. Together with the decline of the *keiretsu*, Keidanren's new policy reflected widespread collapse in Japan's institutions of central control. Both the carrot and the stick were in jeopardy.

There is a rising tide of risk, moreover, for each of the principal players of Japan's former iron triangle. For big business there is risk in the dilemmas of globalization and in the task of maintaining Japan's place in the world economy. For the bureaucrats there is risk in bureaucratic politics at the expense of the national interest. For the professional politicians there is risk in factionalism as usual. In the absence of a national consensus, rising risk leads to an increase in short-term rather than long-term thinking, which itself is risky.

In this milieu, what of communitarianism for the weak? Besides deregulation, transparency, and accountability, a new communitarianism based on fundamental reforms is waiting to be born. These include administrative reform, economic reform (including financial and fiscal reform), education reform, political reform, social welfare reform, distribution reform, science and technology reform, agricultural reform, and decentralization reform. They contain the elements of modern communitarianism. Together they renew Japan's institutions and provide security for both the weak and the strong. Will Japan's wealth be shared in the future as well as its poverty was shared in the past? The essential reforms have been overdue for decades. In their fate lies the answer.

Notes

1. Leon Hollerman, "International Economic Controls in Occupied Japan," *Journal of Asian Studies*, vol. 38 (August 1979), pp. 707–19.

2. In October 1970, industries that permitted 100 percent equity participation in the third round of Japan's inward FDI liberalization program included the following: bars, cabarets, bath houses, coffee shops, dance halls, mah-jong houses, nightclubs, and pachinko pinball parlors. *Journal of the American Chamber of Commerce in Japan,* October 5, 1970 (Tokyo).

3. It took until October 1994 before interest rates on savings deposits were fully liberalized, finally unleashing competition that was not always welcome. In some cases, where small firms were protected by regulations, liberalization was a license for big business to destroy small- and middle-scale firms.

4. See Tomio Iguchi, "Aggregate Concentration, Turnover, and Mobility among the Largest Manufacturing Firms in Japan," *Antitrust Bulletin* (Winter 1987).

5. Fair Trade Commission, Tokyo, June 1995.

6. Noriyuki Doi, "Aggregate Export Concentration in Japan," *Journal of Industrial Economics,* vol. 39 (June 1991), pp. 433–38.

7. Among the means for restricting consumption are protectionist import regulations and zoning laws that reserve urban land for agricultural purposes (about one-seventh of the land in the Tokyo area is owned by farmers or is vacant), rules limiting the height of residential buildings to two floors, and confiscatory capital gains taxes of up to 96 percent on the sale of land. MOF's policy "has been to exempt farmer's heirs from Japan's painful inheritance tax only if they keep their land in agricultural use for at least twenty years after inheritance." Restrictions on living space limit the size of residential property and the market for household furnishings as well as household consumption of energy. In restricting consumption, these regulations promote saving, which increases the supply of capital to industry. Eamonn Fingleton, *Blindside: Why Japan Is Still on Track to Overtake the U.S. by the Year 2000* (Houghton Mifflin Company,1955), pp. 199–202.

8. Both Sony and Toyota plan to produce half of their total output outside of Japan by the year 2000. In the first six months of 1995, Nissan produced 40 percent of its total output abroad.

9. Recently I asked the director general of the Coordination Bureau of the Economic Planning Agency, "What is Japan's strategy for its industrial policy on the international plane?" He replied, "We have no industrial policy on the international plane."

10. Owing to regulatory drag, for example, Japan's financial industry—after a prodigious start in the 1980s—has played a declining rather than a rising role in the world economy. This implies that Japan's capabilities in the financial sector may not be commensurate with those in the nonfinancial sector. For purposes of industrial policy on the international plane it is essential that these be coordinated and harmonized.

11. But MOF usually presents a united ministerial front to the world outside.

12. The Recruit scandal was an influence-buying scheme that exchanged cash and discounted, unlisted shares of stock for favors from top politicians, bureaucrats, and businessmen in Japan. The scheme was financed by Hiromasa Ezoe, founder and chairman of Recruit Co., Ltd., through its subsidiary, Recruit Cosmos Co., Ltd. Ezoe was an "outsider" who sought to quickly penetrate the inner circles of big business and politics in Japan. After Recruit Cosmos went public, owners of its preflotation shares were able to sell them for formidable profits. During 1989–90, scores of influential public figures were implicated. Among those who resigned their positions were the minister of finance, the minister of justice, the director general of the Economic Planning Agency, the chairman of Nippon Telegraph and Telephone Corp., and Noboru Takeshita, who resigned as prime minister.

13. Among the rank and file of politicians, many are opposed to deregulation because in the struggle for votes they are not strong enough to ignore the interests of their constituents. Top-ranking politicians who do not worry about reelection may be more free to act on principle.

14. Notwithstanding, with the exception of a few remaining subsidies, in the complex politics of deregulation MOF has abandoned its paternalistic policy of tax expenditures.

15. For examples, see Leon Hollerman, *Japan, Disincorporated* (Hoover Institution Press, 1988).

16. Concerning Japan as a headquarters nation, see Leon Hollerman, *Japan's Economic Strategy in Brazil* (D.C. Heath & Company/Lexington Books, 1988).

17. The convoy system was also useful in Japan's arguments with the United States about the slowness of its liberalization process.

18. The primary balance equals the amount of principal and interest paid on government bonds minus the amount of government bonds issued.

19. Toshiki Tomita, "Facing Up to Japan's Impending Fiscal Crisis," *NRI Quarterly*, vol. 5 (Winter 1996), pp. 2–17.

Contributors

Frank Gibney
Pacific Basin Institute

Leon Hollerman
Claremont Graduate School

E. B. Keehn
Japan America Society of Los Angeles

Richard Koo
Nomura Research Institute

Charles D. Lake II
Dewey Ballantine

Edward J. Lincoln
Brookings Institution

Koichi Mera
University of Southern California

Masao Miyamoto
Former official, Health and Welfare Ministry

Honorable Yasuhiro Nakasone
Former Prime Minister of Japan

Iwao Nakatani
Hitotsubashi University

Tetsuji Okazaki
Tokyo University

Eisuke Sakakibara
Ministry of Finance

Ulrike Schaede
University of California

John P. Stern
Japan Market Engineering

Edith Terry
Economic Strategy Institute

Christopher Wood
Peregrine Securities International

Taro Yayama
Former foreign correspondent, Jiji Press

271

Index

Agreements, insurance market access, 124–27, 139n
Agriculture sector: bad debt, 226; policy, 102–05
Amaya, Naohiro, 12–13
Antitrust enforcement, 125, 127, 149
AT&T, 56
Auto industry, 97–102

Bad debts, 6, 226–29
Banks: bad debt problem, 226–29; collapse of bubble economy, 220; current state, 6; interest rate bank concessions, 227–28; keiretsu organization, 266; legacy of wartime policies, 26–27; Ministry of Finance regulation, 249–50; prewar, 20; regulatory trends, 248–49; securities industry rivalry, 249–50; wartime regulation, 24–25
Barshefsky, Charlene, 116, 129
Big Bang reform, 5, 13, 132n
Birdzell, L. E., 30
Blood products scandal, 8, 60
Bubble economy, 260; benefits of recession after, 253; collapse of, 6, 220, 250, 262; labor market in, 261–62; negative cultural effects, 81–83; political response to disaster, 7; regulatory response to recession after, 251–52; trade issues, 261
Bureaucratic establishment: accomplishments of, 41; career path, 161–62; competition among ministries, 194–95; deregulation and, 64, 65–66, 71, 73; deregulation power struggle, 257–58; French model, 14–15n; historical development in Japan, 9–10; independence of regulatory agencies, 211; influence of, 41–42; interpersonal relationship networks, 162; linkage with business, 2–3, 35–36, 160; opportunities for reform, 51–52; postretirement employment, 59–60, 106; postwar development, 42–46; postwar model, 10; problems of, 1–2, 45, 46–47, 59–61; prospects for reform, 5; public attitudes, 8–9, 58–59, 61–62; recognition of overregulation, 4–5; response to Bubble disasters, 7; response to Kobe earthquake, 233, 240; self-interest in, 192–94; self-perpetuating tendencies, 71

273